"Without Tom Wheatcroft's enthusiasm and backing, British motorsport would not be where it is today. In rebuilding the Donington circuit, opening the museum and sponsoring drivers he has probably done more for the sport in this country than any other individual. Nobody else has come close to him in the way that he has put money directly into the sport, purely for the benefit of the UK. And all that racing in the Midlands would never have happened without him."
Max Mosley

"From the very beginning, Tom was always very supportive of what I was trying to do at Goodwood and, most kindly, always allowed his cars to come and take part at both the Festival of Speed and the Revival. Also, his advice was always helpful and to the point. I particularly remember a conversation I had with him at one BARC party, when I was discussing the difficulty of getting planning permission to run a race meeting at Goodwood and Tom's response was: "Planning permission, lad? You don't need any of that stuff. Just get on with it." What he meant was – don't give up. Tom had a great dream, which was Donington. He made it happen and that was a great lesson and inspiration to me."
Lord March

"The racing car world owes much to Tom Wheatcroft, not only for the restoration of Donington, but also for the splendid collection of historic racing cars that he has collected over the years. Many of the cars in his collection would have been lost to the country had it not been for his initiative. They will remain as a permanent memorial to his contribution to our motoring heritage."
Lord Montagu of Beaulieu

"I've known Tom for twenty-five years or more, and he is a man I admire enormously. He has achieved so much in his life, largely through sheer bloody-minded persistence and a total determination to overcome every obstacle, to regard every negative as a challenge. Most of those achievements have been not just for himself, but for all of us to enjoy – the circuit, the museum, the racing cars sponsored, the days to remember. Apart from that, he just loves his cars – especially the single-seaters. Howling around his own circuit in his own cars, with a huge grin stretching from ear to ear, he's just like a little boy getting his toys out of their box. Aren't we lucky that he's never grown up!"
Simon Taylor, motorsport journalist and broadcaster

Thunder in the Park

Thunder in the Park

The story of Tom Wheatcroft and Donington Park

Foreword by Murray Walker OBE

LIVE WIRE

Picture credits

First published in 2005 by
Live Wire Books
The Orchard, School Lane
Warmington, Banbury
Oxfordshire OX17 1DE

Tel: 01295 690358
info@livewirebooks.com
www.livewirebooks.com

The right of Tom Wheatcroft to be identified as the author of this work has been asserted in accordance with the Copyright, Designs and Patents Act 1988.

ISBN 0-9542860-5-7

A catalogue record for this book is available from the British Library.

Designed by Dick Malt
Printed and bound in Dubai
by Oriental Press

Front and back cover photographs courtesy of Jim Houlgrave

Section 1 (following p. 48)
Page 4 (top) Morton's; (bottom) sutton-images.com
Page 5 (top) Archiv Auto Union
Page 6 (bottom) LAT
Page 7 (top) *Leicester Mercury*; (middle) LAT
Page 8 (bottom) Eric Richardson

Section 2 (following p. 96)
Page 1 (middle) Paul Boothroyd
        (bottom) Jim Houlgrave
Page 2 (top) Noel Palmer
Page 4 (all pictures) sutton-images.com
Page 5 (top and bottom) sutton-images.com
        (middle) Simon Parkinson
Page 6 (top) John Colley; (middle) Leslie Thacker
Page 7 (bottom) Chris Davies

Section 3 (following p. 144)
Page 1 (top) John Colley; (bottom) Simon Parkinson
Page 3 (bottom) John Colley
Page 4 (bottom left) Simon Parkinson
Page 5 (top) Jim Houlgrave
        (bottom) Simon Parkinson
Page 6 (top) D. Rigley; (bottom) Garry Taylor
Page 7 (top and bottom) *Leicester Mercury*
Page 8 (top) Simon Parkinson
        (bottom) Sean Conboy

Section 4 (following p. 192)
Page 1 (top) sutton-images.com
Page 2 (top) Lyn Chalk; (bottom) Simon Parkinson
Page 3 (top) sutton-images.com; (middle) John Bailie
        (bottom) Paul Debois
Page 4 (top) Simon Parkinson
        (bottom and inset) Jim Houlgrave
Page 5 (top and middle) Simon Parkinson
Page 7 (top) Simon Parkinson
Page 8 (top) University of Derby

Every reasonable effort has been made to establish and contact the copyright holders of all the photographs used in this book. Any errors or omissions are inadvertent and anyone who has not been contacted is invited to write to the publisher so that a proper acknowledgement can be included in any subsequent editions of this book.

Contents

Dedication

For Lenchen, and for Roger Williamson – if things had been different,
how much more might we have achieved together?

Foreword

Like Tom Wheatcroft I've been lucky enough to win a few awards for my endeavours in motorsport, but there is one of them that means more to me than all the rest. It is the inaugural Tom Wheatcroft Award, of which I was the very proud custodian for a year. And the reason it means so much to me is that it came from the man who, next to my beloved father, I like and respect more than anyone else I have ever met.

Tom and I are contemporaries in age to within a few months. We both drove tanks in World War Two, but little did we know at the time that both of us were also amongst the enormous crowds that watched the 1937 and '38 grands prix at the exciting Donington Park circuit, which Tom later came to own and where he was to promote one of the most dramatic and memorable Formula One races of all time, the 1993 European Grand Prix, dominated by the charismatic Ayrton Senna.

Those childhood outings fired an interest in motorsport in Tom that has not only enriched his own amazing life, but also the lives of anyone in the world who is a grand prix enthusiast. For without Tom there would be no magnificent Donington Grand Prix Collection of pristine single-seater racing cars through the decades, no superb Donington Park circuit and, worst of all, no genial presence and friendship from the warm-hearted and affable tycoon himself.

Every so often in life you meet someone who is truly unique and that's Tom Wheatcroft. You will gather from the pages that follow that he is, to put it mildly, an unusual chap. From humble beginnings, he made a fortune in a notoriously tough and demanding business by virtue of his shrewdness, his willingness to take risks that no normal person would even contemplate, his steely determination and inexhaustible energy and his refusal to be mucked about by anyone, anywhere, anytime. Now these are characteristics that seldom result in a lovable personality, but that's not the case with Tom. He may be a tough and demanding, massively astute action man every inch of the way – and I'd hate to try to beat him in a deal! – but he is also so endearingly larger than life that he diminishes virtually everyone in his presence.

His ever-present booming laugh, his infectious enthusiasm for the sport he loves, his kindness and his generosity have made him the friend and benefactor of the great and the good, from Bernie Ecclestone and Professor Sid Watkins to motor racing immortals Juan-Manuel Fangio and Ayrton Senna, plus the multitude of fans who flock to the shrine to motorsport that is the Donington Park complex.

One day, after he had enabled me to achieve one of my life's ambitions by driving his immaculately restored Maserati 250F at Donington, Tom was chauffeuring me at enormous velocity in his BMW when he turned to me and said: "I shouldn't really be doing this Murray."

"Why's that then Tom?" I asked.

"Because I've just had a heart attack," he replied!

God bless you Tom, for being yourself and for all that you've done for all of us. We love you for what you are.

Murray Walker OBE

Silver Arrows

THEY SAY that in moments of sudden and extreme danger your whole life flashes in front of your eyes.

On a beautiful spring morning in 2002, at the age of seventy-nine, I found myself heading straight for a concrete wall at over 70mph in a Ferrari 500. The fifty-year-old grand prix car was completely out of control. I wasn't strapped in – cars of that vintage never had seat belts – and I wasn't even wearing a helmet. As the wall rushed up to meet me, there was nothing I could do except grip the wheel and brace myself. So, what exactly *did* go through my mind in that split second before impact?

Sadly, the historic and hugely valuable Ferrari had only been delivered to Donington that very morning, after months of brilliant, painstaking and expensive restoration work by my old friend Rick Hall. So, all I could think of as I closed my eyes and waited for the bang was: "Ooh, you bugger – Rick ain't half going to give me some stick when he hears about this!" Apart from that, there wasn't even time to offer up a quick prayer, never mind watch an instant replay of the highlights of my life in my mind's eye.

Almost miraculously, I survived the crash to live another day – and even to drive fast cars again, despite the best advice of family and friends! People had been telling me for years that I ought to get my life story down on paper and it was while recuperating after what was just the latest in a long line of narrow squeaks that I began to think that maybe they were right.

To start by putting the record straight, Tom is not my real name. My parents, Ernest and Alice, chose to call me Frederick Bernard, but when I was still very small my mother started referring to me as 'little Tommy Opposite' because, she said, I always managed to do exactly the opposite of what I was told. So, nothing much has changed there over the years! I imagine there must be quite a few council planning officers around who would vouch for that particular characteristic of my personality – although they might not put it quite so politely! The words "b*****d" and "awkward" would most likely figure somewhere in their considered opinions of me, not necessarily in that order. Anyway, the family nickname stuck and I've been Tommy or Tom for as long as I can remember.

I was born on May 8th, 1922 in Leicester, only for my childhood to be disrupted by two major catastrophes that struck before I had reached the age of five. First, when I was still only two, my father was killed in a motorcycle accident. He owned a small garage on the outskirts of Leicester and was on his way home on his motorbike one evening when he lost control coming over a humped-back bridge and smashed head-on into an oncoming car.

I have absolutely no memories of him. I don't even possess a decent photograph – people didn't take family snapshots as readily in those days as they do now – so I have no idea what he looked like. By the time I was old enough to start getting curious about him my mother had remarried, life had moved on and, to be honest, I never really thought that much about him. It was a case, I suppose, of not really missing something that I had never been aware of having in the first place.

It was only much later that I came to regret that I didn't know more about him and what he was like, and to wonder what characteristics, if any, I might have inherited from him; but I had left it too long. My mother had never talked that much about him – perhaps the memories were too painful – and by the time I did start asking questions in an effort to find out a bit more she either couldn't remember or didn't particularly want to. With no other close relatives still surviving from that generation, there was no one else to ask.

I am especially intrigued by the motoring connection. Although I never saw it myself, I was told that he had been presented with some sort of certificate by Ford, along with a quite substantial sum of money, in recognition of a modification that he had come up with for their back axles. So, it seems he must have been quite a talented engineer. Could it be that my own interest in such things is something I inherited from him, something that was in the genes? I like to think so. Rather appropriately, perhaps, the only thing of his that was ever handed down to me was an early Fiat car clock that was apparently a prized possession. I had it specially set in a con rod and it has been on my mantelpiece ever since, my only link with the shadowy figure of my father.

Two years after he was killed, I myself then had a narrow escape. By this time my mother and I had moved into a house just down the road from her parents, John and Agnes Stapleford, that we rented from my uncle, Dick Stapleford. Like my grandfather, who worked as a bricklayer and general foreman, Uncle Dick and his brother were also in the building industry, with a small business of their own, and right next door to the rented house was a timber yard where they used to store some of their materials. I would occasionally sneak out to play there and one day a large log became dislodged from the top of a wood pile and came crashing down on top of me, whacking me on the back of the head.

I still bear the scars of the accident, although I can't remember a lot about it. However, my injuries were serious enough to cause concern that I might have suffered some sort of underlying, long-term brain damage and, as a result, I was kept off school until I was twelve years old. The doctors were apparently worried that I wouldn't be able to concentrate properly on anything and that any undue stress and strain, or another accidental bang on the head picked up amid the normal rough-and-tumble of the playground, could possibly have disastrous effects. So, while all the other kids went off to school my mother would drop me at my grandparents' place on her way to work and I would spend the day with them, running errands down to the corner shop and helping them out in the little local dairy that they operated from a conservatory at the back of the house.

I used to love going out on the cart to do the daily milk round and I remember especially the thrill of being allowed to ladle the milk out of the big churns with 1-pint and ½-pint measures, using them to fill jugs brought out by the housewives. These jugs would be covered with a beaded lace or muslin cloth and stored in a cool pantry – no fridges in those days to keep things fresh! I have since built up a large collection of ladles, measures, jugs and churns that I keep at home as a nostalgic reminder of those childhood days. One classic piece I still want to get hold of is the three-wheel bicycle with a big 17-gallon churn mounted on the front that would often be used for deliveries by some of the smaller dairies.

While I was playing at being a milkman, my mother had got herself a job as the manageress of a local dry cleaner's shop in order to help make ends meet. Not that we were poverty-stricken, by any means, but times were hard for everyone in the depression years of the early thirties. I can remember days when we would have porridge for breakfast, lunch and tea. I can also recall searching along the railway track for any pieces of coal that might have fallen from passing steam trains.

As for my education, it was pretty much non-existent and by the time I was eventually allowed to start school I could barely read and write. However, as somebody pointed out many years later, I never seemed to have any trouble adding up when it came to my business dealings! In fact, I have always had the ability to keep quite a lot of complicated figures in my head.

Despite the oddity of not going to school like everyone else, I was never particularly aware of feeling like an outcast during my childhood. One way and another I was kept pretty busy around my grandparents' house during the day and I mixed with all the other kids in the normal way in the evenings and during the holidays. I certainly wasn't in any sense an invalid. All the doctors' fears proved to be totally unfounded and I never experienced any further problems as a result of the injury. On the contrary, I have never had a headache in my life as far as I can remember.

Physically, I was always powerfully built and more than a match for any of the other lads in a scrap, something I soon had to prove when I did at last go to school and found myself the butt of some mickey-taking on account of my backwardness. It was only then, when I realised just how far I had fallen behind everyone else, that I did begin to feel a bit of an outsider, developing an inferiority complex that was to stay with me for many years and which I was never fully able to overcome until long after I had become well-established as a successful businessman.

There were three lads in particular at school that I used to have trouble with – Roy Bayliss, 'Nadder' Taylor and a kid known as 'Bingo'. I knew I had to stand up for myself by fighting them and that it had to be done properly – and publicly. As it happened, there was a chap living in the neighbourhood who ran a little boxing club along with his two sons, and I started spending some time down there, learning how to handle myself. When I reckoned I was ready, I challenged these three lads to come along one evening and sort it out in the ring and, one after the other, I gave them all a bloody good hiding. I never had any more problems with them from then on – in fact, we became quite good friends.

However, I still wasn't doing too well at school and couldn't wait to get away. The rule in those days was that you had to stay on until you were fourteen – unless you had a job to go to, in which case you could leave at thirteen-and-a-half. The careers master told me: "I don't know who is ever going to employ you, Wheatcroft!" This just made me all the more determined to escape at the earliest possible opportunity.

There was a garage down the road and as I was already getting inter-ested in cars and motorbikes by this time I was forever popping my head around the door whenever I passed, offering to run errands for the gaffer and generally getting to know him. He was obviously quite impressed with me and was always saying that I would be welcome to go and work for him when I left school, so I thought I'd take him up on the offer.

I went home rather nervously to seek approval for my plan. By this time my mother had remarried and we were living in Eastcourt Road, Knighton, a private estate on the outskirts of Leicester. Her new husband, electrical engineer Thomas Freestone, had also been married before and had a son, Fred, who was about twelve years older than me. I got on well enough with my stepfather, but it was Fred I really took to. I think I was probably even closer to him than I would have been to a real brother. Being that much older, he was someone I could really look up to and he responded by taking me under his wing and looking out for me in all sorts of ways. He gave me my first set of initialled cuff links, which I still have to this day, and he also took me for my first-ever ride on a motorcycle.

I'll never forget the excitement of that moment. It was a gleaming new BSA and he was pleased as Punch the day he got it. He brought it home and called out to me: "Come on, Tommy – jump on the back. We'll go for a spin." My mother was anxious, understandably so after what had happened to my dad, but Fred wouldn't take no for an answer. "Don't worry – he'll be fine," he told her. "I'll look after him."

Fred and I even started a little business together to make a bit of extra pocket money on the side. There was an old disused clay pit near us, one end of which was being used as a dump for builders' spoil, and amongst the rubbish you could find quite a few bits of old timber. We would pick it out, chop it up and sell it as kindling and firewood. We had several regular customers who paid us a-shilling-a-sack for it, which was quite a nice little earner at a time when the weekly wage for a labourer was about £2-10s-0d and you could get a packet of five Woodbines for 2d.

Fred was a plasterer by trade and a very good one at that, a true craftsman in the days of lath and plaster, before plasterboard, ready-mix plaster and pre-formed cornices took much of the skill out of the job. Fred used to mix his own plaster, using Buxton lime. This was a laborious process that involved first leaving the mixture to soak for exactly a week; five days and it would be too soft, nine days and it would have started to go off. It would then have to be boiled up in a tub, stirred and put through a sieve. The result was a pure white plaster that took a while to set, giving the plasterer time to do the more intricate, free-hand cornice work. Modern ready-mixed plasters go off too hard and too sudden, which is why corniced ceilings went out of fashion after the war. I don't know a man today who could do what Fred used to do.

By the time I was thirteen, he had already begun taking me along with him on jobs on Saturday mornings and in the school holidays and when

I came back and announced my intention of trying to get a job in the garage he suggested that I ought to think about going on the buildings instead. My mother wanted me to stay on at school and try to catch up, but Fred persuaded her that there was no point. He reckoned that another six months weren't going to make me a genius, so I would be better off getting a job as soon as possible. He said that he would have a word with his boss, Jack Archer, about setting me on.

There used to be an advert you'd see regularly in the local *Leicester Mercury* at that time that read: 'Wanted: A Boy As Big As A Man, To Push A Cart As Big As A Tram.' The wage was ten shillings-a-week, which was exactly the same as what I would be getting at the garage, but Fred managed to get me an offer of 12/6d-a-week from Jack Archer. And so it was that I became a plasterer instead of a mechanic.

Like Fred, Jack was to play a very important part in my life, looking after me like his own son and helping me in all sorts of different ways. He made sure I got all the best jobs, bought me my first pushbike and even helped to pay for my first motorcycle. All this despite the fact that I walked off the first big job he ever sent me on.

This involved going down to South Wales and living in lodgings for several weeks while working on the site of a school for which Jack's firm was sub-contracted to do all the plastering. I wasn't yet fourteen and it was the first time I'd ever been away from home. That wouldn't have been a problem had it not been for the lodgings I was stuck in. They were absolutely filthy and the food the landlady served up was even worse. I'll eat just about anything, but the rancid sausages she used to put in my breakfast sandwiches day after day were so disgusting that I would throw up just about every morning. For years afterwards I couldn't even look at a sausage without feeling queasy.

The clerk of the works eventually took pity on me after he noticed me being sick and came up onto the scaffold to find out what was wrong. When I showed him the sandwiches I'd been given he took one look, pulled a face and invited me down to his office where he handed me some of his own. From then on he got his wife to make a few extra rounds for me every day. One Saturday he even invited me home to stay with him and his wife for the weekend. They were a lovely couple and I have never forgotten their acts of kindness towards me.

The lodgings, however, remained as awful as ever and after about five weeks, when I once again found myself heaving up in the outside toilet following yet another revolting meal, I decided I'd had enough. I went straight out and sold most of my tools to one of the other men on the site in order to raise enough cash to pay for my train fare home.

I fully expected to be sacked on the spot when I got back, instead of which Jack Archer was surprisingly sympathetic. "Was it really that bad, laddie?" he said quietly. "Well, never mind. We've got plenty on back here to keep you busy."

I worked for Jack for the next six years, right up until 1941 when I was eventually called up to join the Forces and went off to war. He was a hard taskmaster, but very fair, and endlessly loyal to anyone who pulled their weight and won his trust – all qualities that I like to think I myself brought to the job when I started running my own business. In that respect he was very much a role model for me.

Jack had all sorts of little sayings that stuck in my mind. "A really good man never walks around with his trowel in his hand during his lunch break or when he's packed up for the day," he used to tell me. "Someone who's been working really hard all day will want to down tools as soon as he gets the chance." He could spot the slackers instantly, simply by their body language. There were occasions when he would set people on at 7.30 in the morning and by lunchtime he'd be taking me on one side to say: "Do me a favour, Tommy. Pop down the post office and get me a couple of stamps – I'll be sacking them two tonight."

I think one of the reasons he took such a shine to me was that he could see what a willing worker I was. I was always very, very competitive, partly, I suppose, because I felt the need to make up the ground I'd lost through missing school. As the youngest of the three apprentice plasterers on the firm, I was determined to be better than the other two and by the time I was sixteen I could lath an average thousand-square-foot house by myself in a single day, lath being the thin board with which stud walls and ceiling were lined before the plaster went on. The going rate for the job was twenty-five shillings per house, which was very good money indeed for a day's work.

Apart from that, I genuinely loved what I was doing. I was always keen to learn how to do the tricky bits and when it came to plastering, this meant the cornice of the ceilings. The trademark of a good plasterer used to be his cornice work, especially in the actual corners – or mitres, as they are known in the trade – and I was lucky to be taught by three of the best in the business, my stepbrother Fred among them. I was very proud of the fact that I could soon plaster a whole room in one go, including all six mitres – the two extra ones being those formed by the chimney breast. Most people reckoned to be able to do only four mitres in a single session.

It was from Fred that I also learned the value of doing things properly and never skimping on the job. I have always been a devil for having everything perfect. One of the reasons I eventually decided to get out of the building business in the late eighties was that really good craftsmen were no longer available. Many of my top men had been with me for life and when they retired there was nobody to replace them. At the same time, I was not prepared to compromise on the quality of materials simply in order to meet competitive price levels. There were a couple of other builders in Leicester who felt the same way, but a lot of the big national house builders we had to compete with were starting to skimp on materials in order to keep prices down. They would then bring in interior designers to tart them up cosmetically so as to draw attention away from the poor quality of the actual building work. I'll never forget an old architect sadly shaking his head and saying to me: "Tom, it took a thousand years to learn how to build and a hundred years to forget."

I look back on my apprenticeship with great pride and satisfaction. However, although I was a hard and conscientious worker I have to admit that I could also be a bit bloody awkward at times. When I came back from Wales, Jack set me to work with Jim, his much younger brother. Jim had obviously been told to keep an eye on me and he often gave me a rough ride. I reckoned he was horrible at the time and often thought seriously about plonking him one. It was only much later, when I was in the Forces, that I looked back and realised that everything he had done had been for my own good.

On one occasion, after he had upset me over something, I foolishly decided to take my revenge by getting hold of his pushbike, putting a nail through each tyre and hanging it upside down from the joists of one of the buildings we were working on. Well, I certainly suffered badly for that!

On every site we used to have a big wooden beer barrel half sunk into the ground under the standpipe tap to catch the water. Jim waited until we were going into the 'mashing hut' for a cup of tea the next morning and then suddenly rugby tackled me, held me up by my legs and dunked me, head first, in this barrel of icy water. Another of his favourite punishment tricks was to tip me upside down on the scaffold, dangle me over the side and swing me, so that the back of my legs thumped against the planking. It was bloody painful and my legs would swell right up afterwards, but I probably deserved it.

While Jim was giving me the big brother treatment, Jack continued to look after me in a very fatherly way. He had already bought me a pushbike soon after I first went to work for him. He said I would have to pay him back at 2/6d-a-week, but at the same time gave me an extra 2/6d in my pay packet each week "for being a good lad". Then, as soon as I reached the age of sixteen, old enough to have a licence, he bought me a motorbike.

I had been saving up for months and was thinking about getting a second-hand AJS from one of the chippies I was working with at the time, a chap named Oliver Neill, but Jack didn't think this was such a good idea. "No sell-on value, lad – much better to buy a new one," he advised me, adding: "I'd go for a 350cc Rudge if I were you." This was a far superior machine, way out of my price range, but when I pointed this out he simply said: "Don't let's worry about the money, let's just buy what we think is best."

He insisted on going with me to the shop in Nottingham, where he managed to knock the asking price right down. I was still £28 short, but to my great surprise he proceeded to pay the whole amount out of his own pocket. Mind you, he managed to get his money's worth out of me in return, regularly using me to ferry one of his labourers from site-to-site all around Leicestershire and generally getting me to run errands for him. Not that I minded that too much. I welcomed the opportunity to roar around on the gleaming machine that became my pride and joy, especially once I had discovered the attractions of the Donington Park race circuit, the thrill of organised motorcycle racing and the beginnings of what was to become a lifelong passion for motorsport.

One of the oldest-established deer parks in the country, with a colourful, aristocratic history stretching back to Domesday, Donington's potential as a site for a racing circuit had first been spotted by a local Derby garage owner named Fred Craner. A former TT motorcycle rider and secretary of the Derby & District Motor Club, Fred was a very forceful and extremely abrasive character – not unlike myself in that respect, according to some people! And when problems arose with the owners of the nearby Syston Park racetrack over arrangements for an event he was trying to organise there, he vowed to set up an alternative venue of his own.

He regularly used to reconnoitre racetracks in a Rolls Royce. Rather cleverly, the company had realised that this would be an ideal way to test-drive their cars and have them really put through their paces by an experienced driving enthusiast and so they employed him to do just that. The sight of Fred, heavily muffled up, at the wheel of a bare Rolls Royce chassis was familiar to motorsport fans and drivers generally throughout the Midlands.

As it happens, he didn't take a Roller with him when he went to do his initial recce at Donington, because he didn't want to draw attention to himself. With its several hundred acres of beautiful, undulating parkland, it was one of several sites in the region that he had identified as being suitable for the sort of circuit he wanted to create. In order to make a closer inspection he simply went along one afternoon as a paying visitor to Donington Hall, one of the first stately homes in this country to open its doors to the general public. After queuing to buy a one-shilling entry ticket, he then slipped away when no one was watching to have a snoop around the estate, pacing out the distances of various carriageways and farm tracks and roughly mapping out a circuit. He was eventually accosted by a patrolling gamekeeper, who angrily demanded to know exactly what he thought he was doing. When Fred told him what he had in mind, the man was so impressed that he straightaway took him to meet Alderman John Gillies Shields, the owner, to discuss the plan.

Shields was a former Scottish land agent who had originally been brought in by the previous owner, Lord Donington, simply to help run the estate. When the old man died, Shields bought it himself, even though he could barely afford it, partly to honour a deathbed promise to his Lordship that he would not allow the estate to be broken up. However, he then had to find a way of paying for its upkeep, which was why he had opened the Hall and its gardens to the public.

An enthusiastic sportsman, albeit more of the old-fashioned huntin', shootin' and fishin' variety, he found the idea of creating what would be the first true enclosed road course on the English mainland quite appealing. What clinched it for him in the end was Fred Craner's confident assurance that it would attract large crowds of spectators who could be charged a shilling-a-head, making it, potentially, a very lucrative venture. He duly gave the go-ahead.

Amazingly, it took just five weeks to prepare a mostly gravel motorcycle circuit of just over two miles in length, much of it through some fairly densely wooded sections of the park. The inaugural event was then held on Whit Monday, 1931, attracting a crowd of nearly 20,000. The organisers had never dreamt that so many would turn up and were so totally unprepared that they actually ran out of tickets at the gate. As huge queues built up, they simply produced buckets and bowls and asked people to chuck their money in as they passed through. Once inside, the crowd watched a programme of twenty races, the main event of the day being won by speedway rider Squib Burton on a 350cc Raleigh, a bike that has recently been loaned to the museum by its current owner, Alf Briggs.

During the next couple of years the circuit was lengthened by 644 yards to two miles 971 yards, widened and improved and a tarmac surface laid down in readiness for the first car race. This took place on March 25th, 1933 and was won by Eddie Hall in an MG Midget at an average speed of 56 mph. Had it not been for a broken crankshaft on the last lap the winner would probably have been another C-Type Midget, driven by Kenneth Evans and owned and raced jointly by him, his brother Denis and their sister Doreen – a car that has recently been traced and which we are also hoping to have on display in the museum sometime soon.

It was two years later, in 1935, that I made my first visit to the circuit. At that time I'd just left school to start working for Jack Archer. Chippie Oliver Neill asked me if I fancied going to a motorcycle meeting there and offered me a lift on the back of the same AJS that he later tried to sell me. Unfortunately, on the way over, he got a bit carried away with his own talents as a budding speedway ace, took a bend on the old A6 between Birstall and Rothley a bit too fast and put us in the ditch. So, instead of spending the afternoon at Donington Park, we found our-selves instead in the Leicester Royal Infirmary being treated for cuts and grazes.

As it happens, that was not my only near miss on that particular bend. The trouble was, it was just a bit too tempting – you could easily take it at a ton if you were in the mood. Many years later I took my wife out for a Sunday afternoon spin in a little two-seater Daimler that was one of the first new cars I ever bought and as we were going round that very same bend at a fair old lick we suddenly came face to face with some bloke coming the other way on the wrong side of the road, overtaking when he shouldn't have done. I dived for the verge and he somehow managed to squeeze through the gap with just inches to spare. It was a very close shave, a bit too close for comfort. In that little Daimler, and at the sort of speed we were going, we wouldn't have stood much of a chance.

The driver of the other car rang me later to apologise. I didn't know him from Adam, but the Daimler, with its distinctive LUT 2 registration, had caught his eye and as he flashed by he somehow managed to make a note of the number and used it to track me down. Although he was apologetic about his driving he didn't sound *too* sorry – all he wanted to talk about was the Daimler! We ended up having a laugh and a joke about it, but from then on I treated that bend with a healthy respect and I was quite relieved when, some years later, they built a by-pass there.

Far from being put off by the accident that had scuppered my first visit, I became even more determined to get to Donington and, when the next meeting was announced, I set out on the pushbike that Jack had just bought me. It must have been the best part of thirty miles from my home, but as a fit young lad I never thought twice about cycling that kind of distance in those days.

From the moment I arrived there for the first time and found myself hanging over the chestnut paling fences I became totally hooked. The cars, the bikes, the sounds, the smells, the huge crowds, the bookies calling the odds, the thrills and spills of the races themselves – I found the whole atmosphere totally intoxicating. It was like nothing I'd ever experienced before.

If you were to ask me for my most abiding memory of those early days I would probably pick out the distinctive smell of the Castrol R racing oil that used to hang in the woods. It is such a strong association. If I close my eyes I can smell it now and it instantly takes me back. In my mind's eye I can still picture the groups of people in trilby hats and flat caps picnicking under the trees in the intervals between races. And the car parks full of MG Midgets, Austin 7s, Wolseley Hornets and all the other small sports cars that were fashionable with the enthusiasts of the day.

I started going to meetings as often as possible. The price of admission had risen by this time to 1/6d for a regular meeting and 2/6d for a grand prix, but I have to confess that I soon found that it wasn't too difficult to find places where you could sneak in without paying. That is why, when I bought Donington and re-opened it as a motorsport venue nearly forty years later, one of the first things I did was to build a solid ten-foot perimeter fence right around the circuit. I didn't want anybody doing what I used to do, coming in on what was known as a 'gap ticket'!

Not content with getting in free, I decided on one occasion to gatecrash the main hospitality area. There used to be a huge marquee set up in front of the Hall itself, which was where the prize giving used to take place. I peeped in and saw all these people milling around, helping themselves to tea and cakes, and thought: "I fancy a bit of that!" I waited until nobody was looking and then slipped in, reckoning that I'd soon get lost in the crowd. But, of course, a rather scruffily dressed fourteen-year-old stood out like a sore thumb among all the toffs in their tweeds. I'd barely managed to swallow a couple of sausage rolls and a cucumber sandwich before I was spotted by a doorman, who was in the act of throwing me out on my ear when a rather distinguished-looking but very kindly old gentleman intervened.

He quietly quizzed me about who I was, where I lived and how I came to be there and when I told him that I had cycled over from Leicester he was clearly impressed. "All that way, lad? On a pushbike? You must be very keen," he said with a smile. He waved the doorman away, telling him: "If the lad's got the cheek to walk in here as if he owns the place, let him stay."

We then got chatting about motorsport generally, my favourite cars and drivers and such like and very soon we were getting on like a house on fire.

It turned out that he was none other than Mr Dalton, then head of the family who owned Silkolene Oil – major sponsors of motor racing at Donington, with a dedicated bridge on the circuit – and our unexpected meeting that day marked the beginning of a long friendship. He arranged for me to have free tickets from then on and, many years later, in the late fifties and early sixties, he even invited me to join him in his suite at Silverstone. As a result, I got to know the whole family very well. I remember being particularly impressed by the fact that they owned a black Ferrari. This was very unusual at a time in the early sixties when Ferraris, traditionally, were always red.

As a mark of appreciation for the kindness shown to me by the family I have always, to this day, made a point of using only Silkolene oil, even though the company has long since been taken over by a German firm. The old man had died by the time I bought Donington, but I also took the greatest pleasure in being able to return some of the many favours he had done me in those early years by inviting his son, Richard, to watch events from my private hospitality suite overlooking the pit lane.

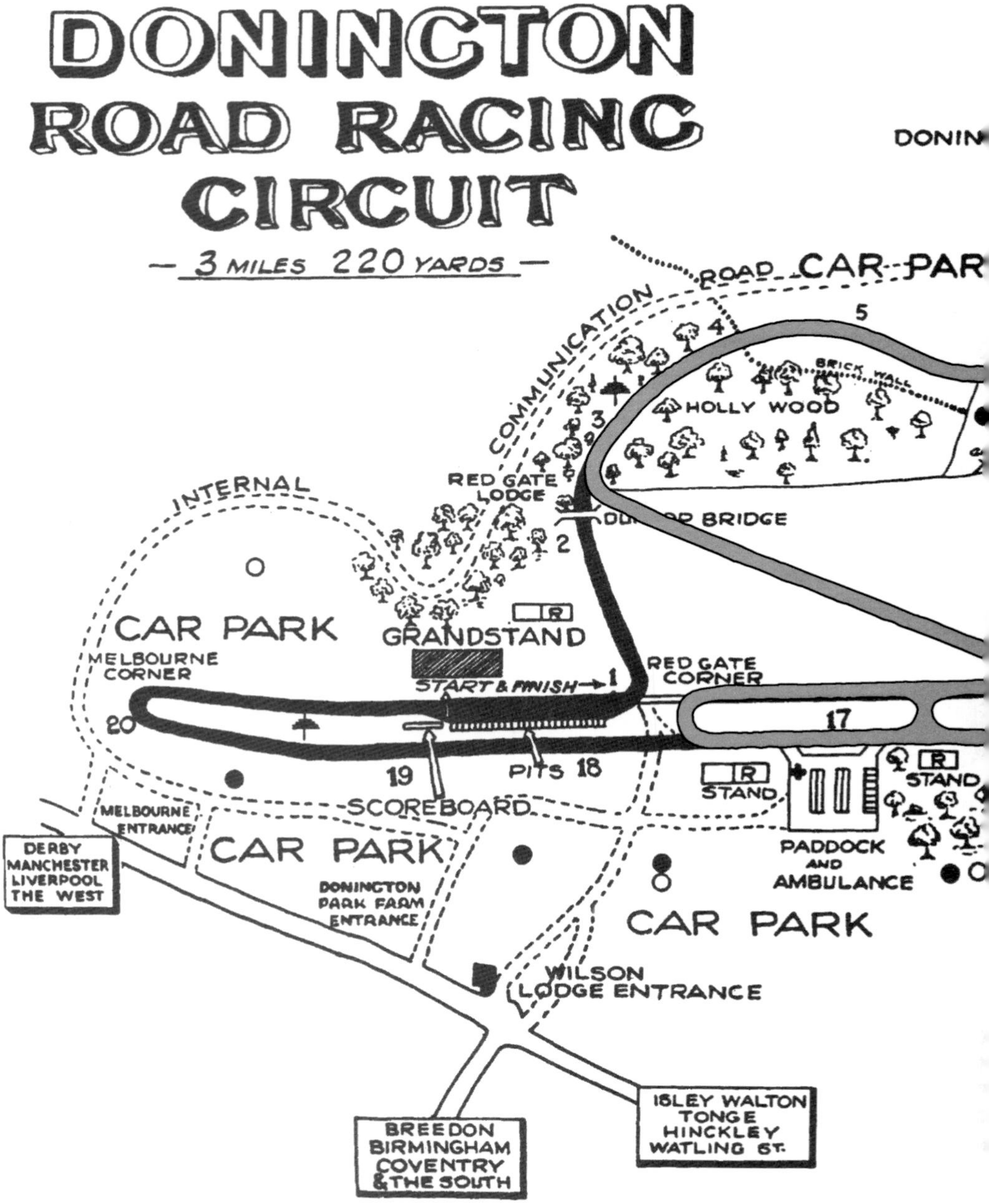

DONINGTON ROAD RACING CIRCUIT

— 3 MILES 220 YARDS —

DONIN

COMMUNICATION ROAD CAR PAR

5

4

3

HOLLY WOOD

BRICK WALL

RED GATE LODGE

DUNLOP BRIDGE

2

INTERNAL

O

CAR PARK

MELBOURNE CORNER

GRANDSTAND

R

START & FINISH →

RED GATE CORNER

20

17

19

PITS 18

STAND R

STAND

MELBOURNE ENTRANCE

SCOREBOARD

DERBY MANCHESTER LIVERPOOL THE WEST

CAR PARK

DONINGTON PARK FARM ENTRANCE

PADDOCK AND AMBULANCE

CAR PARK

WILSON LODGE ENTRANCE

ISLEY WALTON TONGE HINCKLEY WATLING ST.

BREEDON BIRMINGHAM COVENTRY & THE SOUTH

A map of the circuit dating from the 1930s with the present track superimposed.

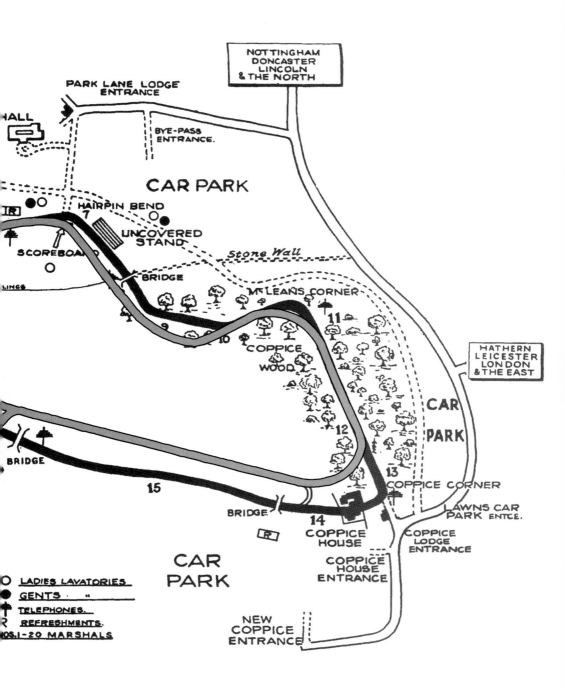

NOTTINGHAM
DONCASTER
LINCOLN
& THE NORTH

PARK LANE LODGE
ENTRANCE

HALL

BYE-PASS
ENTRANCE.

CAR PARK

HAIRPIN BEND

R

UNCOVERED
STAND

SCOREBOARD

Stone Wall

BRIDGE

M°LEANS CORNER

LINGS

11

COPPICE
WOOD

HATHERN
LEICESTER
LONDON
& THE EAST

CAR
PARK

BRIDGE

12

13

COPPICE CORNER

15

LAWNS CAR
PARK ENTCE.

BRIDGE

14

R

COPPICE
HOUSE

COPPICE
LODGE
ENTRANCE

COPPICE
HOUSE
ENTRANCE

CAR
PARK

LADIES LAVATORIES

GENTS   "

TELEPHONES.

REFRESHMENTS.

NOS.1-20 MARSHALS

NEW
COPPICE
ENTRANCE

From the time of the first Donington Grand Prix in 1935 – regarded by many as Britain's first true grand prix road race, since the only previous events had been run on the artificially banked circuit at Brooklands – I have attended every grand prix ever staged in this country. And I can honestly say that for sheer excitement and drama there have been few to match the so-called 'Hitler Grands Prix', staged at Donington in 1937 and 1938.

The 1936 event, won jointly by Hans Ruesch and Dick Seaman, who shared a drive in an eight cylinder 3.8 Alfa Romeo in which they set no less than thirteen new lap records during the race, had also been pretty good. What made the '37 and '38 events so special were the first appearances in this country of the mighty Mercedes-Benz and Auto Union works cars that had already been blazing a trail across Europe, revolutionising motorsport with their unprecedented power and performance. Developed with the enthusiastic but politically-motivated support and encouragement of Adolf Hitler, who could see the propaganda value of a sweeping German triumph 'über alles', the mighty straight-eight, 600bhp Mercedes W125s and the six-litre, V16 Auto Unions were in a different league to anything that had gone before.

A couple of statistics will help to put things into perspective. Until these supercharged monsters made their appearances the highest speeds ever reached down the long Starkey's Straight at Donington would have been about 150mph, 155 mph at the very outside, while the individual lap record, set in the 1936 event by Hans Ruesch in the Alfa Romeo, stood at 73.49 mph. And yet during the 1937 race the Mercedes and Auto Unions were already topping 170mph by the time they were halfway down the straight – and the lap record was raised to 85.62 mph!

As far as the rest of the field were concerned it was simply no contest – like pitting sports cars against F1 cars. Veteran motorcyclist and all-round motorsport enthusiast Charles 'Titch' Allen, a local newspaper reporter at the time and still a regular visitor to Donington in his late eighties, recalls the contrast even more graphically: "It was like seeing jet planes suddenly appear when you'd never before seen anything more powerful than a Tiger Moth," recalls Titch. The nearest anyone got to the

German cars was the legendary Siamese driver Prince Birabongse – B. Bira for short – who came in sixth in a three-litre Maserati. Crossing the line a full fifteen minutes after winner Berndt Rosemeyer's Auto Union, he was so far behind that he couldn't be officially classified!

The build-up to the race had been extraordinary. For motorsport enthusiasts, all roads led to Donington that weekend. The word had gone round that this was one not to be missed on any account. The news-papers and the BBC, who normally gave only scant coverage to such events, were full of it. Even the practice sessions attracted unheard of numbers of spectators and on race day itself there was a crowd of over 50,000. I was lucky enough to be among them, in a prime position secured with the help of my friends at Silkolene.

You had to be there to appreciate the full explosive impact of those awesome 'Silver Arrows', so-called because they had been stripped down to the bare metal to save the weight of paint. From the moment the teams of uniformed mechanics fired up the engines with portable electronic starters – a innovation in itself, as was the introduction of well-drilled, lightning pit stops – none of us had heard or seen anything quite like it. The noise of those engines was deafening, the smell of the special nitro methane fuel they used so overpowering that it made your eyes water. And the power they produced was absolutely breathtaking.

The circuit at Donington had been further lengthened to three miles 220 yards specially for the event, with an extension that ran down from the end of the Starkey Straight to a new 180° hairpin at Melbourne Corner and then back up the hill past the pits and the grandstand, and I shall never forget the sight of those Silver Arrows literally flying through the air as they crested the brow of the hill – the famous Melbourne hump – and took off. At times they must have been a good two feet off the ground. It was electrifying stuff.

After all that excitement one might have expected the following year's event to be a bit of an anti-climax, especially as new regulations had been brought in, reducing maximum engine capacity from six to three litres supercharged and 4.5 litres un-supercharged. In fact, the 1938 grand prix was, if anything, even more dramatic.

This was partly due, of course, to the increasingly tense political situation in Europe. The race had originally been due to take place on October 1st, but as Hitler started massing his troops on the Czechoslovakian border during late September and threatened to invade, war seemed so imminent that the German teams, who had already arrived at Donington by then, packed up and started heading home.

When the Munich Agreement and Mr Chamberlain's piece of paper appeared to have averted the crisis, Fred Craner entered into hurried negotiations with the team managers and succeeded in re-arranging the event for October 22nd. The added publicity created by all this to-ing and fro-ing ensured even greater awareness of the race and this time 60,000 people flocked to the circuit. I rode there on my new Rudge motorbike and as the sun broke through the early morning mist at the start of what was to be a perfect autumn day, all the approach roads were already solid with traffic.

The line-up of drivers included Dick Seaman, Manfred von Brauchitsch, Hermann Lang and Walter Baumer in the V12 supercharged Mercedes W154s, with Hermann Müller, Rudolph Hasse, Christian Kautz and the great Tazio Nuvolari in the D-type Auto Unions. The race was due to be flagged off at 12.00 and as the cars took their places on the grid and the final countdown to high noon began, with the noise of the revving engines rising to a deafening crescendo, the atmosphere of excited anticipation reached fever pitch.

The race that followed went down in motorsport history for one defining moment of brilliance. At around the halfway mark the engine of Robin Hanson's Alta blew up on the far side of the circuit between Holly Wood and the Hairpin – the section I later named Craner Curves in memory of the great Fred Craner – spraying oil all over the tarmac and effectively turning it into a skating rink. Nowhere in contention, Hanson had just been into the pits to re-fuel and had rejoined the race only seconds ahead of the leaders, who were right on his heels and closing fast when the incident occurred. As a result, there was no time to warn them of what lay just ahead.

One after the other they hit the oil slick and went into a skid. Dick

Seaman and Rudolph Hasse both spun right off the track, while von Brauchitsch, Baumer and Lang just about managed to keep control. However, it was Nuvolari, the first to encounter the hazard, who reacted in the coolest and most effective way. As the car went into a violent slide, he realised instantly that there was no way of holding it on the track through the approaching corner and decided that rather than trying to fight it, he would simply allow it to follow its own erratic skid path across the grass before judging the exact moment to regain control and guide it back onto the tarmac. This masterful piece of driving was generally acknowledged to have clinched victory in a race that he went on to win by a margin of one minute and thirty-eight seconds from second-placed Lang.

I didn't actually witness the oil-spill incident – I was at another part of the circuit, up near the grandstand. But, along with the other spectators, I listened breathlessly as the whole drama unfolded over the public address system, described by an increasingly hysterical race commentator. Interestingly, when we came to resurface the circuit in the seventies we found that the stain left by that oil spill was still clearly visible. We cut out a small section to keep as a memento and my son, Kevin, has incorporated it into a pathway in his garden at home.

My other outstanding memory of that day is of Nuvolari being presented with the trophy at the prize-giving ceremony in front of Donington Hall. The little Italian was so tiny that they made a joke of trying to stand him in the huge trophy. It turned out later that he'd driven the race with a cracked rib, a painful injury received during practice when his car hit and killed a full-grown stag, one of a herd of several hundred deer that had roamed Donington's ancient royal deer park since 1066. They had the head stuffed and mounted and presented it to him as a souvenir, now on permanent display in the Nuvolari museum in his home town of Mantua.

One way and another it had been a gloriously memorable day and I rode home a happy young man, already looking forward to the 1939 event. Fred Craner did actually announce the details in advance, even getting so far as to take deposits of £500 each from the German works teams. When the Derby & District Motor Club was wound up many years later they discovered an amount of German marks lying, long forgotten, in a special client account. But, of course, the war finally intervened to scupper all Fred's plans. How could I ever have imagined then that the next time a grand prix was held at Donington, I would be the owner of the circuit? And that I would open the proceedings with three laps behind the wheel of one of those very same W154 Mercedes Benz Silver Arrows that I had watched thundering around the circuit in such awesome fashion that day in 1938.

Meanwhile, whenever I wasn't watching motorsport I was working overtime on the buildings. Thanks to its flourishing footwear and clothing industries, Leicester was booming in the mid-to-late-thirties – it was actually named the second most prosperous city in Europe at the time in a League of Nations statistical report. And with a lot of slum clearance going on and new estates springing up there was plenty of work around for builders.

I was always a very hard worker. I didn't have that much of a social life and although I certainly enjoyed the odd pint with the lads I was never a great one for going to dances and all that sort of thing. I was keener on working and making money. I was very ambitious in that way. By the time I was eventually called up at the age of nineteen, I actually had several hundred pounds in the bank, three suits in my wardrobe, two pairs of shoes and a motorbike and was generally doing quite well for myself – a right little 'Rajah Wallah', as we used to say. And all that on a basic wage of 11d-an-hour! I was very proud of the fact that this was 2d-an-hour more than the average tradesman got at that time.

The war came as an unwelcome interruption, but in many ways it was to be the making of me. The Tom Wheatcroft who finally came back more than five years later would be a very different character from the raw young lad who left home in 1941 – tougher, wiser and absolutely determined to make up for lost time.

Tom and Jerry

ONE BY ONE, friends and workmates had been disappearing off to war at regular intervals for the previous two years so it didn't come as that much of a shock when my call-up papers eventually dropped through the letter box in the autumn of 1941. They informed me that I had been assigned to the Royal Artillery as a gunner, with the number 1130868, and I was ordered to report for duty to the 51st Anti-Tank Training Regiment at Catterick on October 23rd, 1941.

It was a truly motley crew that assembled on the bleak, chilly parade ground that day, a mostly rather bewildered bunch of lads, many of whom, like myself, had hardly been away from home until then and had no idea quite what they were in for. In some ways it was a bit like your first day at school, when nobody's quite sure where to go or what to do. The people you warm to in those first few hours as you try to get your bearings and find your way around often go on to become your best mates. As a bellowing Sergeant Major lined us up, still in civilian clothes, and marched us off, three abreast, to the quartermaster's stores to get kitted out, I found myself in the middle rank, flanked on one side by a fresh-faced lad called Copperwheat and on the other by a hard-bitten Mancunian named Ben Warr. Once we had been given the order to fall out, we introduced ourselves and got chatting and from that moment on the three of us became pretty much inseparable until we were finally demobbed some five years later.

Copperwheat, who came from Raunds, in Northamptonshire, was about the same age as me, while Ben Warr was a good twelve years older, already in his early thirties. A swarthy, six-foot-two-inch ex-miner, he had joined the regiment fresh from Strangeways prison, where, as he revealed once we got to know each other a little better, he had been doing time for holding up the box office of a cinema in Manchester. Physically that much bigger and tougher than the rest of us, Ben was also a great deal more worldly wise and street sharp, a real hard man who knew how to look after himself. He was, in every sense, a man amongst boys.

In the years that followed I came to think more of him than anybody else in the world, despite the fact that he had a violent streak and could be totally and cold-bloodedly ruthless in certain circumstances. He reminded me of a fox in some ways, with a cunning that always kept him one step ahead in the fight for survival. He knew everything there was to know about working the system and he was extremely practical; no matter what the problem was, he could always find a way around it.

The age difference between Ben and I was almost exactly the same as that between me and my stepbrother, Fred, and in some respects I suppose we ended up having much the same sort of relationship. I certainly looked up to Ben and he, like Fred, took me under his wing. Recalling one or two of the nastier situations that we encountered at various times during the war, I think it is quite likely that had it not been for his cool head in a crisis I might not be here today. At the same time, it has to be said that he was also a very bad influence in other ways. In particular, he had an utter contempt for all forms of authority, an attitude that rubbed off on me and became very much a part of my own make-up. Not that 'little Tommy Opposite' needed much pushing in that direction!

As a soldier, I always did my best when it mattered and I am very proud of my war record. During the five years that we were away, we were in action everywhere from Madagascar to India and over to the Caucasus, down to the Middle East and North Africa, across to Sicily, up through Italy and from there to Holland and up through Germany as far as Lubeck in the north. We took part in three sea-borne invasions and half-a-dozen major river crossings and were heavily involved in some of the bloodiest fighting of the entire war at Anzio. So, one way and another we certainly had our fair share of muck and bullets. At the same time, some of the escapades that Ben, Copperwheat and I and some of our other mates in the unit got involved in along the way were more like something out of *Catch 22* or *Kelly's Heroes*. I often found myself in trouble as a result and had actually managed to amass so many 'penalty points' by the end of the war for various minor misdemeanours that my final demob was delayed by a year to make up for all the time I would have spent in detention in normal circumstances!

In this respect, I opened my account early on, being docked half of my fourteen-day embarkation leave just before we first left England in March 1942 after getting into a fight. It was no more than horseplay, really. A bunch of us in the unit were boarding a bus when this other lad, with whom I'd already locked horns a couple of times, pushed in front of me in the queue. I couldn't let him get away with that – it was a matter of saving 'face' – so, I yanked him out by his coat collar. That led to a scuffle and, before we knew it, we were both on a charge.

All very silly, of course, but the sort of thing that is bound to happen when a bunch of lively nineteen and twenty-year-olds are suddenly thrown together in a strange, repressed and rather uncomfortable environment. Inevitably, some adapted better than others to the rigours of Army life and, as it happens, I was actually one of those who found it easier to cope. It's the little things that can often make the difference in that sort of situation. For instance, a lot of people had trouble with their boots – and there's nothing more miserable than having to march around with blisters on your feet. But having already spent quite a few years working on building sites, I was well used to wearing heavy-duty boots, so my feet were hardened to it and I didn't suffer in that way at all.

Working alongside people in all sorts of different trades also proved to have been useful, helping to make me both practical and good at improvisation. At the same time, the little bit of mechanical experience I'd gained as a result of having to keep cement mixers running, along with the basic engineering I'd picked up through maintaining my motorbike, gave me a head start as a trainee driver/mechanic in the Royal Artillery. I did very well and was even considered for promotion to Lance Corporal until I made it clear that I wasn't interested in having a stripe. My new friend Ben would have held me in complete contempt! I just wanted to stick with the lads.

After six months' training at Catterick, we were assigned to the 52nd Anti-Tank Regiment and in March 1942 we sailed for India, via Madagascar, en route to Burma. For someone who had scarcely ever ventured beyond the Leicestershire county boundary before, and who had certainly never even seen the sea, this was a fairly daunting prospect.

Still a few months short of my twentieth birthday, I was the youngest member of our unit. As we lined up on the dockside at Liverpool and prepared to board the troopship, they ordered anybody under twenty to fall out and for a moment it looked as though I might not be going after all. But when I stated my exact age as nineteen years and nine months I was told brusquely: "You'll be twenty before your knees are brown, lad. Fall back in line."

From Liverpool we steamed up to the Clyde to pick up more men and equipment before setting off as part of a convoy of more than forty vessels. Altogether, there were several thousand of us crammed aboard what was a converted Dutch cruise liner named the New Holland – but this was certainly no pleasure cruise. The ship, which was later sunk off Tobruk, had been completely stripped out and we had been herded in like cattle. If I close my eyes I can still vividly recall the awful stench that hit you as soon as you went below deck, the odour of stale sweat from all those tightly packed bodies mingling with the lingering evidence of widespread seasickness to create a nauseous fug.

That seemingly endless fourteen-week voyage was one of the more unpleasant episodes of the entire war as far as I was concerned. I couldn't believe the sea could be that bloody big! Apart from the sheer discomfort and the ever-present threat of marauding German U-boats, the boredom of being cooped up for so long in cramped surroundings led to irritability and frayed tempers. In these difficult circumstances I didn't make life any easier for myself by constantly getting into hot water, partly out of

devilment and partly from an increasingly bolshie disregard for authority. I got used to hearing that traditional army warning: "If you don't
watch it, Wheatcroft, I'm going to put you somewhere where the birds
can't shit on you!" Looking back, I make no excuses for myself.
I was a handful – and I probably deserved everything I got.

It is surprising how often food figured in it somewhere. Growing lads,
we never seemed to get quite enough to eat and what we did get was not
always very appetising. One way and another, we were always hungry and
a great deal of energy and initiative was exhausted in trying to find any
means, fair or foul, of supplementing our rations.

On one occasion, word filtered up from the galley that the officers on
board were having some sort of special roast chicken dinner, a luxury
that most ordinary people only enjoyed at Christmas in those days. It
didn't take me long to work out that there was a vantage point just above
the gangway leading from the galley to the officers' Mess where one could
lie in wait and then lean down and pluck a chicken or two from the trays
as the orderlies went by with them on their shoulders. Needless to say, we
got caught and as I was the one who was actually pinching the chickens
and passing them on to the others, I was the one who was punished, even
though I never got to enjoy a single mouthful myself. I got fourteen days
for that.

Much more serious was the custard incident. At mealtimes we sat
seventeen to a table in the Mess, eight down each side with an NCO at the
head, and it so happened that our NCO was the very same bombardier
who had been given the Lance Corporal's stripe that I had turned down.
A biggish bloke, he was cocky with it and thought he knew everything –
the sort guaranteed to put anybody's back up, mine especially.

The trouble started after he insisted that I do an extra stint as Mess
Orderly, a duty that involved collecting the food from the galley and
bringing it to the table. I had been quick to volunteer for this chore on the
way up from Liverpool to the Clyde, anxious to get it out of the way early
on. But then, shortly after we had set out from the Clyde, we ran into
some rough weather and the man whose turn it was to be on duty got
seasick, whereupon the L/Cpl ordered me to stand in for him. I pointed

out that I had only just done my stint, but he wouldn't have it and so I had to do as I was told. It was as I was bringing a huge metal jug of custard to the table that he pushed me just a bit too far. The jug weighed very heavy and was cutting into my fingers so that I couldn't wait to set it down as I arrived at our table. "Don't put it down there," he barked instantly. "Put it over here!"

Well, that was it. Without another word, I picked up the jug and emptied the entire contents over his head. For good measure, I then jammed the upended container down on top of his head. He struggled to his feet, with custard running down his face, and as he lifted the jug from his head, I hit him. I was still only nineteen, but a strong nineteen, and I plonked him good and proper! I got another fourteen days for that and they stuck me in a cell on the port side of the ship.

At that point I think they would probably have liked to throw away the key, but after I'd been there for a day-and-a-half there was a submarine alert and the captain of the ship ordered that nobody was to be locked in the cells, so they had to let me out. They had me scrubbing the deck instead, with a Sergeant standing over me, prodding me with his swagger stick every now and again. Unfortunately, I had not yet learned my lesson. Some of the lads had assembled on the deck above and were cheering me on. As I waved and shouted back the Sergeant rapped me across the knuckles with his stick. Again, the red mist came down. I picked up the dixie, full of dirty, slimy water, and tipped it neatly over his head.

Of course, that brought an even louder cheer from the lads above, but I was now in real trouble. This time I was sentenced to twenty-eight days' solitary confinement and because they couldn't put me in the cells they stuck me down below in the hold, at the sharp end of the boat. That was even worse. It was pitch black in there. From time to time you would hear scurrying sounds and if you looked very carefully you could see the eyes of the rats glinting all around you in the darkness.

The lads did their best to look after me, smuggling extra food down to me from the galley. Then, after six days, a delegation led by Ben Warr went to see the captain to complain on my behalf. He was horrified when they showed him where I was being held and ordered my immediate release. He said it was an inhuman way to treat anybody and, to make up for it, he allowed me to sling my hammock up on deck, where the fresh breeze was wonderful after the stinking atmosphere below.

We stopped off only briefly at Madagascar, taking no more than four or five days to secure control of the island, the French colony having sided with the Vichy government. We were greeted by a few big guns firing as we went in, but they were very quickly silenced by the Royal Navy and after that there was very little resistance. Once things had been sorted out there, we continued on to Bombay, where we were immediately put into quarantine for three weeks as one or two people had picked up blackwater fever in Madagascar. We then moved on to Poona.

At this stage we still had no real idea of what our final destination was likely to be. In these modern days of instant radio and television communication we take it for granted that everybody involved always knows exactly what's going on and what the political situation is worldwide, but back then there was no easy way of finding out what was happening anywhere outside your own immediate vicinity. All you had to go on were the snippets of information passed down the line by word of mouth. Most of the time we were pretty much left in the dark.

On the way over, the savvier ones among us guessed that we would probably be going to Burma and that was certainly the original plan. From Poona we went by train all the way up the Assam border. We were herded into cattle trucks and every now and again everybody would have to get out and push the train round bends. At Agra we stopped off at the Taj Mahal, where we were warned that on no account were we to take a dip in the lake, despite being hot and filthy dirty after chugging along for hour after hour in our cattle trucks. Of course, we all dived straight in. And every time the train stopped to take on water we would all strip off and race up to the engine in the hope of getting doused from the overhead filler hose.

When we eventually reached our destination we soon discovered that the worst thing about life out in the bush in that part of the world was the risk of disease. I was among the many who went down with malaria, but, thankfully, I managed to avoid the dysentery that was also rife.

Now, there is nothing in the least bit funny about dysentery – but it did lead indirectly to one dreadful practical joke that raised a few sniggers. Our latrines consisted of an open trench with a couple of poles on which to perch and, for obvious reasons, they were located some distance from the main camp area. The problem with this was that there were a lot of snakes about and at night you could sometimes hear them slithering around as you sat there with your trousers round your ankles. Consequently, nobody was too keen to go up there in the dark unless it was absolutely necessary, so they would put it off until the very last moment, often getting caught short as a result. This infuriated the Colonel, who was convinced that people were deliberately trying to avoid going all the way up to the latrines out of sheer laziness and he ordered that anybody found guilty of this offence would get an automatic 'fifty-six' – a 56-day detention.

Well, it was all right for him because he had his own private lavatory, a very superior sort of commode made from old wooden field ration boxes and located inside a curtained off cubicle. So, when the whisper went round that he himself had got the runs in a bad way we waited until the coast was clear and then nipped in and nailed down the lid of his fancy thunder box. Sure enough, his next emergency visit was accompanied by howls of frustration and bellowed curses that could be heard all round the camp.

Meanwhile, the situation in Burma having changed, it was decided that we weren't needed there after all, so we were turned round and sent all the way back across to what was then Persia, now Iran. Our job was to help bolster the defences on the Russian border against the threat of the Germans trying to break through the Caucasus to the Persian oil fields in order to fuel their Eastern Front offensive as they launched the ill-fated advance on Stalingrad.

Here we had to endure extreme discomfort of a completely different kind from that experienced in India, swapping the sweltering heat for sub-zero temperatures. It was so bitterly cold that we had to dig pits in the ground over which to pitch our twelve-man tents in order to give ourselves added protection from the icy winds. In addition, we were short of rations, existing on virtually nothing but rice. Any fresh fruit and vegetables that did find their way up to us were rotten by the time they arrived.

This combination of terrible weather and a poor diet was probably to blame for the boils that suddenly erupted on the back of my neck. The size of eggs, they were extremely painful and eventually turned septic, adding to my general discomfort. Being a young lad, my main worry at the time was that I was going to be scarred for life.

My condition only started to improve when I was dispatched down to the Iraqi capital of Baghdad a couple of times as part of a small convoy charged with bringing back truckloads of sheepskins for the Russian troops, who were very poorly and inadequately kitted out and in danger of freezing to death.

The drive down the Paitak Pass in our big GMC lorries was pretty hair-raising, with a combination of steep gradients and tight bends on the perilously narrow road that wound down through more than 3,000ft. However, it was worth every bone-jarring, wheel-wrestling mile just for the chance to get a bit of warmth and enjoy some decent grub, even the odd bottle of beer. On each trip, we managed to find a good excuse for staying a day or so longer than was strictly necessary.

In February 1943, after almost a year in India, Iran and Iraq, we moved down to the Middle East, Egypt and North Africa. By the time we got there the Germans were already on the run following the battle of El Alamein and we were only really involved in relatively routine mopping up operations during our seven months in the region. In fact, the nearest I got to any serious combat throughout the whole of this time was during a 24-hour leave in Haifa. It was then that I got a rather chilling glimpse into Ben Warr's darker side.

He, Copperwheat and I had just emerged from a bar and were strolling down a street quite late at night when we were suddenly confronted by three military policemen who were clearly looking for trouble. As they came up to us their leader twirled his swagger stick like an aeroplane propeller, threw it up in the air, caught it and then flicked Ben under the nose with it by way of stopping him dead in his tracks. I held my breath as

I waited for Ben's reaction, knowing instantly that he would never let anyone get away with doing something like that to him. Even so, the sheer speed and ferocity of what happened next was quite shocking.

I was only too well aware of Ben's fearsome talents as a street fighting man. During our time at the training unit in Catterick one of the sergeants, who happened to be a former Services middleweight champion, decided to keep us all entertained on wet afternoons by organising boxing sessions. At the end of the first session he asked if anybody fancied going a round or two with him and as I looked round to see who would be foolish enough to accept such a challenge he tossed the gloves to me and called out: "Come on, Wheatcroft, you'll do." I think he had already taken a dislike to me and had decided that I needed taking down a peg or two because he proceeded to give me a right pasting.

After that, I spent the next few weeks going regularly to the gym to train, determined to challenge him again and give a better account of myself. However, although it wasn't quite so one-sided the second time around and I did manage to get in a few good punches, I still ended up getting a good beating. Ben was outraged, insisting that the Sergeant was a bully who had taken unfair advantage of somebody much younger and less experienced than himself. He decided that when the time was right he would exact retribution. He waited until the very last afternoon session before we left the training unit and then called out casually: "Come on then, Sarge, I'll have a little go with you."

And, oh my word, he *was* good! He was so quick and powerful, throwing punches like a machine gun as he smashed through the sergeant's defences to give him a terrible thrashing. I'll never forget the way he finished it off, hitting him so hard that he knocked him clean out of the makeshift ring that had been set up and straight through the wooden door of a wardrobe that was standing nearby. It was an impressive demonstration of sheer animal aggression.

Even though there were three of them, those MPs in Haifa never really stood a chance. It was all over in a blur of violent action as Ben, single-handedly, laid all three of them out cold. In the blink of an eye, he nutted the one who had dared to tap him on the chest and he went down like a sack of spuds. The other two were gone in seconds. Then, as the first one struggled to his knees, Ben beckoned him up, muttering "Come on, my boy, up you get" before grabbing his head in both hands and kneeing him in the face. Even then, he wasn't satisfied. As the man lay groaning help- lessly on the ground, he planted one boot on the side of his head and kicked back sharply with his other heel in a deliberate attempt to smash his jaw. "It'll be a while before he'll be wanting to eat anything," he mut- tered as we slipped away back to camp, me feeling rather uneasy about what I had just witnessed, although still very much in awe of the man.

Any misgivings I might have had about the incident were soon pushed to the back of my mind by more immediate thoughts of self-preservation as our unit suddenly found itself preparing to get involved in front-line action once again. At the end of June 1943 it was announced that we would be moving out of the Middle East. As usual, we were not told in advance exactly where we would be going, but as soon as we assembled on the dockside at Haifa and saw the fleet of amphibious landing craft being loaded aboard the troop carriers it became obvious that we were to be part of a major sea-borne invasion force.

A mood of tense, nervous anticipation descended on the ship as we slipped our moorings and steamed out of the harbour, wondering what lay ahead. It was only at the very last moment that we were told that our destination was to be Sicily. The night before the invasion, the Colonel called us all up on deck at 0100 hours to reveal that we would be going in at dawn the next morning, landing on three separate beaches along the coast near Syracusa.

I was still only just twenty-one and as we took up our positions in the landing craft, along with our tanks, our half-track armoured vehicles and our two-pound and six-pound guns, waiting for the order to go, I expe- rienced real fear for the first time in my life. The hairs were standing up on the back of my neck and I had so many goose pimples that I felt I must look like an oven-ready Christmas dinner.

We had all been offered a tot of rum to steady our nerves before we went down to the landing craft and while some people were too tense to drink anything at all, others swallowed as much as they could lay their hands on. Everyone reacts differently at such moments and each man has his own way of dealing with it. Some become very talkative and try to crack a few jokes while others fall silent; some become so terrified that you can see them visibly shaking, others appear icy calm; some pray to God while others put their faith in lucky charms or little rituals. There were quite a few I knew who were forever working out the percentage risk they faced, but I never believed in that sort of thing. The way I looked at it, you just had to get on with things and hope that no shell or bullet had your name on it.

Conditions were far from ideal that morning, with a rough sea whipped up by a strong offshore wind that proved too much for the gliders that had been sent in, many of them dropping nearly a mile short of the beach. We could see the bodies of drowned parachutists floating in the water as we headed for the shore, which didn't do a lot for our confidence.

We came under fire early on from some heavy artillery located above the beach, shells splashing into the sea all around us, but these big guns were very soon silenced with a heavy barrage from a Navy destroyer lying three miles offshore. Then a lone enemy dive-bomber suddenly appeared, swooping low over the bay, and we watched in stunned horror as it scored a direct hit on the landing craft that had left the mother ship immediately ahead of us. One moment it was there, the next there was blinding explosion and, when the smoke cleared, it had vanished. There was nothing left of it to be seen.

It seemed to take an age before we eventually made it to the beach, but once we got there things weren't nearly as bad as I'd feared. I'd expected there to be somebody waiting for us behind every tree and bush and thought that we would have to fight our way through a continuous hail of machine gun fire, but there actually turned out to be surprisingly little opposition. That may have been because there were no German troops there, only Italians – and, let's face it, they have never been exactly famed for their fighting qualities. Whatever the reason, we were able to make pretty rapid headway.

Within a month, we had swept through the entire island. One of my most vivid memories is of marching up Mount Etna with the infantry. My little legs were no good for marching at the best of times and I remember fantasising, as we flogged up this hill, about how much nicer it would be to drive up there in an open sports car. Little did I ever imagine then that one day in the future I would have the opportunity to do just that.

Once Sicily had been secured, the Allies turned their attention to mainland Italy. Following the downfall of Mussolini, the Germans had poured huge numbers of reinforcements into the country in an attempt to stem the Allied advance, leading to some of the bitterest and bloodiest fighting of the entire war. And we were right in the thick of it.

From Sicily we invaded across the Straits of Messina, landing at Reggio. At least, that was where most of our unit landed. Unfortunately, our crew got lost on the way over and ended up somewhere quite different. We never did know quite how it happened. We were sent across in American DUKW amphibious landing craft, setting off at twenty-minute intervals to cover the two or three miles across the Straits. All we had to do was follow a compass course and I can only think that the metal in the extra cans of petrol we had smuggled aboard affected the compass in some way, because we somehow managed to miss the heel of Italy altogether, ending up miles further round the coast. As dawn broke we scrambled ashore and then had to spend several anxious days hiding out in an olive grove, behind enemy lines. The welcome arrival on the scene of an advancing Canadian unit allowed us to break cover and we made our way back to our own unit in a 'borrowed' 15cwt truck. "Had a nice holiday have we, Wheatcroft?" sneered the Sergeant Major suspiciously when we eventually turned up.

During the next few months we fought our way through southern Italy to Naples, from where we took part in a sea-borne landing at Anzio. Here, during the early part of 1944, we spent four months dug in just above the beach, pinned down in our trenches by a fairly relentless artillery bombardment. Using my building site experience and some 7x4 timber that had been washed up on the beach and which we managed to salvage during lulls in the shelling – having first driven a small herd of cows across the beach to make sure there weren't any mines buried there – I had constructed a superior, reinforced dug-out of which I was extremely proud. I reckoned it would probably withstand even a direct hit from the regular 88mm stuff that the Germans were throwing at us most of the time, although I certainly couldn't have guaranteed its survival against the might of Anzio Annie.

Anzio Annie was one of five huge, train-mounted K5 superguns built for Hitler by Krupp and designed, originally, with the aim of making it possible to hit London from across the Channel. The one targeted on the Allied positions at Anzio was sited just outside Rome, more than 30 miles away. The 550-pound shells it fired were so huge that they had to be loaded with cranes and they made a distinctive and quite terrifying howling noise as they came over.

It was said that after the war one of these guns was found hidden at the Krupp's factory, bricked up in one of the giant furnaces with its great 70ft barrel pointing vertically upwards inside the chimney. Many years later I happened to see Anzio Annie herself in a railway siding in America, on her way to permanent display at a museum in Maryland, and I made a point of sneaking round the back and peeing against one of the wheels, a token gesture of contempt on behalf of myself and the rest of the lads who had suffered her bombardments.

We were still at Anzio when, on May 8th, 1944, I celebrated my twenty-second birthday. As things turned out, it was almost my last. I had decided it would be nice to mark the occasion by treating myself to a clean shirt for the first time in weeks and had ventured outside the trench, wearing just my shorts, to wash the only one I possessed at that time, having first soaked it in petrol to kill off any lice!

I was in the middle of doing my little bit of laundry when yet another bombardment began. I was so keen to get the job done that I hung about outside for just a moment too long before diving back into my trench, at which point a shell exploded nearby, spraying red-hot cordite all over my bare back. The stuff sets on you like melted candle wax and when you try to peel it off it takes your skin with it, just as if you have been rather badly sunburned. Ben Warr immediately took charge, picking twigs from a bush and using them to roll up and remove the dead skin as gently as possible before treating the burns with iodine. It was painful, but as always in those situations, you were happy just to have survived.

The Allies suffered appalling losses at Anzio and almost every day word would be passed on about casualties somewhere just up the line. "Have you heard? So-and-so's copped it! He didn't quite get back in his hole in time and a shell caught him." Or: "Did you know about such-and-such a unit? A shell landed right in the middle of their trench and killed four of them."

These were the only clues we had as to what was going on in our immediate vicinity. As for what was happening further afield and in the war generally, we really had no idea at all. Odd rumours and bits and pieces of news would occasionally filter through – if, for example, a big ship like the Hood had gone down. Apart from that, all we knew for sure was that we were stuck in a hellhole in the middle of Italy, going nowhere fast.

I felt reasonably secure and comfortable in my bunker – I even had an old sprung mattress that I'd picked up from somewhere – but it could still be very unnerving at times, especially during a creeping barrage when you would hear the shells gradually dropping closer and closer to you. We had a young signaller with us who suffered very badly with his nerves and on these occasions I would sometimes have to sit with my arm round his shoulders as he shook uncontrollably, re-assuring him as confidently as I could: "Don't worry, kid, we're going to be all right."

Not that it was all one-way traffic, by any means. I'll never forget watching a 1,000-bomber allied raid on the German positions at Monte Cassino. It was an awesome sight. There were so many planes going over that they literally blotted out the sun, as if a dark cloud were moving across it. I hate to think what it must have been like to be on the receiving end of a bombardment like that.

I could just about handle being under fire in the circumstances we experienced at Anzio. What frightened me most were invasions and river crossings. For one thing, I'm no swimmer. Apart from that, you knew that beaches and riverbanks were always likely to be mined and that you could be blown up at any moment. I especially hated river crossings. Even in an amphibian, they could be extremely unpleasant. As it entered the water, the amphibian would dip right under the surface and as it came up the other side the entire soft underbelly of the craft would be exposed as it crested the bank, making a very tempting target for the enemy. Because of the angle as it lurched up the bank, all you could see from inside was sky and, for a moment, you would just hold your breath and hope you weren't in somebody's sights. On foot, it was worse still and even if you made it across safely, there was nothing more miserably uncomfortable than being both cold and wet, your boots full of water and your damp uniform chafing your skin until it was red raw.

For me, one of the nastiest experiences by far was a sneak attack we mounted across the River Garigliano in Italy, on our way up to Anzio. We were part of a detachment that had been sent ahead under cover of darkness as a diversionary tactic to draw attention away from a major attack that was to take place three miles up river. There were mines everywhere and the water was very fast flowing, so that we had to grab hold of floating branches to help us get across.

As usual, Ben, Copperwheat and I had stuck close together. We were among the first over, but then the flares went up and suddenly the place was like a bloody fairground. As all hell broke loose, with machine guns chattering left, right and centre, it was Ben who sized up the situation in an instant. Pointing to some rocks up ahead, he yelled at us to make a dash for cover behind them. I thought at first that he'd gone mad because this put us right under the noses of the Germans, so close, in fact, that we could quite clearly hear them talking above us. But there was no doubt that he was right. We wouldn't have stood much of a chance out in the open, trying to scramble back.

We remained stranded behind those rocks, undetected, for three full days, hardly daring to speak as we waited for an opportunity to slip back across the river under cover of darkness. I remember being terrified that one of us might suddenly sneeze and give our position away. On the fourth night, with heavy cloud covering the moon, we decided the time was right to make a silent dash for it, hoping that the Germans might have relaxed their guard, assuming that no survivors of the raid were still left on their side of the river.

Once safely on the other side we came across a six-wheel Albion heavy artillery truck that had been abandoned in the middle of a minefield, with its left front wheel blown off. I very carefully backed it about a mile out of the minefield, along its own tracks, with Ben lying in the back to guide me. He had attached lines to each of my arms so that he could give a little tug to indicate whether it should be left hand or right hand down a bit.

Once clear of the minefield, we switched one of the double back wheels to the front and then drove off to find the rest of our unit. We eventually located them camped about five miles away in the courtyard of a large, deserted house, their presence indicated in the pitch darkness by a four-gallon petrol drum with the unit number stamped out in perforations and illuminated by a lighted candle inside. We arrived to a heroes' welcome, having been listed as missing in action along with a number of others who never did make it back from that particular sortie. Once again, I had good reason to feel indebted to Ben Warr and his unerring instinct for self-preservation.

The stubborn German resistance at Anzio and Monte Cassino was only finally overcome after one of the bitterest and bloodiest confrontations of the whole war and the way was then open for the Allied advance on Rome. At one point, I remember, our unit stopped to brew up right outside the Colosseum.

By now, having been together for more than two years and having traipsed half way round the world, we had developed a special camaraderie. Among us were all the stock characters you might get in any classic war film: The Colonel – the 'Old Man' or 'The Mad Mullah' as we called him (his name was actually Muller) – a professional soldier and one of the few officers whom we all treated with respect; Peter Webb, the easy-going and rather reluctant Lieutenant in charge of our particular crew who was like a fish out of water, having been pitched into the war from a cosy niche in the family business, but who was well-liked because we could twist him round our little fingers; Sergeant Quinn, full of bluster, but not too bad, as sergeants went; radio operator Frankie Mole, a tailor in civvy street and the 'brains' of the unit, a man who seemed to know everything there was to know about anything and who lectured us all on the historical background to each phase of the war; Duffy, amiable but a bit slow; Copperwheat, boyish and good-natured; Harry Hinge, the good-looking ladies' man; and, of course, Ben Warr.

Ben was a law unto himself. He could be a hero one moment – as when he broke cover during a fierce gun battle in an Italian village and dashed across a road to rescue a child that had strayed into the crossfire, snatching it to safety amid a hail of bullets; or, again, during another of those dreaded night-time raids across a river, when an airburst shell exploded near Duffy and blew off one of his legs. Under heavy fire, Ben not only stayed cool and calm enough to sever the dangling remains of the shattered limb with his penknife, but then somehow managed to carry Duffy back across the river to safety, an incredible act of bravery.

At other times he could be a cold-blooded killer. He was the only one of us who carried a rifle, as against the usual Tommy gun. He called it his 'Betsy' and he was deadly with it. Again in Italy, we were involved in an action to take a village when we spotted the body of a dead British soldier from another unit lying on top of a wall about two hundred yards away from where we had taken cover. As we waited to move forward somebody noticed that a boot had suddenly been removed from the body and then, as we watched, a hand sneaked over the wall and started trying to remove the other boot. You could only just see the top of the head of whoever it was who was trying to steal it off the body, but that was quite enough of a target for Ben. He took aim and – bang! That was it. "Another one bites the dust," he growled, carving a further notch on the rifle butt.

Early on in the Italian campaign, our Padre, for whom Ben had great respect, had been fatally wounded in a grenade attack. He died in Ben's arms and Ben swore then that before the war was over he would kill one of the enemy for every one of the Padre's fifty-six years. As we rolled through Italy and then Germany in our Sherman tank, he would sit up top while I drove, keeping a watchful eye out for likely targets and, to be truthful, I'm not sure that he was always too particular about who strayed into his sights. As far as Ben was concerned, you were either with us or you were against us – in which case you were fair game.

In all sorts of ways, war then was a much dirtier business than it is

The model soldier, shortly before going off to war in 1942, aged nineteen, and (below) the earliest surviving picture of the young Wheatcroft, centre, taken during an Easter weekend visit to a Derbyshire farm owned by a couple who were friends of the family.

The gang's all here! With other members of my unit outside Frau Renschall's hotel in Walkenried shortly after VE Day in 1945. Standing on my right, with arms folded, is Ben Warr. On my left is Copperwheat.

With Lenchen in Germany (above) and (right) Lenchen in the yard behind her home in Walkenried, pushing our daughter Jill in an antique pram that looks as though it should perhaps be on show in the museum at Donington!

Lenchen in the two-seater Daimler, the 'little red bomb' that nearly got me into trouble with the taxman.

With Mick Higgins and the first cement mixer I ever owned, brought out ceremonially to launch every new project and (left) my trusty 1948 Bedford truck outside a redevelopment site in the early sixties.

Three views of the
Craner Curves – (top)
during one of the first
motorcycle events in
the early thirties, (right)
still lined by military
vehicles in the late
forties when the re-
opening of the circuit
after the war was first
considered and (below)
obscured by spray
during the
extraordinary first lap
of the 1993 European
Grand Prix.

Tazio Nuvolari (left) in his trademark red helmet and yellow jersey and (above) leading the 1938 Donington Grand Prix.

(Below) The aftermath of the fatal accident that occurred at Holly Wood during a twelve-hour race in 1937.

(Above) My growing collection of cars in 1970. (From nearest the camera) H16 BRM, Lowline Cooper, Flat Eight Porsche, Sir Stirling Moss's 1961 Monaco-winning Lotus, Flat Four Porsche, Tec Mec, Lotus 16, 250F Maserati (also pictured, right, at Donington), Aston Martin, 4.5 litre Osca and Maserati 8CM.

(Left) Legendary motorsport journalist Denis Jenkinson in the Mercedes W 154 loaned to us by the Czechslovak National Technical Museum of Prague in 1974.

(Above) Great to be back! Me shortly after I had bought Donington in 1971.

(Right) Motorsport journalist Philip Turner in the 8CM that made a 'squatter' see red.

(Below, right) Starting work on re-building the track and (below, left) me helping to map out the half-mile grand prix extension in 1980.

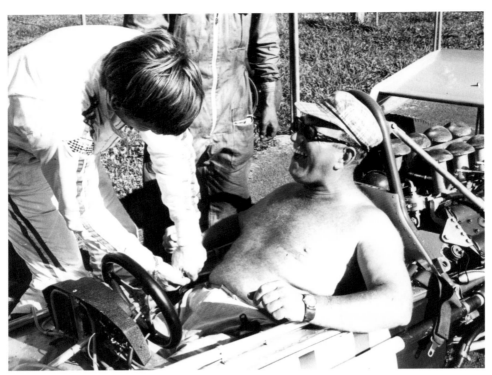

Derek Bell helping me to squeeze into the Brabham BT26 (above), a rare light-hearted moment during our ill-fated Tasman Series in 1970 and (left) the full team in New Zealand during the same Series.

(Below) Re-united with Derek and the Brabham at the Historic Motorsport Show at Stoneleigh in 2005.

today – when there is quite likely to be a television team right behind you – and, like any invading army, we didn't always play strictly by the rules. For instance, moving about as much as we did, we were often short of food and in those circumstances we never hesitated to live off the land. If you passed a likely looking farm with a few chickens clucking around the yard you would simply go in and help yourself. If the farmer objected, a warning burst from a Tommy gun would usually persuade him to be more co-operative.

Sometimes you would find more than you had bargained for. Towards the end of the war, by which time we were in Germany itself, I went into a farmhouse one day to have a look round and noticed that the farmer's wife kept throwing anxious glances towards the stairs. When I then crept up to check, I found an SS man in full uniform, lying fast asleep on a bed. I guess he was a deserter, possibly the woman's son. I wasn't interested in him, I was only after food, and so I simply relieved him of his Luger and left him where he was. Afterwards I thought how silly I'd been – he might well have had a rifle hidden somewhere in the house and could have picked me off ever so easily as I walked away.

On another occasion we spotted a pig in a farmyard and decided to snatch it. "Just think, Wheaty, we can have bacon for breakfast every day for weeks," chuckled Ben, smacking his lips. However, when we went inside the farmhouse it turned out that somebody else had beaten us to it. We were explaining to the nervous old man we found in the kitchen that we were taking his pig – we always used to ask nicely first! – when all of a sudden we heard screams from upstairs.

When we went to investigate we found a soldier from another British unit chasing a young girl around the bedroom. Ben had grabbed a large smoked ham from the kitchen ceiling on the way up and he now used this as a weapon, whacking the squaddie over the head so hard that I feared for a moment that he must have killed him. Here was another example of Ben's strangely inconsistent sense of outraged morality. As we left the house he apologised profusely to the old man for the would-be rapist's behaviour. Then, turning to me he said: "Put the pig back in the sty, Wheaty. We won't be taking that with us now."

I have to confess that he and the rest of us were not always quite so high-minded. From Italy, we had been transferred to Belgium and we then spent the final few months of the war fighting our way up through Germany, eventually ending up in Lubeck, on the Baltic coast. The situation there was especially chaotic as the British, the Americans and the Russians all converged on this key strategic port simultaneously.

At one point we came under a fierce bombardment from our Russian allies, who mistook us for the enemy. It was a couple of hours before they realised their mistake, by which time we had already endured the worst stonking we'd had since Anzio. Amid this sort of confusion, the whole place was pretty much ransacked by the conquering armies, especially marauding bands of renegade Russians, so when presented with the chance to relieve a small bank of the contents of its vaults, I'm afraid that we didn't think twice.

We were on our own, rumbling down a street on the outskirts of town in the Sherman when Ben spotted the bank building, which looked as though it had been abandoned. His eyes lit up. "I think we should definitely have a look in there, boys," he said. "You never know what we might find!" It turned out that the manager lived in the house right next door. When we found him and ordered him to open up he pretended at first that he didn't have the keys. When he continued to refuse our polite requests, we simply swung the Sherman around and, in true *Kelly's Heroes* fashion, put an armour-piercing shell straight through the main door. As a builder, I remember being quite upset about the awful mess the tank tracks made of the lovely marble steps leading up to the entrance of the bank. The manager, meanwhile, had suddenly had second thoughts about letting us in and produced the keys to the vault. A few minutes later we were walking out with armfuls of German banknotes.

There was so much of the stuff that it weighed the tank down when we loaded it aboard, making the thing so back-heavy that I could drive it quite easily using just one finger! When we came to share the money out there was far too much to count so we just split the notes into roughly equal piles.

"I never thought I'd come out of this war a millionaire," said Ben. And, of course, he didn't. Apart from anything else, he made the mistake of being too greedy and stacking his pile with higher denomination notes. It turned out that the Reichmark had been so heavily devalued that the higher denomination notes weren't worth the paper they were printed on. And, anyway, you couldn't take it back with you to the UK. You had to change any local currency you had into sterling at the dockside before you got on the ship and there was a limit of £50 worth per man. When it was my turn to go home on leave I kept slipping round the back to rejoin the queue, going round quite a few times during the one-and-half-days it took to go through the formalities of embarking everybody. As a result, I did actually manage to come back with enough cash to set myself up in business after the war.

Looking back now, people might say we were completely out of order, but at the time it didn't really occur to us that we were doing anything that wrong. However outrageous this may sound today, you have to think of it in context. As far as we were concerned, the Germans were the enemy we had been fighting through six years of bitter warfare and we didn't feel under any great moral obligation to respect their property. Looting was widespread. Everybody was at it. "Not really cricket is it, Wheatcroft?" remarked one of our officers. But that didn't stop him from readily accepting his share.

As for me, personally, I nearly didn't get to enjoy any of my ill-gotten gains. On May 8th, 1945 – my 23rd birthday and the day after Germany had surrendered unconditionally – I almost managed to get myself killed by what I reckon must have been one of the last shots fired in anger any-where in Europe.

Back to Blighty

I ACTUALLY HAD not just one, but two close shaves in the hours immediately following the peace announcement, the first of them at the very instant we learned that the war was finally over.

We were in the port at Lubeck, busy checking through one of the many German ships that had been abandoned there to see if there was anything worth 'salvaging', when a motorbike despatch rider arrived on the quayside looking for "Witt, Warr and Wheatcroft".

"Who wants them?" we asked suspiciously.

"They've got to report to HQ – they're going back to Blighty," he replied. "The war's over – it's official, as of three o'clock this afternoon – and arrangements are already being made to send people home on leave. For some reason they've decided to start at the bottom of the alphabet and work backwards, so those three are right at the top of the list."

We barely had time to take all this in before we heard the sound of an approaching aircraft. "Don't worry, it'll be one of ours," said the messenger, glancing skywards. Even as he spoke, the plane rolled into a dive and, with engine screaming, swooped low over the harbour, strafing the quayside from end to end. Clearly, nobody had told the pilot it was all over. We all dived for cover. I grabbed hold of a mooring rope and jumped over the side of the dock while the messenger himself pulled a bucket over his head and scrambled under a horse-drawn cart that was standing nearby.

When the attack was over I was left dangling helplessly from the rope and had to be hauled to safety by the others. The despatch rider, meanwhile, had got his head stuck firmly in the bucket. "One of ours, eh?" said Ben sarcastically, giving the bucket a whack with the butt of his rifle, which must have left the poor chap with a terrible headache.

Back at HQ, the first person we ran into was our battery commander, Lt Peter Webb. "Where do you lot think you're going with those stupid grins on your faces?" he demanded.

"We're going back to Blighty, sir," we chorused smugly.

"Not yet you're not," he said. "There's a German armoured unit out there that won't give up and we've got to go and fetch them out."

"Not us, sir," we insisted. "We're going back to Blighty. It's official."

The look of utter contempt that crossed his face when he heard this was terrible to behold. "If that's your attitude, then go to Blighty," he said scornfully. "But after all this time with the unit I would have thought you'd have had the decency to stick with your mates until we get the job done."

The way he said it made us feel so ashamed of ourselves that we threw our kitbags into his jeep there and then and headed back with him to where the unit were preparing to move out. There were about fifteen tanks in the column, led by a Stuart M5 light reconnaissance tank with me at the controls and Peter Webb riding up in the turret. We were out in the country, some distance outside the town, when I suddenly spotted the muzzles of some anti-tank guns protruding from the edge of the forest up ahead. No sooner had I called out a warning than we took a direct hit from what turned out to be the only shot they fired before surrendering.

Fortunately for us, it was a straightforward high explosive round rather than an armour piercing shell. Had it been the latter then I very much doubt that I would still be here to tell the tale. As it was, the shell exploded on impact, stopping the tank dead in its tracks and hurling us about violently inside. Up above, Peter Webb was slammed back against the turret, breaking several ribs, while down below I hit my head and was severely concussed. The next thing I remember was waking up in a hospital bed, complete with clean white sheets – the first time in nearly four years that I had enjoyed the luxury of sleeping on sheets. Fortunately, my injuries weren't serious, although it emerged much later that the cordite from the shell had left my eyesight permanently impaired. It still bothers me to this day.

During the next few months Ben and most of the other lads were sent back to England to be demobbed, but my return was delayed for more than a year, partly because of the punishment time I had to serve out. In the end, I was actually keen to stay on in Germany a little longer than I needed to because, by then, I had met and fallen in love with a local girl.

I had almost literally bumped into Helena Morgenstern in the street. As part of the occupation force, our unit had been moved 150 miles south to an area in the Harz Mountains, close to what was to become the East German border, and I had gone ahead with Peter Webb to do a recce and to sort out some suitable accommodation in the vicinity. We came eventually to a small mountain village called Walkenried am Harz, and as we turned through an arch into the main street our tank skidded slightly, hitting the kerb and startling Helena and her mother, who scurried into a doorway. We jumped down to apologise and I made a big fuss of Helena, much to Peter Webb's indignation.

"Wheatcroft! Behave yourself!" he warned. "She's hardly out of school."

"Don't be like that, sir," I replied cheekily. "You're only jealous because you're too old." We had a bit of a laugh about that before he reminded me that any fraternisation of that kind was still strictly forbidden at this time.

With our few words of German we then did our best to explain why we were there and what we were looking for and were directed to a couple of small hotels in the village. At the same time, I made sure I got a fix on exactly where Helena and her family lived. I was one of about twenty-four of us who were eventually billeted in the hotels, which were actually more like hostels, used in peacetime mostly by tourists who came to walk in the mountains. As we settled in I mounted a sort of one-man diplomatic offensive in an effort to win over the locals, who, quite understandably, were very wary of us at first. Our duties with the unit were fairly light during this period, which meant that I was able to spend quite a lot of time around the village, trying to make friends – especially with Helena and her family. In this respect, my rather unorthodox prowess as a hunter helped to break the ice.

There was a general shortage of food in the village and fresh meat, in particular, was in scarce supply. There were plenty of deer and wild boar in the surrounding forests, but they weren't always that easy to shoot – unless, that is, you went after them with a Bren gun! I returned from my first hunting trip with a three-ton truck loaded with enough venison and boar meat to keep the entire village fed for weeks. From then on, my standing in the community rose significantly.

I was especially popular with Frau Renschall, the proprietor of the hotel where we were living. She also happened to own the butcher's shop next door and soon found herself doing a roaring trade. Apart from that, I won further Brownie points by saving her dog, Reif, from summary execution after he bit one of our officers.

The officers, who were living in a big house some distance away, would occasionally carry out spot checks at night to make sure we were all present and correct. They knew that several of us had got girlfriends in the village by this time. Despite the strict ban on 'fratting' with German women just about everybody was courting by the time we'd been there a few months and it was suspected, quite rightly, that we weren't always sleeping in our own beds. You could usually fool the duty NCOs by putting a kit bag and a tin helmet under the covers. It suited most of them to turn a blind eye because they were at it themselves. The officers, however, were a bit more conscientious, especially the new ones who were starting to come in as replacements for those who had been demobbed.

On this particular occasion the raid was carried out by a newly-arrived young Lieutenant who made the mistake of sneaking round the back of the building, whereupon Reif, a very large and extremely effective guard dog, went for him. As the Lieutenant angrily nursed his wounds I was ordered to take Reif out and shoot him, instead of which I managed to spirit him away, arranging for him to be kept at a farm some distance away until all the fuss had died down. I thought nobody outside the family knew what I'd done until some time later, when the officer who had ordered Reif's execution said casually: "Oh, by the way, Wheatcroft, you can bring the dog back now, if you like."

The Renschalls had two sons, both of whom had been away, fighting in the German Army. By some extraordinary coincidence it then turned out that the younger of them was being held at a PoW camp just outside Leicester. He was still there when I eventually got home on leave and so I went to visit him. As well as passing on messages from his family, I was also able to thank him for the loan of his motorbike, which I'd been borrowing to ride around on while I was in Walkenried. He was delighted when I told him that I'd given it a thorough overhaul down at the unit motor pool.

In the meantime, his brother, who had been reported missing, presumed dead, on the Eastern Front, had suddenly turned up out of the blue after nothing had been heard of him for three years. You can imagine his parents' joy when, without any warning, he appeared on their doorstep one morning.

Sadly, there was to be no such happy ending for Helena's family, her brother, Gerhard, having been lost at Stalingrad in especially harrowing circumstances. Four years older than Helena, Gerhard was killed just a few days before Christmas, 1942, when he stepped on a tank mine twelve miles outside Stalingrad. A man's weight would not normally have been enough to detonate a tank mine, but Gerhard, a radio operator, happened to be carrying an 80-lb radio on his back at the time. The explosion literally blew him to pieces. No remains were ever found and so he had no grave.

Partly because of this tragedy, my courtship of Helena – known to everyone by her family nickname of Lenchen – had been progressing rather slowly. I got on well with her father, partly because he was working for a little local building firm, which meant that we had something in common that we could talk about. However, her mother, not surprisingly in the circumstances, was very protective of her daughter. When I did eventually manage to arrange a 'date', which amounted to no more than an innocent walk in the countryside, mum insisted on coming too.

By now, the rules on fraternisation had been relaxed and our romance gradually blossomed. Not even the obvious language difficulties got in the way. I'd had one steady girlfriend back in England who wrote to me regularly when I first went away to war, but nobody had ever had quite the same effect on me as Lenchen.

A petite figure, with dark brown hair and hazel eyes, she was the prettiest girl in the village by far. And as well as being stunningly attractive she also had the kindest heart and the sweetest nature. Quite what she saw in me, I'm not sure. As one of our closest mutual friends used to tell her many years later: "You could have had the pick of the British Army, Lenchen, and yet you had to go and choose Wheaty! Whatever came over you?" She used to love that. She would just smile and say: "I know – I must have been mad!"

Getting involved with me certainly didn't make life easy for her. Harry Hinge had started going out with her best friend, Lucy, and the four of us would sometimes have a meal together in the hotel. However, Frau Renschall was always careful to put us in a back room where nobody would see us because, despite my best efforts at a charm offensive, there were still plenty of locals who objected very strongly to any sort of fraternisation with the enemy. On top of that, Lenchen also had to cope with the fact that her mother, still grieving over the death of her son, was becoming increasingly fearful at the prospect of her daughter going away to live in England. This possibility was made even more painful for her by the fact that Lenchen was actually a twin, whose sister had died at birth.

It had got to the point where I was virtually living with the family. When our unit was then moved to the former German army camp at Fallingbostel, half-a-day's drive away, Frau Morgenstern must have hoped that the relationship would naturally fizzle out, but by then I was too smitten to be put off that easily. Being responsible for servicing the unit's vehicles and for taking them out on road tests gave me the perfect opportunity to organise unofficial transport to and from Walkenried for me and Harry and any of the other lads who had girlfriends there – "fratting wagons" as they became known. We had devised a way of using electric drills to wind on the mileage clocks so that we could account for the extra petrol rations needed for these trips.

Life in our unit had by this time settled into a routine that would probably strike a chord with anyone old enough to remember the popular American TV comedy series 'Sgt Bilko'. I, in particular, had established a very cosy set-up for myself in the motor pool, leaving me with plenty of scope to carry on various black market activities that involved everything from Lugers and Leicas to vintage wines and silk stockings.

On one occasion I was sent out with a mate of mine named George Viles to retrieve a truck that had crashed after being shot up by the Russians as it tried to smash through the newly-established border between East and West Germany, which, as I have already mentioned, ran very close to Walkenried. When George and I reached the abandoned vehicle and opened it up we found that it was packed with a large consignment of thimbles, scissors, lengths of suiting – and thousands of pairs of silk stockings.

Faced with this unexpected windfall and not quite sure what to do with it – any kind of looting had been strictly forbidden once hostilities were over – we first hid it in a nearby sandpit before towing the empty truck back to base. To our horror, it then began to rain very heavily and, realising that our valuable prize was in danger of being completely ruined, we had to sneak back in a three-tonner to fetch it out. Desperately trying to think of a new hiding place, I eventually came up with the idea of stuffing everything into a couple of Army water bowsers that we had standing round the back, unlikely to be used. I made some steel plates and screwed them down under the hatches so that nobody would stumble across our cache by accident. Over the next few weeks George and I became the most popular chaps in the unit as we handed out pairs of stockings to all and sundry, including Lenchen and all her friends in Walkenried. I also managed to send a whole lot back home to England in parcels that I smuggled out in one of the ration trucks so as to avoid having them opened by the censors.

Shortly after this I was offered the chance to be demobbed earlier than originally planned in line with a scheme that gave priority to anyone who was in the building trade in an effort to ease the labour shortage back in the UK, where post-war re-building was getting under way. However, mainly because of my relationship with Lenchen, I was quite happy where I was, so I turned the offer down, opting instead to stay on and serve out my full time.

This decision was smarter than I realised. As it turned out, not everyone in the truck containing the silk stockings had been killed when it was shot up by the Russian border guards. One of the four men on board had managed to escape and when he then gave himself up to the British authorities he revealed what had been inside the lorry. This led to a full-scale investigation and it wasn't long before George and I were identified as the prime suspects. We were both interrogated at length and the MPs even raided Lenchen's home. There they found what they thought was incriminating evidence – a jacket that was identified as having come from the looted truck and which happened to have a silver three-penny bit in the pocket. However, Lenchen's father insisted that he had got the jacket from somebody else and nothing could actually be proved. When I then turned down the chance to go back to England, my CO took it as a clear sign of my innocence and even went so far as to apologise for ever having suspected me!

Eventually, in August 1946, I was told that I would be going back to the UK in six weeks' time to be demobbed. I had already made up my mind to get married and I went back that very same day and popped the question. I can't remember now whether Lenchen answered 'Yes' or 'Jawohl'. Either way, we decided to get married straightaway, agreeing that she would then stay behind in Germany while I returned to England alone to find myself a job and get settled in. She would follow me over as soon as I had got everything set up and once the various formalities involved had been sorted out.

That was easier said than done and we actually ended up having to get married twice over. First, there was a church wedding that took place in Walkenried. Peter Webb, by now promoted to Captain, was my Best Man and quite a few of the lads from the unit were there, including Copperwheat. Ben, unfortunately, could not be there, having already returned home to Manchester by then. The large quantity of wine that I had managed to get hold of through black market connections in Hanover ensured that the reception was a pretty lively do.

Later, we were informed that for various bureaucratic reasons connected with the war, the marriage could not be considered legally valid back in England, so when Lenchen eventually came over in 1947 we had to go through a second ceremony at a Register Office in Leicester. At least that gave us a chance to celebrate with members of my family.

By then, the first of our seven children, Jill, had already been born in Germany. For Lenchen, the wrench of leaving her home and her family behind to come and make a new life in England was obviously very stressful, but it proved even more traumatic for her mother. When I told her about our plans she replied that she wouldn't dream of standing in the way of her daughter's happiness, but added tearfully: "If Lenchen goes, I'll be dead in eight weeks." Sure enough, six weeks after Lenchen had come to join me in England, we received a telegram to say that she had died suddenly. It turned out that she had actually been suffering from a coronary condition for some time, but Lenchen couldn't get it out of her head that she had died of a broken heart. It preyed on both our minds for some time.

Along with baby Jill, we had moved in with my mother at Eastcourt Road. My stepfather had died during the war, as had both the grandparents with whom I'd spent so much time when I was growing up. Then, immediately after the war, my stepbrother decided to move permanently to London, where there was plenty of work to be had repairing bomb damage. This meant he wanted to sell the house. He offered me first refusal, but although I was keen to buy it from him, I needed a mortgage – and getting such a thing was almost impossible for someone in my position. I had still not been finally demobbed at that point and you normally had no chance of getting a mortgage while you were still in the Forces and without a regular job.

There was only one hope. Before the war, I had done some work in my spare time for the boss of the local Earl Shilton Building Society. The Society had repossessed four pairs of unfinished semi-detached houses from a builder who had gone bust and I had helped to finish them off, putting in fire grates and doing all the tiling. I had got on well with the boss, who was impressed with the way I worked and who told me at the time: "If there's ever anything I can do for you, just let me know." I decided that this was a perfect opportunity to find out if he really meant it.

As soon as I next got home on leave, I jumped on my motorbike and rode the twenty-odd miles to Earl Shilton to see him. After six years I wasn't even sure if he'd even remember me, but he actually greeted me like a long-lost son, hugging me and pumping my hand. And when I then explained the situation he straightaway sat down with me and helped me to fill out the application form. By the next day, I had a cheque. I think it must have been one of the quickest mortgages ever done!

I came home for good shortly after that, but it was another year before Lenchen came over with Jill, then just a few weeks old. I, meanwhile, had set myself up as a jobbing builder, using my £50 gratuity and what remained of my share from the Lubeck bank raid and various other black market activities to invest in an ex-WD jeep and trailer, some bits of scaffolding, various tools and a cement mixer. I still have that first mixer to this very day. Built like a tank, I had it brought out ceremonially as a sort of lucky charm to christen each new building project right up until the late eighties and it is now a museum piece, restored and maintained in perfect working order as a permanent reminder of how it all began for me.

I started off in a very small way, fixing broken chimney pots, replacing fallen tiles and making good ceilings brought down by floods resulting from burst water pipes. The terrible winter of 1947 ensured that there was plenty of that kind of work around and right from the start I was able to earn quite a reasonable living for myself in this way. In fact, all that was holding me back at this stage were the restrictions imposed by the post-war rationing of building materials. Licences were required for everything from timber to plaster and at one time the amount anyone was allowed to spend on new materials for use on an extension or other home improvement was limited to just £10. That didn't give you much scope, even at a time when the average wage for a labourer was no more than about £9-a-week and when a three-bedroom semi could be had for less than £1,000.

The controls on the building of new houses were even tighter. You had to get a licence for each individual house and despite the huge demand for new homes after the war, these licences were only issued very sparingly and were extremely hard to come by unless you were a large, well-established builder, with good contacts in the local planning department. For someone like me, there was no chance.

The only consolation was that with so few new houses being built, a lot of people had no option but to stay where they were, extending and improving their existing properties instead of moving. So, if you were prepared to bend the rules and could find ways around the £10 limit, your services were much in demand. I soon had more than enough to keep me busy and in 1948, after about a year, I formally registered the company as Bernard Wheatcroft Ltd.

Around this time, I was driving home in the drizzle after work one day when I happened to spot a man walking along the road whom I recognised as someone I'd worked with on building sites before the war and I stopped to offer him a lift. I remembered Mick Higgins as the best and hardest-working labourer I'd ever seen. As we chatted away, I explained how I was just doing odd jobs but that my ambition was to start building new houses and added: "The minute I get some licences, I'd love you to come and join me."

That would suit him fine, he told me, because he was not very happy with the people he was working for at the time. "As soon as you want me, I'll be right there," he said. "In fact, I'd come tomorrow." And that's exactly what he did. He was the first man I ever employed and, like a lot of other people who came to work for me over the years, he stayed with me for life.

One of the great secrets of my success as a builder was the quality and the loyalty of my workforce. I picked the top men in every trade and then made a point of looking after them very well, to ensure that they stayed with me. As a result, I built up a team of people who were so good and so trustworthy that even when I was running several different sites at once, I never really needed foremen. I would just go round the sites myself in the morning, tell them what needed doing and then leave them to it.

Mick was a classic example of the sort of man I admired and valued most, the salt of the earth. He may have been only a labourer, but he turned even that into an art form. He had a rhythm and a method when he was working that was a joy to watch, as steady as a pendulum. As with anybody who is really good at what they do, he made it look easy. He never seemed to rush at anything and yet he always got finished quicker than anyone else.

I clearly remember the first job we did together after he had joined me. It involved digging a foundation trench and we agreed that we would start at either end and stop for a tea break when we met in the middle. I was a fit, strong 26-year-old chap and he was a good bit older, so I reckoned I would have no trouble keeping up. But after a couple of hours Mick suddenly stood up and announced: "Right, that's it. Time for a break."

"But we've not got to the middle yet," I protested.

"Well, I've done my half," said Mick with a grin. And, of course, he had. I, on the other hand, still had quite a way to go.

He was certainly the hardest worker I ever employed. I remember another occasion in the early days when he single-handedly unloaded a full lorryload of 3,500 bricks and ran them up the scaffold in the space of one afternoon, carrying them up on his head sixteen at a time. Most 'bricknobbers' – as we called them – couldn't manage half that number in a whole day.

I became very fond of Mick over the years. I've never been one for bringing back presents for everyone when I go abroad – not even the family. But I often used to get something for Mick, usually a pipe to add to his collection – even though I have always heartily disapproved of smoking. I really thought the world of that man, partly, I suppose, because he'd been there with me right from the start. And he was there to the very end, still working for me when he died suddenly, in his seventies. I have kept his last shovel as a memento of a very special man. At his funeral I was horrified to see that his grave had been dug very roughly. When Mick dug a trench the sides were so smooth and straight that it was as if they had been plastered. I told the vicar: "If the lid of his coffin weren't nailed down, Mick would get out and finish that hole properly before he got in!"

In the months after Mick joined me, back in 1948, more and more business started coming my way – mostly extensions and alterations – and, before too long, I found myself employing seven people. But I was still no nearer getting a licence to build a house. Even though I had bought a piece of land and had got planning permission for a pair of semi-detached houses, it made no difference. When I went to see about getting a licence I was turned down out of hand with the dismissive comment: "Come back in ten years' time."

That was the moment when my patience finally gave out. "I've just wasted five years of my life in the war," I snapped back. "I'm not going to waste another ten!" And I decided there and then that I would go ahead and build without a licence.

There's no doubt that I had come back from the war with a big chip on my shoulder. Although I'd only been away five years, it felt more like twenty in my head. And after everything I'd gone through in that time, my general attitude was that I was never again going to be buggered about by anybody, man or beast.

This showed through very clearly in a little incident that took place almost as soon as I got back to England. When the six men in our gun crew got together in Germany for the last time before starting to be demobbed, having gone through the whole war together and survived, we made a vow. We promised that as each of us finally got back to Blighty and to our home towns, we would go straight into the nearest pub, order a pint and drink to the other five – and to those of our mates who had not made it.

As soon as I got back to Leicester I duly went into the first pub I came to, intending to do just that. It was lunchtime, the place had just opened and there was nobody in the bar. I walked in still carrying my kitbag, ordered a pint and handed the barman a £1 note. He turned away, put it in the till and gave me the change from ten shillings. I said: "I think you've got it wrong, m'duck. I gave you a £1 note."

"Don't you try that one on with me," he replied, rather too aggressively for my liking.

I took one or two sips of my beer, which, as it happened, didn't taste too good, and said quietly: "This beer's off – and I'm telling you now that I'm not leaving this place until I get my pound back."

"Oh, I see – it's like that, is it?" he sneered, making it clear that in no way was I going to get any more change out of him.

Without another word, I simply picked up my pint and poured it over his head. Then, as he stood there dripping, with a rather surprised look on his face, I walked round behind the bar and opened the till. As I half-expected, my £1 was the only note in there. I took it and marched out without a backward glance. Caught out on the fiddle, there was no way the barman was going to do anything about it. The pub, as it happens, was called The Bricklayer's Arms.

Looking back now, I'm not particularly proud of myself for the way I handled that situation, even though I was in the right. I think it was probably just indicative of how a lot of us felt when we came back from the war. After everything that we'd gone through, and having lost a lot of friends along the way, we weren't about to take any nonsense from anybody. On top of that, my years in the Forces and my hero worship of Ben Warr had left me with a total contempt for all rules, regulations and any kind of authority. Given all of that, it was hardly surprising that I soon found myself in open conflict with the local council planning officials and what I regarded as their petty-minded formalities.

The plot of land on which I built that first pair of unauthorised houses was in Wigston. As I say, I had already got planning permission and had dug the footings before my request for a licence was turned down and I calculated that I wasn't actually taking too much of a risk in going ahead regardless.

Even if I was taken to court, the penalty for building without a licence was only £40-a-house, which wasn't a lot. And, given that there was such an acute shortage of housing in the country at the time, I didn't think it was likely they would ever dare try and force me to tear them down once they were up. At the same time, I didn't have to worry about any potential problem in selling them on because I initially intended to move into one of them myself, while my stepbrother, who had decided to move back from London by this time, was going to have the other one.

As it turned out, I had people queuing up to buy both of them long before they were finished. One chap was so determined to have the one that I had earmarked for myself that he came by almost every day as it was going up to badger me about it. I had to point out to him that not only did I not have a licence to build the house, but that there was also the added difficulty that when I got planning permission I had managed to avoid paying the usual development charge on the grounds that I was going to live there myself.

Despite this, he wouldn't take no for an answer. He reckoned that nobody would bother to check up on who was actually living there and that if they did then he would happily pay the development charge himself. I was still a bit reluctant to sell, partly because I had been putting in all kinds of little extras for my own benefit – which was partly why this chap was so keen. But in the end he made me an offer that I couldn't refuse and paid me on the spot, in cash, pushing a roll of those big, old-fashioned £5 notes into my hand.

Having got away with it once, I decided to try my luck again. This time I moved inside the boundaries of Leicester itself, to a plot that came with planning permission for nine houses. It belonged to my uncle, who had got hold of it before the war with the intention of building on it himself, but had never got round to doing anything with it. He agreed to sell it to me under an arrangement whereby I would pay him in instalments, as each house went up. Once again, the idea was that I would have the first one myself.

By now, however, the authorities had twigged what I was up to and I was summoned to the town hall to explain why I was building without a licence. Dressed as smartly as possible in my ill-fitting demob suit, the jacket of which was so tight that I could hardly button it up across my chest, I set off with every intention of being on my best behaviour, in the hope that I might be able to sweet talk my way out of trouble. Unfortunately, I then got off on completely the wrong foot by losing my temper and getting involved in a furious row with the officials in the outer office before I'd even got into the meeting at which my fate was to be decided.

I couldn't help myself. As I waited to be attended to, a woman in the queue immediately ahead of me was presenting some technical drawings for approval and I couldn't believe how rudely she was treated by the planning officer behind the counter. In the end I couldn't listen to it any more without saying something. "I don't think you'd talk to this lady like that if her husband were here," I told him.

"What's it got to do with you?" he said pompously, looking me up and down as if I'd just crawled out from under a stone.

A heated argument then ensued during which I swept all his papers off his desk and called him a horrible little bastard. From then on, it all got rather silly. "Would you care to repeat that in front of a witness?" he spluttered. I told him that I would be glad to do so, whereupon he disappeared into a back office and returned with the head of the department. They were like Laurel and Hardy, but without the sense of humour, the first one small and thin, his boss big and fat.

"Is it right – what you just called my man here?" demanded the fat one. "Because if it is, then you are going to have to apologise to him."

There was then a further shouting match, which ended with me shaking my finger at him and saying: "The only apology I'll make to him is that he's obviously not as big a bastard as you are!"

After all this, I was prepared for the worst when I was eventually shown into the oak-panelled office of the council bigwig with whom I now suspected that I was going to have a very awkward interview. Instead of which, I got a very pleasant surprise as I walked through the door.

Some months beforehand, one of my brickies had come to ask me if I could do a favour for someone. He explained that his father worked as a gardener for the City Surveyor of Leicester, a wonderful chap named John L. Beckett, famed as the man mainly responsible for re-developing the city after the war. He had a young son who had broken his back in an accident, as a result of which he had to wear a metal corset and as part of his therapy the boy had to be walked on a pony. His father had bought him a pony for this purpose, along with a small portable stable unit, and he needed someone with a truck to dismantle the stable, transport it the fourteen miles to his home and re-erect it in a paddock behind the house. The gardener had suggested that as we had a four-ton lorry we might be able to help.

It snowed heavily during the weekend that we did the job, which turned out to be much harder than we expected, the truck sinking into the sludgy, snow-covered paddock at one stage and getting stuck. Anyway, we eventually got it all finished around Sunday lunchtime and Mr Beckett made it clear how grateful he was, thanking us profusely. He even insisted on paying me extra for the use of the truck, despite me saying that it wasn't necessary. Unbuttoning the breast pocket of the battle dress jacket I was wearing, he tucked three crisp, old-fashioned £5 notes inside.

He then suggested going down to his local pub for a drink. It was dead on closing time when we got there and yet he still managed to get in a couple of pints for each of us. That was quite something at a time when most landlords were very strict about last orders. I remember being very impressed. Not only was he a gentleman – but a gentleman with clout!

It was the same Mr Beckett who now faced me across the desk at the City Hall. "Don't I know you?" he said with a smile, as soon as I walked in.

When I reminded him where we had met before he smiled and leaned forward to press a button on his desk. This rang a little electric bell in his secretary's office and when she came running in to see what he wanted he asked her to make two cups of coffee. I was very impressed with that little bell. In fact, I used to go on about it so much that years later somebody bought me one just like it as a present, so that I could have it fitted in my own office – although I never had the nerve to use it! Another little thing that stands out in my memory about that meeting is that I was offered sugar with my coffee, a real luxury in those days of rationing.

After glancing through the reports in front of him, Mr Beckett looked up and said: "You're in a bit of trouble here, aren't you? Tell you what, though. If I call these two chaps in, would you apologise to them?"

"I'm sorry, sir, but, to be honest I don't think I can do that," I said. "They really are a right pair of bastards."

He shook his head and sighed deeply. "Look, I know that as well as you do," he said. "But you don't need to go and tell them to their faces! Now, leave it to me and let's see if I can sort things out."

He then called them in and said very pleasantly: "Gentlemen, you've put me in a very difficult position. Mr Wheatcroft here happens to be a personal friend of mine and has recently done me and my family a great favour. So, I wonder whether on this occasion you could possibly over-look this rather unfortunate incident? I'm sure it was just things said in the heat of the moment."

"Of course, sir," said the fat one, bowing and scraping and almost wringing his hands in oily deference.

"Oh – and by the way," added Mr Beckett. "Mr Wheatcroft has just come out of the Forces. He's starting out on his own as a builder and he badly needs some licences. I wonder if you could look after him?"

When I walked out of the building an hour or so later I had nine licences in my pocket, each of them worth a premium of £200 extra on top of the price of a new house to prospective buyers desperate to have one. From that moment on I never really looked back.

Fastest Man Backwards

To be really successful in business, you need a bit of luck. Hard work alone is not always enough. Getting those licences, against all the odds, gave me a flying start and I took full advantage of that, wasting no time at all in getting those nine houses up. I then had another stroke of good fortune.

As planned, I myself had moved into the first of the nine houses and within a year it almost doubled in value. At around the same time I happened to be driving along Welford Road, just off the main A50 out of Leicester, when I spotted a For Sale notice going up outside what appeared like an extremely interesting property. Closer inspection revealed a large, late-Victorian house, surrounded by about six acres of land and one glance was enough to tell me that it would not only make a wonderful home for my growing family, but that there was also bags of potential for development in the extensive grounds. Properties at that time were being snapped up the minute they came on the market, selling so quickly that some 'For Sale' signs were reversible, with 'Sold' already written on the other side in anticipation of an almost instant turn-around. I surreptitiously switched this one round to deter any other prospective buyers before going straight off to the estate agent to negotiate and by five o'clock that same evening I owned the place.

The asking price was £3,500 – the equivalent of about £700,000 today.

This was a hefty amount and more than I could really afford at the time, especially as the nine-bedroom house, which included a fifty-foot lounge and a vast cellar, needed a great deal doing to it. I nevertheless decided to go ahead, confident that it would prove to be a sound long-term investment. Just how sound became clear only a matter of weeks later when it was announced that the A50 was to be widened into a dual carriageway, mainly to cater for the heavy traffic going in and out of the USAF base at nearby Bruntingthorpe, and that this would necessitate taking a slice of my land, bringing the boundary of the road much nearer to the house itself on one side.

The amount of compensation calculated under the terms of a proposed Compulsory Purchase Order was paltry and so I, along with a local garage owner who was going to lose his forecourt, made it clear that we were prepared to fight it through the courts, at which point the County Council offered to negotiate a settlement in order to speed up the process.

I argued strongly that with the main road coming that much closer the house would be ruined and would immediately lose most of its value. That might have been true had I been going to keep it as it was – a big house standing alone in its own grounds. But, of course, I already had major development plans in mind for the land. So it was an unexpected bonus when the Council finally caved in and agreed to pay me exactly £3,500 for the bit of land they were after. Having effectively got the whole place for nothing, I then went on over the years to build no less than ten houses on the remaining land, with planning permission for another five, while still retaining a sizeable garden for myself. All in all, it turned out to be one of my more profitable ventures.

That house, known as The Firs, remained the family home for the next eighteen years, right up until the early seventies. By then, all seven of our children had been born, Jill, the eldest, being followed by Susan, David, Joy, Kevin, Tina and Mandy. The house itself is still there, although it has since been converted into offices – and, sadly, one landmark feature has disappeared altogether. There used to be a large holly tree, clearly visible from the main road outside, which I had trained up a special metal frame so that it was in the shape of a perfect Christmas tree. Every year we would decorate it with about a thousand fairy lights that would come on automatically at dusk and go off again around midnight. People from miles around used to make a point of driving past to show their kids. What nobody ever twigged was that an electrician had somehow managed to hook the lights into the power supply in the road outside, which was why they always came on and went off at exactly the same time as the street lighting. Whilst I obviously knew about this, I rather cheekily figured that as the display was helping to provide a bit of entertainment for the public, it was only fair that the council should make a small contribution!

It was shortly after we moved into that house that my business really started to take off. The abolition of the licence system and the ready availability of building materials once rationing ended in the early fifties had opened the floodgates for development. As far as I was concerned, it was really just a matter of being in the right place at the right time – and with the right attitude. I was full of youthful drive, energy and ambition, along with a headstrong readiness to ignore the risks and go for the main chance. At a time when other builders were quite content to build one house a month, I was already thinking of completing one a week. I remember the bank manager scoffing at me when I first told him this.

"I know big firms that have been in business for twenty years who have never got anywhere near building that many," he said dismissively.

My solicitor was equally sceptical at first. I had gone to him to ask if he could complete the sale of nine houses within ten weeks and after pausing for a moment to mull it over he replied: "Well, yes, I think we should just about be able to manage that. Have you got the names of the purchasers?"

"Oh, no," I said. "We can't even go on the ground until Monday!"

He looked at me cock-eyed, thinking that I must be joking. But when I got those houses finished exactly nine weeks later he couldn't wait to tell me: "Listen, Tom, we've always got plenty of cash in our private client account, so if you ever need to borrow anything from now on just let me know and you can have it at a very low rate of interest."

I was building all over the place by this time – although never outside the Leicestershire county boundary. That's always been my policy. I've always stuck to my own patch, which I know like the back of my hand. Such local knowledge can give you a big advantage when it comes to identifying and buying up the best potential building plots before everyone else cottons on. I was always quite shrewd in that respect. I started with small developments of six, nine or twelve houses and from doing one house a week I was soon up to a pair a week. Then, in 1958, I set my sights even higher with the purchase of a much larger site where there was already planning permission for an entire estate of one-hundred-and-twenty-five houses.

This was quite a gamble. No other private builder in the area had ever tackled a single project of that size before, but having weighed it all up I was confident that I could do very nicely out of it as long as I got the whole lot finished within a year. That way the money wouldn't be out too long before I started getting a return. In order to achieve that, however, I had to double the size of my workforce and invest in extra plant. I also had to streamline all our working systems.

At the yard in Aylestone Lane, between Leicester and Wigston, where my fast-growing company was now based, I set up a joinery workshop in which we started making our own staircases, doors and window frames, thereby saving time and money as well as guaranteeing a constant supply. I also had the logistics at each site worked out very precisely, so that instead of all the materials simply being dumped at a central collection point, everything, right down to the last bag of cement, was carefully delivered to various strategic areas, exactly as and when it was needed. This helped to cut out waste and to ensure maximum efficiency. All that kind of thing is now routine, but in those days it was quite a new concept.

From the mid-fifties onwards the soaring demand for new homes was such that we could still scarcely build them fast enough to keep up. We certainly never had to advertise and didn't even need a show home. People would come to the office and put their names down as soon as they saw the foundations going in. For any builder who really knew what he was doing it was like a licence to print money, so much so that at times it seemed almost criminal. That's how I felt about it – and it seemed I wasn't the only one who formed that opinion. My nearest neighbour, also a builder but not quite in the same league, became so jealous of my success that he committed the unforgivable sin of getting in touch with the Inland Revenue to tip them off about what he considered to be my over-extravagant lifestyle, suggesting that they should perhaps take a closer look at my affairs.

The first I knew about it was when I was summoned to a meeting with the Inspector. This was held in an ex-Army depot down in Woking, the sort of place where even the valves on the central heating radiators had been polished until they shone. As I walked in I thought to myself: "Ooh, you bugger, this is serious!"

I had gone along accompanied by a small army of advisors, including a taxation QC, my accountant and my solicitor. The Inspector had also lined up his own team of investigators. As the interview got underway, I couldn't believe how much they knew about me. Almost the first thing the Inspector said to me after we had shaken hands and sat down was: "Now, tell me, Mr Wheatcroft, how's that expensive £5-a-square-yard carpet of yours wearing?"

Well, even I didn't know exactly how much it had cost. I knew it was top quality Wilton, but Lenchen had been in charge of all the furnishing and interior decoration at the house and I had settled the bills without paying too much attention to the price of individual items. I tried not to appear too surprised. "As it happens, we're very pleased with it," I said nonchalantly.

"And how's that little red bomb of yours going?" he inquired, obviously referring to the brand new two-seater Daimler sports car that I had recently splashed out on.

"Very nicely, thank you," I replied, as calmly as I could.

It went on like this all morning until about 12.30pm, when we were told that there would be a ninety-minute break for lunch. "There's a very nice restaurant across the road that might suit you," said the Inspector, adding pointedly: "We can't afford that. We go to a little café nearby."

"Well, that seems a pity," I said. "Perhaps I could invite you to join us in the restaurant?" I didn't think I was doing anything wrong, but received a hefty kick under the table from my QC. However, the Inspector and his team immediately accepted. In fact, the hearing lasted just over three days altogether and I ended up taking them to lunch every day.

Then, on the Thursday morning, the Inspector suddenly announced that he would be prepared to settle for £100,000 in additional tax. This, I was told later, is a routine ploy. They offer you a deal just to see how you react. If you seem a bit too keen to accept, it suggests you might have much more to hide.

Anyway, my QC turned the offer down flat, insisting that I didn't owe them a ha'penny. That, as far as I concerned, was absolutely right. To be frank, I was always too busy running the business to bother about trying to fiddle my tax. Even so, I was taken by surprise when the Inspector, without further ado, closed the file in front of him and turned to me with a smile, saying: "OK, Mr Wheatcroft. That's fine. I'm pleased to say that your books are perfect. We've been through everything and it's all in order. I shall be happy to give you a clearance notice."

As we all prepared to leave he thanked me for the lunches, adding: "I enjoyed that bit very much, but I wouldn't like to say that I look forward to seeing you again."

I replied that I certainly shared that sentiment, adding that the whole experience had been a bit of a strain.

"Were you seriously worried, then?" he asked.

I admitted that although I was sure I hadn't done anything wrong, I had, of course, been anxious. "The problem is that I've got no foremen," I explained. "I do everything myself. So, all the while I've been down here being grilled by you lot, there's been nobody looking after the business."

As we shook hands he assured me: "Well, you don't need to worry any more. You just keep on earning the money and let these fellows sort the paperwork out for you."

I had come to admire that man. He was tough, but he was fair – and he played everything by the book. Except, that is, in one respect. As he explained to me right at the end, he was not allowed to reveal where the tip-off had come from. However, he then very pointedly left the papers that included the informant's name lying on top of the table, in full view, while he went out of the room, saying: "I've got to spend a penny – I won't be a minute." So, of course, I peeked. And that's how I found out who it was who had shopped me.

I was quite shocked by the discovery. I never would have believed it of that man. He had always seemed very friendly and had even asked me on several occasions if I'd like to go into partnership with him. I never let on that I knew it was him who had done the dirty on me. However, I made sure I got my own back, going along to land auctions and bidding against him so as to push the price up, without having any serious intention of actually buying.

I suspected that it was probably my growing collection of cars that had prompted his jealousy. Shortly before all this happened I had actually bought two Daimlers at the same time – a Conquest Century drop-head saloon and the two-seater DS 18, the "little red bomb" referred to by the tax inspector. The cars came complete with the distinctive registration numbers LUT2 and UT3, which had no particular personal significance, but were kindly given to me by Daimler as a bit of a bonus for a valued customer. At that stage, I already had a Mercedes 220S – one of the earliest examples of this particular model to be imported into this country after the war – with the registration KUT 1. And I must admit that I did take great pride in lining them all up outside the house, so maybe I was asking for trouble.

From the moment that I started making serious money, cars were my only real extravagance. I've never been one for yachts or private jets or villas in the Caribbean; I've never even had particularly grand houses. And wherever I've lived, the garage has always been one of the most important features. Before I opened the museum at Donington I had a split level bungalow built in the grounds of The Firs, with the lower level converted into a two-tier garage for my collection of classic sports and grand prix cars. Later, when I moved house, I drained the large swimming pool of the new place and turned it into a three-tier stacker.

I don't know where this passion came from originally. For as long as I can remember, I have always been fascinated with cars and motorbikes. It is as if I was born with petrol in my blood. The first car of any kind that

I ever owned was a Jeep that I bought, along with a trailer, at an army surplus sale in Sheffield, for £15. I did 104,000 miles in that Jeep. It was brilliant, capable of pulling anything up to a ton in weight. To plaster a pair of houses you needed a ton of lime and a ton of plaster – everything I needed seemed to come in measures of a ton at that time – so it was ideal. After that I bought an old Humber armoured car, also for about £15, took the body off and converted it into a shooting brake. That pulled an even bigger trailer, capable of taking three mixers if need be.

My first brand new saloon car was a Vauxhall Velox, followed by the 2-litre Mercedes 220S. That was one of the best cars I ever had, about 15% better in performance than anything else on the road at the time. Only six were allowed into the country at first, two of which went to the Nottingham dealers B&K Thomas. I had been doing some work for them and they tipped me off in advance that they were coming in, which was how I managed to get hold of one.

I had always been a big fan of Mercedes, ever since getting to drive one or two of them in Germany at the end of the war, and over the next few years I built up a collection of sixteen – including several of the same model in different colours and styles. Among them were two 220Ss, two 190SLs (a white hard top one and a black soft top) and no fewer than five of the six-cylinder, 3-litre 300SLs. That has to rate as one of the sexiest sports cars ever built; there was certainly nothing to touch it in its day. I had one in black, one in red and one in white.

I also had two of the special gull wing models, including what was only the second one ever to come into this country – the first having gone to the great motorsport enthusiast and renowned private entrant Rob Walker. It was actually that very same 300SL that Rob was driving on the fateful night in 1959 when he and Mike Hawthorn raced each other along the Hog's Back section of the A3 in Surrey and Mike ended up losing control of his Jag and crashing to his death. Mike had apparently come up behind Rob quite by chance and it has been suggested that the sight of his old friend in the German sports car might have been like a red rag to a bull to the patriotic Hawthorn, seized with an instant determination to prove the superiority of his British Jag.

I was so well in with Mercedes by the time that I ordered the first of my 300SLs that I actually managed to get it a fortnight before the car's official launch date. To my great embarrassment, I then managed to write it off within days of taking delivery and had to send it back to the factory in two halves. Later, I decided to have a second one in black, as well as the original silver one. I suppose that was a bit over-the-top, but I certainly did make full use of them all. The only problem was that it got so confusing at one time that I ended up being warned for having two cars on the road simultaneously with the same KUT 1 registration! I was in the process of switching this from one 220S to the other and, without thinking, made the mistake of taking them both out on the same day, only to be spotted by an eagle-eyed traffic policeman.

Also among my collection at this time were a 38/250SS and a 500K that had been specially custom-built for the legendary pre-war racing driver B. Bira – Prince Birabongse Bhanutej Bhanubandh to give him his full title. A member of the Siamese royal family, the Prince first got into motor racing while a student at Cambridge University and went on to become one of the stars of the immediate pre-war era, the highest placed 'also ran' behind the Mercedes and Auto Unions in the 1937 Donington Grand Prix.

My own interest in motor racing had been revived in 1950 with a visit to the first post-war British Grand Prix at Silverstone. The circuit had been open less than two years at that time and the grandstand, I remember, consisted of little more than scaffolding. Since then, I have never missed a single British Grand Prix or any other non-championship Formula One event held in the UK.

Of all those early fifties events, it was the one held at Silverstone in 1956 that stands out most vividly in my memory. The winner, in a Lancia Ferrari D50, was Juan-Manuel Fangio. The great man was already in his forties by then and little did I ever imagine as I watched him drive to victory over Peter Collins that afternoon that he was destined to become a close friend during the course of the next forty years, inviting me on several occasions to stay with him at his home in Argentina.

The friendship started when I made one of my first visits to the

Argentinian Grand Prix and got introduced to him there. From then on we regularly bumped into each other at various events around the world and later, after I had bought Donington, he came there on several occasions to make guest appearances and to look around the museum. We were of the same sort of vintage, with a shared passion for classic grand prix cars, and we just got on very well right from the start. He didn't speak much English, but we seemed to understand each other perfectly, conversing with a lot of gestures and sign language.

I loved every moment of being with him, partly because I admired him so much but also because he was blessed with such a wonderfully warm and generous personality. I remember talking to Jackie Stewart about him one day at some event at which Fangio was also present, and saying to Sir Jackie: "It's a funny thing, you know, but whenever I'm in a room with him I get this warm feeling – as if I'm glowing." And Sir Jackie replied: "Tom, I'm exactly the same."

The last time I saw him was when he invited me to be a guest at his 80th birthday party in Buenos Aires. That was an extraordinary experience, not least because he was such a hero in his own country, treated like royalty wherever he went. He had arranged to meet me at the airport and when I flew in I was amazed to find myself being whisked straight from the tarmac to his waiting car, by-passing customs and all the other airport formalities. At one point a customs official came chasing after us, but the man who was helping me to carry my bags had a quiet conversation with him, during which the only words I recognised were 'Fangio', 'amigo' and 'El Presidente', whereupon the official saluted smartly and waved us through.

Fangio himself then drove me the four hundred miles to his home village and I was reminded of a story I'd read of how, at the very peak of his fame, the whole village would turn out to welcome him home after each new triumph on the world's grand prix circuits. The village children would scan the distant horizon for the telltale plume of dust raised by his car as he sped along the gravel roads and as soon as they spotted it the excited cry would go up: "Here he comes – look at the clouds!"

He had grown up doing long-distance 7,000-mile races in South

America, driving on loose mountain roads where he would be going sideways all the time, just like a rally driver. That's how he developed his natural hand, eye and foot co-ordination and his lightning reactions.

I've got a favourite photograph of him in action that, for me, sums up his whole life story. It was taken at Rouen during the 1957 French Grand Prix, at a spot on the circuit just a few yards from where you went from a tarmac surface into a cobbled hairpin, with a thirty-foot drop down an embankment on one side. And there you see him, flat out, sliding sideways on opposite lock, with a big dent in the nose cone. Whenever I look at that picture I think to myself – that was Fangio, from the day I first watched him race to the very last time I ever saw him at that 80th birthday party in Buenos Aires.

What an occasion that was! The guests included everybody who was anybody in Argentina – right up to and including the President himself. But when Fangio made his entrance, he got an even bigger standing ovation than El Presidente. And there, too, was I, hardly able to believe that I had been placed on the top table. It was one of the proudest moments of my life.

I have a very special and lasting personal memento of my friendship with Juan-Manuel. Throughout his whole career he only ever used two helmets. I happened to mention in passing how much I would like to have one for my collection and it arrived almost by return post. Unfortunately, we were in the middle of the Falklands War at the time and it was intercepted by Customs, who rang me to say that as it had come from a country with which we were at war it would have to be destroyed. I explained what it was and who had sent it, but they weren't impressed. They were about to burn it!

I was horrified. I told them: "Hold on! Whatever happens, that helmet must not be burnt. I'm going to do every mortal thing possible to make sure that it is given clearance. I've got contacts in the Government and if necessary I'll go right to the top!" As it turned out, I didn't have to go quite that far. I got in touch with my MP and he sorted it all out.

That helmet remains the pride of my collection, along with the one worn by Nuvolari when he won the 1938 Donington grand prix and the one that Sir Stirling Moss was wearing when he had the horrific crash at Goodwood in 1962 that ended his racing career. The collection, which has an estimated value of over £500,000, also includes those worn by Alberto Ascari, Froilan Gonzales, Mike Hawthorn, Graham Hill, Niki Lauda, Nigel Mansell, Ayrton Senna and Michael Schumacher.

Back in 1956, that same British Grand Prix won by Fangio was also memorable for a blistering performance from Stirling Moss in a Maserati 250F. Having started in pole position, he recorded the fastest lap and led for much of the race before unluckily being forced to retire near the end with a broken back axle.

Stirling was another of the great drivers I got to know well over the years after that and his 1961 Monaco-winning Lotus Climax 18 was one of the first cars I bought for my grand prix collection. It also featured prominently in one of my more embarrassing moments. It had only just been delivered to the yard at Aylestone Lane, where I had set up a workshop to restore and service my fast-growing collection of classic cars, and I was so excited when the mechanics got it fired up that I couldn't wait to take it for a spin. As it happened, I had to pop down to one of my sites at Oadby, about five miles away, and I rather foolishly decided that it would be fun to go in the Lotus.

People in the street were doing double takes and walking backwards into lamp-posts as they turned to gawp at the sight of a full-blown Formula One car crackling along the suburban road. Amazingly, I got almost all the way to the site before an incredulous traffic cop pulled me over.

"What on earth do you think you're doing?" he demanded, taking off his cap and reaching for his notebook.

"Ooh, I am sorry, officer," I said, rather sheepishly. "I've only just bought this car and when we got it started up I felt like a kid again. I couldn't resist the temptation to have a little go in it."

We then got chatting and it turned out that this copper was a bit of a racing fan himself, so I invited him to sit behind the wheel. By now some of the lads from the building site had gathered round and it looked as if I might have talked my way out of trouble – until the officer went to get out and burned his arm on the hot exhaust pipe. That put him back in a right bad mood and, of course, he threw the book at me – driving without lights, without tax, without insurance, you name it! I think I was done on eighteen counts altogether. So it turned out to be an expensive joyride, but I reckoned it was worth every penny.

Another highlight of the 1956 season for me was a visit to Sicily for the Syracuse Grand Prix. Tony Brooks had won a sensational victory there the previous year in a B-Type Connaught – one of which I later acquired for my collection – eclipsing the might of the full works Ferrari team to become the first British driver since Sir Henry Segrave in 1924 to win a Continental grand prix. I drove down through Italy in the Daimler DS 18, curious to revisit the scene of my wartime landing of 1943 and bent on realising the dream I had had, while marching up Mount Etna all those years earlier, of driving up that same road in a high-powered sports car. To be able to do just that was a deeply nostalgic experience – although the climb wasn't quite as steep as I remembered it.

There was an even more poignant moment for me during the weekend. Les Leston had a bad crash in practice when his drive shaft snapped, sending his car spinning into a low stone wall and over it into a neighbouring cemetery, where it burst into flames. Les jumped out with his clothes on fire and was taken off to hospital, but he insisted on returning the next day, all bandaged up, to watch the race from a stretcher. It was this accident that inspired him soon afterwards to start the successful business that pioneered the development of flame-resistant clothing for drivers.

It happened that there were quite a few lads from our unit buried in the cemetery where the car ended up and when I walked round it later I was terribly upset to see names that I recognised on some of the gravestones. This brought a lot of sad memories flooding back. The experience actually affected me so deeply that I vowed never again to visit a war cemetery. Later, when I was with a group of friends at Anzio, I stayed in the car while they went to look at the war graves there. I couldn't bear to join them.

That 1956 Syracuse Grand Prix was again won by Fangio, with Luigi Musso in second place and Britain's Peter Collins third, all of them in

Lancias. The following year I went back to see Peter Collins win from Musso, both of them in Lancia Ferraris, with Stirling Moss third in a Vanwall. Moss, who might have won but for problems with his pit stops, duelled excitingly with the Italian Piero Taruffi for third place, just pipping him on the line.

The best bit about that particular trip by far was that, having got to know Tony Vandervell quite well by then, I actually got the chance to drive Stirling's Vanwall – the first time I had been behind the wheel of a grand prix car. It was practice day and I was invited to move it from the garage to the paddock. This should have involved no more than about a couple of hundred yards on the track itself, but as I entered the circuit I pretended not to notice the marshal who was directing me to turn left and straight along to the paddock. Instead, I turned right – and managed to sneak a complete lap. That was the greatest thrill of my life up until the moment when I actually acquired an historic grand prix car of my own.

That came about, quite by chance, in 1963. I hadn't originally intended to buy such a car – I simply wanted a painting of one. By this time I was a fully-fledged motor racing fanatic, regularly travelling all over Europe and even further afield to watch the main events, and I got to thinking that it would be rather a nice idea to commission a top motorsport artist to do me a portrait of one of my favourite historic cars – the Ferrari 125.

I was quoted a price of £900 and although that was quite a lot of money at the time, I was about to give the go-ahead when I happened to be flicking through *MotorSport* magazine one day and noticed an advert offering what was described as Peter Whitehead's 1949 Ferrari 125 for sale for £1,000. So, for an extra £100 I could have the real thing! The only slight hitch was that the car was in Australia, which meant that I would have to buy it unseen. However, when I contacted the vendor, a chap named Harwood, it all sounded legit, so I did the deal and arranged to have it shipped over.

There was great excitement at Aylestone Lane a few weeks later when the car arrived in a large packing case. Unfortunately, we found when we got it out that although it looked fantastic, it was not quite the genuine article. Instead of the original 1.5-litre V12 supercharged engine that had been in it when Luigi Villoresi drove it to victory in the 1949 Italian Grand Prix and when Peter Whitehead later bought it and raced it Down Under in the Tasman Series, it now had a 5-litre V8 Chevrolet engine.

I was obviously disappointed, but there was not much I could do about it at that stage so we decided to go ahead and start it up. That proved impossible at first because the sea air had got to it during the six-week voyage from Australia and it just wouldn't fire up. Even when we cleaned all the plugs and points, it still wouldn't catch. At that point we decided to give it a push.

From outside the workshop, the yard at Aylestone Lane sloped all the way down to the main gate about one hundred yards away, perfect for a bump start. I got behind the wheel, the lads gave an almighty shove and within a couple of wheel turns the engine spluttered and then roared into life.

Well, of course, I had to put on a bit of a show, didn't I? So I gave it some welly, leaving a couple of nice black lines on the yard. But then, as I came up to the gate and dived for the brake, I found that the clutch plates wouldn't disengage – again, they must have been affected by the sea air. As a result, I shot straight out across the road – which, almost miraculously, was deserted at the time – went straight through the wooden gates of the house opposite and ended up stuck in a flowerbed halfway up the drive, thankfully stopping just short of the garage doors.

The woman who lived there was a rather awkward customer at the best of times, always complaining about noise and such like and, even though I immediately promised to put right all the damage, she created merry hell, threatening to sue me and all sorts. I eventually managed to calm her down, but the car, meanwhile, was in a rather sorry state, the nose dented and the underside grazed where it had banged over the kerb. I was heartbroken. I'd hardly unwrapped my new toy before breaking it. It wasn't to be the only time that happened!

Undeterred by this early setback I went on to have enormous fun with that car, not to mention several more narrow squeaks. I've never officially raced any of my grand prix cars – at forty-two I was already a bit too old by the time I started collecting them and my eyesight had never been that good since the incident at the end of the war. However, I've had just about every one of them out on a circuit at some time or another.

The main problem with the Ferrari 125 was that the Chevy engine was too powerful for the car. As a result, it was very twitchy once you put the power on and, given the slightest excuse, it would spin like a top. I soon lost count of the number of times I'd spun it. I don't think there is a corner at Oulton Park where I didn't go off in it at one time or another.

Until I bought Donington, Oulton was where I did most of my driving, regularly booking time for myself on the track there. First time out in the 125 I had the biggest spin of my life. I was going flat out down the back straight when, suddenly, she just went. I thought for a moment that I could catch her, but she spun and spun and spun. It was sheer luck that I missed everything, actually going clean under the bridge and somehow managing to stay on the track.

The next time I was up there, I found myself sharing the circuit with members of the Jaguar Club, including a chap who held the lap record for a sports car with a lightweight aluminium E-type. The atmosphere was quite competitive and there was a lot of friendly banter. I set off like a bomb, but, true to form, I didn't even make it round the first lap before coming off after giving it a bit too much welly through one of the corners. However, I had a lovely day's racing and was quite proud of the speeds I'd done, knocking the E-type's lap record into a cocked hat.

Afterwards, the Jaguar Club crowd held a dinner and prize-giving at a local restaurant up the road and very kindly invited me to join them. It turned out they had organised a little surprise, presenting me with a cake that had been decorated with the message 'Fastest Man Backwards'!

We all had a good laugh about that. At the same time, the E-type owner whose record I'd broken gave me a serious, though good-natured, warning. "You're going to kill yourself if you're not careful," he said, with genuine concern. "You're going into the corners 15/20mph quicker than the car's made for."

As this chap was a top insurance broker and no doubt well versed on the subject of risk management, I should, perhaps, have heeded his advice more closely than I did. As it was, it took a really bad crash to convince me that I really should slow down a bit. This followed very shortly after another incident in which I had once again gone off at Oulton Park and into a tree, albeit very gently. I had almost come to a stop and was only doing about 5mph, so the impact was very slight. There was virtually no apparent damage and I thought nothing of it.

The next time I had the car out was at Silverstone. I was first off, early on a beautiful summer's morning. I had this lovely wide track to myself and I was thinking: "Ooh, ain't this grand!" Then all of a sudden, halfway down the straight, I noticed that although the wheels were wobbling, I couldn't feel anything through the steering wheel. I hardly had time to register that something was seriously wrong before the car slewed wildly out of control, turned over and started rolling. The next thing I knew I was sitting in the middle of a cornfield, slightly stunned, with the car nowhere in sight and Roy Salvadori bending over me, anxiously asking if I was all right.

When we did a post mortem on the wreckage of the car, we discovered that the collision with the tree at Oulton, gentle though it had seemed at the time, had actually caused fatal damage within the steering column, twisting the splined steering rack without quite causing it to snap right off. Although there was no visible sign that anything was drastically wrong, it was only just holding and, of course, as soon as I took the car out at Silverstone and there was any kind of pressure, it sheared clean off.

I was extremely fortunate to get away with that. As I lost control, the car apparently somersaulted several times, end over end, throwing me out as it did so. It finished up some distance from where I was eventually found, dazed and confused, my disorientation made worse by the fact that I'd lost my glasses and couldn't see properly. First on the scene was Roy Salvadori, who happened to be testing that day. Having witnessed the whole rather spectacular accident at close quarters, he was pleasantly surprised to find me still in one piece. Amazingly, nothing was broken and my only injuries were severe grazing of the knees and elbows.

At that point I decided that it was time to retire the 125 from active racing duty. But that was by no means the end of the story. Many years later I succeeded in tracking down the original 1.5-litre engine and managed to buy it back. It had been installed in a powerboat down in Australia and although the block had been painted green in order to protect it from the seawater, it was still in pretty good condition.

I found it with the help of the man from whom I'd got the car in the first place. Mr Harwood and I were never the best of friends after I discovered that he had sold me a bit of a pup. Our relationship wasn't improved when, at around the time the museum at Donington was opened in 1973, I gave an interview to an Australian journalist in which I told the whole story of how I'd acquired the Ferrari, making it clear that I felt I'd been conned. The next thing I knew, I had a solicitor's letter from Mr Harwood, threatening to sue me for libel unless there was an apology in the next issue. I cabled him immediately with the message: "Don't bother to wait for the next issue because there will be no apology. I meant what I said." And I added: "If you want to sue, go ahead. I just hope you have more luck than I do when suing. I've always found it very hard work!"

I heard nothing more about it after that until I went down to Australia some time later to take part in a 2000-mile rally, driving a 1922 Sunbeam – one of two that I had acquired in New Zealand. That, in itself, was quite some car. Originally built for the 1921 French Grand Prix, it finished fifth in the Indianopolis 500 that same year and then won the Brooklands three-litre Scratch Race with Sir Henry Segrave at the wheel, setting a lap record there of 102 mph. It also achieved the fastest lap at the 1922 Isle of Man TT.

Beautiful to look at and fun to drive, the biggest problem with it was that it was a pig to start. You had to crank the handle and then run round to catch the throttle in time to warm her up very slowly or a great flame would shoot out of the exhaust, which was very short, and if she then coughed back it could very easily catch fire. Some years later, I was taking part in the Genevieve 500 Rally in Australia with John Bentley as my co-driver, when, without warning, the car suddenly burst into flames as we were actually driving along.

John was at the wheel at the time. We were still going at quite a lick as the flames started shooting up around the gear lever, but he immediately bailed out, stamping on my elbow in his frantic effort to get clear. I wasted no time in following suit and ended up rolling into the ditch at the side of the road, where my main concern was the poisonous snakes that I feared might be lurking there. Amazingly, neither John nor I was hurt, apart from a few grazes and bruises, but the car was a bit of a mess. It turned out that excessive vibration had caused the main fuel pipe to rupture and the undertray had then acted like a sump for the leaking petrol, which eventually exploded.

Anyway, it was while I was standing around in the paddock, just before the start of the earlier, 2000-mile event that I was approached by a very odd looking character in long baggy shorts and pith helmet. Hello, I thought, we've got a right one here! At which point he stuck out his hand and announced: "I say, old man, I always thought we'd bump into each other one of these days. The name's Harwood." It took a second or two for me to register exactly who he was, after which I immediately proceeded to give him some real stick about the 125 he'd sold me!

My booming voice does tend to carry and by the time I'd finished there couldn't have been anybody in the paddock who didn't know exactly what I thought about the Ferrari deal. To his credit, he did tell me where I could find the original engine and even offered to pay half the cost of buying it back. However, I reckoned I'd already had my money's worth just through being able to vent my feelings about him face-to-face.

And anyway, by that time a lot of water – and a lot of cars – had flowed under the bridge.

Fun and Games

THE CONTINUING boom in the building industry throughout the sixties and the rapid expansion of my business during this period meant that I was able to indulge my growing passion for motorsport to the full. Between 1963 and 1973 – by which time I had a workforce of several hundred and had started building factories, hotels and shopping centres as well as private housing estates – I bought and restored more than thirty historic grand prix cars.

One of my first acquisitions after the Ferrari 125 was a Maserati 250F. Out of more than one hundred and fifty exhibits now on display in the Donington collection, this remains one of the most pleasing to look at, its sleek and perfectly proportioned profile conforming to most people's image of a classic, old-fashioned racing car.

Apart from its looks, I had another reason for putting the 250F at the top of my early wish list, and that was its association with my great hero, Fangio. For it was in a 250F that Fangio won his fifth and final World Championship in 1957, with victories in the Argentine, Monaco, French and German Grands Prix.

Of the thirty that were built between 1954-57 – and numbered 2500 to 2530 – mine is No. 2515, a 1955 works car. Driven at various times by Cesare Perdisa, Roberto Mieres and Peter Collins, it then passed into the ownership of Count Ottorino Volonterio, one of the directors at

Maserati, and it was from him that I bought it in 1967 after seeing it advertised in a magazine.

I went to the factory in Modena to pick it up. The Count wanted to drive it one last time, so we went up to the company test track where he did five laps before finally handing it over. I'll never forget the look on his face as he got out; it was obvious he could hardly bear to part with the car. For a moment I thought he was going to burst into tears. I sometimes wonder how he must have felt a few years later when the market for classic cars was at its peak and a 250F similar to the one he had reluctantly sold to me for £3,500 changed hands for £1 million!

As it happens, I don't think that the one that fetched £1 million was as good as mine, which had never really been out of factory ownership until I got hold of it. Probably the only better example is the later lightweight Piccolo version that provided Fangio with the last drive of his career in the 1958 French Grand Prix at Reims. I was there that day and saw it run, so I was extremely disappointed when I missed out on the opportunity to buy that as well. One of only three ever made, it was also priced at £1 million when it came up for sale. I offered £750,000, but, without giving me the opportunity to raise my bid, the vendor then sold it to somebody else for £800,000. It turned out that he was buying a new house at the time and needed the money urgently so decided against getting involved in an auction.

Another very valuable early acquisition was Tazio Nuvolari's 1934 Maserati 8CM. One of twenty-three 2.9-litre 8CMs that were built, this is generally acknowledged to be the most original and best preserved of any 1930s grand prix car. It also has the distinction of having been driven by the little Italian ace regarded by some as the greatest racing driver of all time. What's more, he actually drove this very car in pre-war races at Donington.

I acquired it from fellow collector Colin Crabbe for £9,500. Several years later I had an offer of several million pounds for it from a well-known Italian car manufacturer, but I would never sell that 8CM. I have simply had too much fun in it over the years and have driven it in special demonstrations all over the world.

As with quite a few of my cars, I have also had several hairy moments in it, including two separate incidents during a trip to Switzerland. The first of these occurred when I took part in a speed hill climb. As we came back down afterwards I was following a little Alfa Romeo driven by Alain de Cadenet, father of the glamorous so-called 'It girl' Amanda de Cadenet. I was getting a bit of a move on, trying to catch up with Alain, when all of a sudden I came upon a railway level crossing.

I was doing nearly 100 mph at the time and knew immediately that I had dropped a clanger. I could feel the car starting to cock over as it hit the ramp formed by the crossing and then it took off. Out of the corner of my eye I saw a photographer drop his camera and run for cover. My heart was in my mouth for a split second, but although the car snaked alarmingly as it came down I just about managed to hold it on the road. The moment was captured for posterity by another photographer who happened to be on the spot and got a spectacular shot of the car flying through the air about four feet off the ground. That framed picture now hangs on the wall of my private suite at Donington.

During the same trip, I took part in a Flying Mile at a circuit in St Moritz. The 8CM is quite a tricky car to drive until you get used to it because it has a fluid flywheel rather than a regular gear change, which means that you pre-select your gear on a column-mounted lever and then just jab the clutch to change up or down. It had also begun to rain just before I started my run, making the track a bit slippery. Despite all this, I got off to a brilliant start, without a hint of wheelspin, so I was feeling very pleased with myself.

The trouble is that when you're only doing a mile you very quickly get to the other end. My eyesight is not brilliant at the best of times and it was even worse with raindrops on my visor. What with that and having to concentrate hard on my gear changes I failed to see the man with the flag until the very last moment. I suddenly became aware of people ahead of me scattering in all directions and I thought to myself: "Ooh, you beauty, I'm not going to be able to stop here!" All I could do was put it sideways into a slide, to scrub off some of the speed and, thankfully, I did manage to stop before I'd done any serious damage.

However, things got even more embarrassing when I then took a wrong turn off the circuit and suddenly found myself driving through the centre of town. I thought I'd be able to find a way back onto the circuit, but I couldn't. So, I just carried on until I came across a multi-storey car park near the hotel where I was staying and parked it there.

My friend Rick Hall, the former BRM engineer and restoration expert who has worked on many of the cars in my collection and who accompanied me on this and many other similar jaunts, has never let me forget either of these little episodes. As he puts it: "You're such a plonker, Wheaty! You only seem to know one way to drive – and that's flat out!"

I didn't always get away with my mishaps quite as lightly as I did with the Ferrari 125 and the 8CM. One of my more spectacular early prangs involved a very rare beast indeed – the 1958 Studio Tecnica Meccanica. Known simply as the Tec-Mec, this was a smaller, lighter version of the Maserati 250F, developed by Maserati's former chassis designer, Valerio Colotti, after the company had decided to withdraw from racing in mid-1958. Colotti had been working on the design before Maserati's decision to pull out, which had been prompted by financial problems, and he then set up his own company, Studio Tecnica Meccanica, to complete the project. In the end, the Tec Mec only ever made one, rather inglorious grand prix appearance – at the 1959 United States Grand Prix at Sebring, an airfield circuit in Florida. Driven by Brazilian Fritz d'Orey, it retired after just seven laps. By then, the 2.5-litre formula had been changed and apart from a brief appearance at Daytona the car was not seen again until the late sixties when it was discovered in a garden in Florida, where it had been left to rot away.

Having had it fully restored, I took it out for a day's testing at Silverstone, along with several other cars from my fast-growing collection, including a 1966 BRM P83, a 1969 four-wheel drive Cosworth and Colin Chapman's 1963 Lotus Climax. I was trying each one in turn and eventually came to the Tec Mec. We'd been having a lot of trouble with it blowing head gaskets but seemed at last to have sorted that problem out, one of the mechanics having already done ten full laps in it that morning without any problems.

I jumped in and soon had it going really well. There were a couple of F3 cars just ahead of me and as I came down the straight towards Woodcote I fancied that I might be able to overtake them. I was right on their tails at a full 6500 revs when I suddenly realised that I wasn't actually going to be able to get past at that point. In the same instant it dawned on me that with their wide modern tyres they still had time to scrub their speed off before the corner whereas I, in my 1958 car, did not. That realisation came a fraction too late for me to rescue the situation.

The mechanics were watching anxiously from the pits, along with my youngest son, Kevin, who was then aged about nine and had been taken along for the day as a special treat. The others could already tell simply from listening to the way I was going down through the gears that something was not quite right. Then, to their horror, they heard the car suddenly open up again just as I went into the corner. What had happened was that I had momentarily forgotten, as I wrestled frantically to keep the car under control, that it had a central throttle pedal and amid all the excitement I had hit that by mistake, instead of the brake. I was told afterwards that as soon as they heard the engine open up again, all three of the mechanics instinctively leapt off the pit wall as one with a shout of "Oh, shit!" and, without waiting for the inevitable bang-crash-wallop, started sprinting down to Woodcote, with young Kevin at their heels.

In those days, the circuit's ambulance driver, known to one and all as 'Silverstone Sid', used to park his old ex-Army Bedford ambulance in a little lay-by on the outside of Woodcote. As I slid out of control, I just clipped the front of the ambulance, taking off the front wing, the bonnet and the headlight (I've still got the invoice for the repairs that had to be carried out!). The impact threw the Tec Mec round and it then somersaulted twice, hit the banking and barrel-rolled about six times, throwing me out before finally coming to rest the right way up.

Arriving on the scene a few seconds later, the mechanics and Kevin feared the worst when they first caught sight of the wreckage, with nobody in it. Then, as they ran through the clouds of smoke and steam, they saw me some distance away on my hands and knees, clawing at the grass with my bare hands and complaining loudly that everything was uphill, despite the fact that I was actually on flat ground. I remember having the feeling that petrol was pouring on me and that I needed to roll as far as possible away from the car only to find that whichever way I tried to roll it seemed to be steeply uphill. It was like one of those dreams where you are desperately trying to escape from something and your legs turn to lead. The effect of spinning and rolling so violently had obviously left me dazed and disorientated.

As I dusted myself down, a quick check revealed that, quite miraculously, I had once again managed to escape from a fairly spectacular crash without serious injury. My glasses were smashed and I had lost my watch – we reckoned that the Perspex of the windscreen must have sliced cleanly through the watchstrap without breaking the skin on my wrist. Apart from that, I was left without so much as a single cut or graze. However, after about half-an-hour I had stiffened up so much that I could hardly walk and I had to be lifted bodily into my car and driven home.

Most of the stiffness wore off after a few days and I thought no more about it. It wasn't until quite recently, shortly before my eightieth birthday, that X-rays taken following a fall revealed how close I had actually come to breaking my neck all those years before. The X-Ray pictures showed clear evidence of much earlier damage to five of the vertebrae, fractures that could only have been caused by that accident. The doctor was astonished that it had gone undetected for so long. It helped to explain the back trouble I'd suffered from time to time over the years, although I had never allowed that to cramp my style.

They say that life begins at forty and as my forties coincided with the Swinging Sixties, I think this was doubly true in my case. A large part of my youth, between the ages of nineteen and twenty-five, had been sacrificed to the war. But I certainly made up for that with all the fun I had in the decade following my fortieth birthday in 1962, much of it revolving around motorsport and an awful lot of it enjoyed in the company of my great friend Brian Hecks, known to one and all as 'Hecky'.

Hecky and I first met when I was fourteen and he and his family came to live near me in Leicester. We picked up our friendship again after the war and, at the same time, Lenchen also became the best of friends with

Hecky's wife, Cynthia. The four of us were so close that for years we made a habit of going out together for a meal every Thursday night without fail. And, in between times, Hecky and I saw a lot more of each other, either going to motor race meetings together or, more often, simply getting together for a drink at the local pub that I had persuaded him to buy.

Up until then, he and his younger brother had been running a very successful family hosiery business together, but Brian had decided he wanted to retire early and did a deal whereby his brother bought him out. I then convinced him that he would soon get bored doing nothing and talked him into buying the Bath Hotel, just down the road from us at Shearsby. He proceeded to turn this into one of the busiest and most popular pubs for miles around and it became my second home, especially after I built the Gun Club premises round the back just so that Hecky and I and our chosen friends would have somewhere where we could drink legally after hours.

The Gun Club became the venue for many a long night of conviviality and the starting point for some fairly wild escapades. Among the regulars was the Commanding Officer of the USAF base at Bruntingthorpe, the main gate of which was only about half a mile down the road. I had got to know him in rather unusual circumstances after I gate-crashed the airfield security system in a veteran 1912 Fiat that had once belonged to the Dame of Sark.

This all started when Hecky and I went down to Monza for the Italian Grand Prix. There were a couple of Yanks sitting next to us in the grandstand and as we got chatting to them there was a fair amount of banter about who was going to win the race. They were rooting for Phil Hill, the only American in the race, and we were ribbing them about how there had never been a Yank who was any good at Formula One level. Bets were struck and it was like taking candy off a baby. Anyway, they were great fun and good sports so we treated them to dinner afterwards on our winnings. During the meal one of them asked casually: "I don't suppose you guys know a place in England called Bruntingthorpe, do you?"

They couldn't believe it when we told them that Hecky owned the pub next door and that I lived only six miles away. They then revealed that they were USAF pilots and that they were due to fly into Bruntingthorpe the next day with one of the first B52s to arrive in the UK. When we heard this we naturally arranged to meet them at the Bath Hotel for a drink, after which they became regulars throughout the time they were stationed at the base. One of them actually met his wife-to-be in the bar there. An American herself, she was hitching round Europe with a friend and had popped in for a drink. On their wedding day I drove her to the church in the Dame of Sark's old Fiat, which had only eight hundred miles on the clock when I bought it.

Afterwards, there was a big reception up at the base during which the Yanks were boasting about their security systems. We'd been telling them how we used to take a short cut across the airfield to get to another favourite pub and they had pointed out that there was no way we would be able to do that any more. "We've got radar here that can detect a rabbit running across the runway," they drawled. "Any intruder would get picked up within seconds of setting foot inside the perimeter fence." Well, it wasn't long before Hecky and I were going round with a hat saying: "How much will you bet us we can't drive that old Fiat the length of the runway without getting stopped?"

We then waited until the very early hours of the morning, when nearly everyone else had gone home, before sneaking off to where the car was parked, jumping in and heading for the runway. It was supposed to be the longest runway in the UK at the time and the ancient Fiat had a top speed of about 13mph, at which point it vibrated so violently that you felt it was in danger of shaking itself to bits, so we didn't really expect to get too far. But we'd had a few drinks by then so we were game for anything.

Sure enough, it wasn't very long before a jeep full of guards came racing after us, with somebody firing warning bursts from a machine gun into the air. However, they quickly realised that these two rather drunken and dishevelled Limeys, still wearing their wedding suits, did not constitute a major security threat, so they allowed us to carry on to the end of the runway before escorting us back to the guardhouse, where they locked us in a cell for what was left of the night, insisting that it was for our own safety. "We wouldn't want you driving home in that condition," they smirked.

(Above) Getting airborne in the Maserati 8CM during a hill climb in Italy.

Taking things a bit easier in the Mk II BRM V16 at Donington (right) and (below) spinning the Lancia Ferrari D50.

(Above) The 200 mph, twin-engined Alfa Romeo Bimotore in which I have driven demonstration laps at circuits right across Europe.

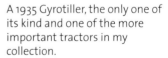

A 1935 Gyrotiller, the only one of its kind and one of the more important tractors in my collection.

A rare traction engine discovered on a farm in the Australian outback.

My great friend 'Jumbo' Goddard (above, right) in Australia with Bentley restoration expert
Rod Warriner and Rod's three-litre Bentley.

(Left) Preparing to take Gavin
Strang, then Minister of
Transport, for a spin in
Jumbo's record-breaking
Bentley and (above) the 1922
Sunbeam in which I nearly
came to a hot and sticky end
during Australia's Genevieve
500 Rally.

(Above) A quiet word with Roger Williamson just before the start of a race during those two very successful 1971/72 F3 seasons when he swept all before him, winning a string of more than thirty victories and establishing himself as Britain's most exciting young driver.

Roger during his tragic final race at Zandvoort in 1973 and (left) me with his sister, Barbara Upton, at the unveiling of his statue in the Memorial Garden at Donington. He will always have a very special place in my heart.

(Above) Formula Classics in action at Donington. The idea never really caught on quite as well as I had hoped but I still have the cars in storage and one of these days we might try to resurrect the project.

Neil Corner on his way to victory at Silverstone in the BRM P25 in 1974 and (right) with me and mechanic Arthur Birchall at Donington.

With my great hero, the late Juan-Manuel Fangio, who became a friend and demonstrated his skills during a special event at Donington in 1979 (below), when he put Neil Corner's Mercedes 125 through its paces in breathtaking style.

(Right) Me in Fangio's Mercedes W196.

Hanging on for dear life as Gunnar Nilsson gives me a high-speed lift in his John Player Special Lotus during a special appearance at Donington in 1979 and (below) posing a little more comfortably in front of the Ferrari 500 in which I was to have my worst accident.

(Left) Outside the museum with the Ferrari 125, the first grand prix car I ever bought.

The CO himself came down to release us a couple of hours later and that was the start of a great friendship. The Colonel was a great character who became not only a regular at the Bath Hotel, but also an honorary member of the Gun Club. He even gave orders for one of the giant hangars up at the base to be cleared out so that we could have indoor clay pigeon shoots up there. The same hangar also became the venue for a famously successful series of special public party events that the Gun Club laid on.

Billed as 'A Night To Remember', these originated as a way of paying Hecky back for the way he had been ripped off by members of the Gun Club, who had been signing the slate for their drinks in the clubhouse with a whole lot of fictitious names, such as Mickey Mouse, Tom Mix, Elvis Presley and so on. It was all meant to be a bit of a joke at Hecky's expense. We took great delight in winding him up – it was worth it just to see his big nose literally twitching whenever he started to smell a rat. As far as the drinks bill was concerned, we had always intended to settle up with him in the end, but then, when the total amount owing had reached about £4,000, the book suddenly and mysteriously went missing.

Rather than try to work out who owed what from memory, we decided we'd have to find some other way of raising the money. The clay pigeon shoot had been so successful that we thought it would be a great idea to set up a whole series of games and entertainments in the hangar, with everything from go-kart racing to ten-pin bowling, plus a bar and a band, and then throw it open to everybody on the base and the general public as well. The Colonel was very enthusiastic and gave us the go-ahead. And, of course, everybody wanted the chance to meet the Yanks – especially the local girls! So, once the word got round we had people coming in by the coachload. The venture proved so popular with everybody that we repeated it several times, attracting more than two thousand people at a time and making more than enough money to pay Hecky back and still show a handsome profit.

Meanwhile, the Colonel had become a family friend. My girls used to go and play with his daughters and when he eventually left to go back to the States he sold me their three ponies – Cockade, Poppy and Pretty Nellie. The deal was done one night in typically rumbustious Gun Club style. I kept knocking the price down and when we'd finally agreed a figure I suggested that he might like to cut the cards to double or halve the amount. Well, Hecky and I had doctored the pack so that I couldn't lose. After that it was darts, and again we fixed it so that I won. By the time we finished, I owed him virtually nothing.

Later, I rang him to explain how we'd been fiddling him all along and to tell him that I would be sending him a cheque for the full amount that we'd originally agreed. "Oh, don't do that," he said. "I'm not as daft as you think. I knew exactly what you lot were up to – in fact, I had a job to stop from laughing. The truth is, I always intended for your girls to have the horses because I wanted to be sure that they were going to a good home, so I was planning to give them to you anyway."

After he left and went back to the States I didn't see him again for thirty years – and then it was in rather sad circumstances. He had been diagnosed with terminal cancer by then and, knowing that he didn't have much time left, he came over to re-visit the area that held so many nostalgic memories for him. I spent a week driving him round to all our old haunts and reminiscing about some of our more outrageous exploits at the Gun Club.

One of the stories he loved to hear me tell involved yet another of my motoring mishaps. I was on my way back home in the very early hours after a long session at the Gun Club, during which one of the main subjects of conversation had been a bit of magic from Stirling Moss at Aintree the previous weekend. Going over Melling Crossing, Moss seemed to lose control, spun the car three times one way, three times the other and then flicked the wheel and carried straight on as if nothing had happened.

This was very much in my mind as I drove home along the deserted country roads. I was in the Mercedes 220S and as I swept through the centre of Wigston Magna, still going a great deal faster than I should have done, I suddenly felt the back start to slide. At that moment I very rashly decided to see if I could do a Stirling. I couldn't! The car spun across the road and smashed into the local Co-op store, demolishing the main window and leaving behind the bumper, the radiator grille, one of the front wheels and the number plate before rebounding backwards across the High

Street and uprooting a Belisha beacon, losing the boot lid in the process.

The village was like a ghost town at that unearthly hour and as no other vehicle was involved, and as nobody had emerged to find out what all the commotion was about, I felt that it would be wise in the circumstances to make myself scarce and come back later to get things sorted out. Amazingly, despite the extensive damage, the car was still just about driveable and I somehow managed to nurse it the short distance home.

Lenchen was not amused when I crawled into bed at about 4.00 a.m with the muttered apology: "I'm sorry I'm so late, duck, but I've had a bit of an accident in Wigston. I've broken a shop window."

"Don't you come home at this time in the morning, lying to me," she snapped, turning her back on me.

The next thing I know she was shaking me awake, crying: "Tom, Tom – the police are here! You've had a crash. You've knocked the Co-op down in Wigston!"

"I know I have not!" I protested indignantly.

"It's no good you lying now," she said. "You left your number plate behind! And have you seen the state of the car? It's only got three wheels left!"

The bobby was very understanding. "Perhaps you could pop up to the station when you've got dressed, Mr Wheatcroft," he said politely, handing me the number plate, the boot lid, the front wheel and various other bits and pieces.

Today, of course, they would have hauled me off in handcuffs there and then, locked me up and thrown away the key. And quite right, too. But things were a lot different in the days when you were only considered too drunk to drive if you were incapable of walking straight along the white line in the middle of the road.

When I presented myself at the local station and made it clear that I would, of course, pay for all the damage, the Sergeant helpfully suggested that the accident had probably been caused by an icy patch on the road – despite the fact that it was the middle of May!

"You'd better go and square up with the manager of the Co-op," he said. "He's a bit upset because he's only just had the whole shop re-fitted. And by the way, you'll also need to talk to the lady on the other side of the road. She's on the warpath because the Belisha beacon you knocked down flew straight through her dining room window like an arrow and embedded itself in a valuable antique sideboard!"

I eventually managed to pacify everybody, sending a team round to rebuild the Co-op and finding a French polisher to repair the sideboard. After that, I heard nothing more about the incident. I had had a very lucky escape in more ways than one. From then on, I confined my Stirling Moss impersonations to the racetrack.

By the second half of the sixties my interest in motor racing and the quest for further historic cars to add to my collection were regularly taking me all over Europe and America and, in 1967, I made my first visit to Australia and New Zealand for the Tasman Series.

From the moment I set foot 'Down Under' I fell in love with the place. The pace of life, especially in New Zealand, is rather as one remembers it being in England years and years ago. Going there is like stepping into a time warp, with the added attraction that the weather seems to be stuck in perpetual summer. The people are lovely, the food is great and for anyone interested in collecting old racing cars, both Australia and New Zealand are treasure houses – at least, they were before I went down and plundered just about everything they'd still got that was worth having!

The reason there was so much stuff down there is quite simple. After the war, British and European drivers would routinely migrate to the other side of the world during our winter to take part in the hugely popular Tasman Series and at the end of the season there they often found that it made more economic sense to sell their cars and spares rather than go to the considerable expense of shipping them back again. As the Aussies and Kiwis were mad keen on their motorsport, there was never any shortage of enthusiastic buyers. An awful lot of classic cars ended their days in this way and, because of the climate there, they tended to remain very well preserved.

The only difficulty has always tended to lie in tracking them down. As you might expect, the people with the money in that part of the world tend to be the farmers and, especially in the Australian outback, where your nearest neighbour may be twenty or thirty miles down the road, some rare and exotic items can often be found gathering dust in a remote barn somewhere in the back of beyond. In many cases you only learn of their existence through word of mouth. Occasionally you stumble on them purely by chance.

One extraordinary example of how that can happen occurred when I was driving through the outback with 'Jumbo' Goddard, a fellow English car enthusiast and collector who had gone to live in Australia. Jumbo became a great friend during my regular visits there over the years. On this occasion a raging bush fire forced us to make a three-hundred-mile detour during which Jumbo decided that we should drop in on a farmer he happened to know in the area. "He's got a few interesting pieces stashed away," promised Jumbo. The place was about 400 miles from Melbourne. We got off the main road and drove for miles down a dusty track to the farmhouse and after the obligatory cup of tea that you are invariably offered in Australia if you are a 'Pommie', we were led out to an incredibly cluttered workshop in one of the outbuildings.

As we were being shown round I spotted a familiar steering box hanging from a rafter. I recognised it instantly.

"That looks to me like the steering box off a 1948 1.5-litre Ferrari 125," I said. "I wouldn't mind buying that off you."

"I'm sorry, it's not for sale," replied the farmer. "But how did you know what it was?"

I told him about Peter Whitehead's 125, how the steering had failed, how we'd then had to strip it down and how, as a result, I knew exactly what the steering box looked like.

He heard me out before revealing with a grin: "Well, that's a coincidence – because that box up there came out of that very same car. I used to work as a mechanic for Peter Whitehead when he was racing over here, which is how I come to have it."

Before we left, I took him and his wife out for a meal in Melbourne as a thank you to them both for looking after us. As we were sitting in the bar, waiting to go to our table, he suddenly produced the steering box and handed it to me. "I think you'd better have this," he said. "It seems to me like you're the rightful owner." And he gave it to me. He wouldn't take a penny for it.

Such generosity is quite rare amongst classic car collectors, who tend to guard every spare very jealously. For some reason, this seems to be especially true Down Under. In New Zealand I got to know a couple of enthusiasts who were near neighbours and also very good friends – until, that is, it came to their precious collections. As far as those were concerned, they were ruthlessly competitive and would go out of their way to thwart each other.

I discovered the full extent of their bitter rivalry in this respect after I had acquired the basic components of my extremely rare 1936 Alfa Romeo Bimotore from one of them. Originally a twin-engine car, built and run for Alfa Romeo by Enzo Ferrari before he went out on his own and generally regarded as the first Ferrari, the extraordinary 200 mph Bimotore was a pig to drive, Tazio Nuvolari being one of the very few who could handle it competitively. Later, it was acquired by an Englishman named Charles Aitken, who converted it into a single-engine car and raced it quite successfully both in Europe and in the Tasman Series before finally selling it off down there. Known as the Alfa Aitken Special, it then disappeared and was never heard of again until, quite by chance, I discovered it lying hidden under a tarpaulin in this New Zealander's barn, in bits.

I couldn't believe my luck. Only two Bimotores had ever been made – this one and a smaller 2.6 version built for Louis Chiron – and as far as anyone was aware, neither of them had survived. So, this was an extremely valuable car. I was even more pleasantly surprised, therefore, when the Kiwi agreed to swap it for one of two relatively insignificant Ford P68 sports cars that I had been given by Ford's Research & Development people, who were desperate to find a home for them after an order came down from on high that they should be scrapped.

The restoration of the Bimotore to its original twin-engined form was to be one of the biggest and most complex projects ever undertaken for me by Rick Hall. Altogether, it took more than five years and involved having to work from photographs when reproducing the bodywork and various other missing parts for which no original drawings were available. Rick and panel beater John Cole eventually did a brilliant job and the end result was well worth the wait. It's a fantastic piece of equipment and people can hardly believe it at first when you take off the covers to reveal these two whacking great straight eight engines. The noise they make when running at full revs is phenomenal – not the high-pitched scream of the BRM V16s but a deep-throated roar. Over the years, I have driven it with great pride on demonstrations throughout Europe and it has always given me a great thrill.

Anyway, the point of this particular story is that after I had done the deal to buy most of the main components of the car from the Kiwi owner who had had them under wraps for so long, I went to visit his friend and fellow enthusiast who lived no more than five miles up the road and, lo and behold, hanging there on the workshop wall were a set of Bimotore brake drums. When I remarked on this coincidence, explaining how I'd just bought the rest of the stuff from his mate, he told me gleefully: "Oh yes, he's been after those brake drums for years – but I wouldn't let him have them!" It then turned out that he'd also got a few more spares hidden away, including the prop shaft that joined the two engines together and various other bits and pieces. He agreed to give me the whole lot – but only after making me promise that I wouldn't, in any circumstances, give any of it to his pal!

Even more extraordinary is the story of the two collectors in the South Island who, between them, bought a job lot of components that included the basic parts for two much sought-after Alfa Romeo P3s. They shared these out, each taking turns to pick various bits. All was well until it later turned out that the chassis chosen by one of them actually belonged to the car that, famously, had been driven by Nuvolari when he beat the might of the big new Mercedes W25s at the Nurburgring in 1935. This history immediately made that particular car potentially much more valuable than the other and this almost inevitably led to bad feeling between the two of them. It soon got to the point where, out of spite, they refused to lend each other parts to copy, so that instead of both of them being able to build a complete car, they ended up without one between them!

I don't know what it is with those New Zealanders. They can be a funny lot in that way. You hear all sorts of rumours about wife swapping among the more isolated sheep-farming communities out there – something to do with the pioneer spirit, or so I'm told! If that is true, then all I can say is that they are obviously a great deal more relaxed about sharing their wives than they are about sharing their cars.

As well as historic cars, I have also built up quite a large collection of steam engines and antique farm machinery over the years and much of this, too, has come from Australia and New Zealand. Among the more interesting items are a 1935 Gyrotiller, a massive thirty-ton tractor-cum-rotovator of which mine is the only surviving example, an extremely rare three-wheeled Glasgow tractor, of which only three still exist, and a giant traction engine known as a Z7 that we have only recently finished restoring, after working on it for eight years.

The Z7s were made originally for Tate and Lyle for use in their West Indian sugar plantations. Here they would work in pairs, pulling a special plough several hundred feet wide that was strung between them. Then, immediately after the war, the same plans were used to make an even bigger pair for the specific purpose of sweeping mines from the Normandy beaches. These two were later shipped right across the world to Tasmania where they were used very successfully to clear a particularly virulent and fast-spreading weed from thousands of acres of countryside, dragging a weighted wire that would cut a swathe one hundred yards wide, ripping the weeds out by the roots.

The one I've got came from the West Indies, while its sister engine ended up at the bottom of the Zambesi river, having sunk while being floated to a new location on a special raft. I was keen to acquire the Tasmanian pair as well and actually got as far as agreeing a price over the telephone. Unfortunately, the Australian I bought them from then reneged on the deal and sold them behind my back to somebody else who had come up with a better offer. I then had a further disappointment when the Australian Government brought in a new regulation banning the export of any machinery that dated from before 1920. As a result, I had to leave behind a lot of the stuff I had bought, much of which is still stored on a friend's farm.

Meanwhile, back in Leicester in the early seventies, my collection of grand prix cars was growing steadily, to the point where I was running out of space in the two-tiered garage that I'd built behind the house in Welford Road. Here, I would occasionally amuse myself of an evening by going in to sit behind the wheel of my favourite cars, savouring their histories and driving imaginary grands prix. This was fine until one night when I found myself in a rather awkward predicament that convinced me I would have to make alternative storage arrangements.

I had just acquired the 1962 Porsche 804 in which Dan Gurney won the French Grand Prix at Rouen, despite famously likening the power and handling of what was actually a very sophisticated car to that of a VW Beetle! I managed to insert my rather bulky frame into the narrow cockpit only to find when I went to get out, after a few fantasy laps, that I was wedged behind the wheel, completely unable to extricate myself.

This was all because of an injury sustained in an accident I'd had while on holiday in Bermuda shortly beforehand. I had picked up the local newspaper there one day and read a story about the wreck of a First World War German warship that had been discovered just offshore with a quantity of live ammunition still aboard. This had become so unstable that it couldn't be removed safely so the authorities had decided that the entire wreck would have to be blown up where it lay, in a controlled explosion. I fancied watching that and tried to hire a car in which to drive across the island to the spot where it was all going to happen. Unfortunately, there were no hire cars available. All I could get was a motor scooter.

I started riding this around the bay fairly sedately and then, in typical fashion, decided once I had got used to the controls that I would open it up a bit. I was zipping along, thinking to myself: "This is lovely, this is grand!" when all of a sudden I came round a bend and hit a patch of water where the waves had come over the sea wall. I lost it completely at that point and ended up in the gutter with a broken collarbone. This took some time to heal completely and in the meantime I couldn't put any heavy pressure on it, which was why I was unable to lever myself out of the Porsche.

It was late at night, the garage was some considerable distance from the house and however much I shouted I couldn't attract anybody's attention. I was trapped there for several hours until, at about one o'clock in the morning, car headlights sweeping across the garden signalled the return home of my then teenage daughter, Joy, after an evening out with her boyfriend. I bellowed even louder at that point and she did eventually hear me.

"What on earth are you doing, dad," she giggled as she edged into the garage rather apprehensively to find out what all the fuss was about.

"Never mind what I'm doing! What do you think you're doing coming home at this time in the morning?" I demanded angrily, relief at being rescued – not to mention the desperately urgent need for a pee after being sat there for nearly three hours – momentarily replaced by nagging parental concern about a seventeen-year-old daughter's moral well-being. Instead of being thanked, poor Joy found herself being gated for a week.

It took almost that long to get me out of the car! Lenchen arrived on the scene and, between them, she and Joy tried to lever me out with the help of a broom handle placed under my arms. That attempt was abandoned when the broom handle snapped. Eventually, a couple of neighbours had to be summoned to provide the extra manpower needed to hoist me out.

I never sat in that car again. More to the point, the incident did help to concentrate my mind on finding a more satisfactory way of storing and displaying my collection, which numbered around thirty cars by this time. My first idea was to lease a showroom from a car dealer I knew in Leicester. I thought that such an arrangement would suit us both, providing an attraction that would pull more customers in for him, while giving me a city centre location. Unfortunately, the sort of rent he was looking for, along with the administrative expenses that would be involved, made it uneconomical.

I then identified a site not far from where the M6 now joins the M1, a spot that I thought would be perfect for a combined museum and hill climb complex. It was easy to find and the access couldn't have been better, but the council would not consider it because it was out in the country. They wanted me to put it somewhere within Leicester itself, but land there was far too expensive.

It is no secret that I have spent most of my professional life at war with planners. To my way of thinking, they are the enemies of progress, all too often holding the country back with their negative approach towards exciting and imaginative enterprises that could benefit the local community and the general public. I have wasted months of my time and millions of pounds on appeals and inquiries over the years, most of which I won in the end. And in that time I have met very few planning officers for whom I had any real respect. I'm not suggesting for one moment that they should simply rubber-stamp every plan that is put before them, but at the same time I do believe that a culture has grown up in many planning departments whereby the automatic reaction to any project is to find a way of saying no.

One of the few exceptions to the rule was the Leicestershire County Council planning officer, Maurice Pettifor. He was no pushover, but I always thought that he was a very fair man. More important, in my view, he could usually be relied upon to take a positive approach, suggesting ways in which projects could be made acceptable within the existing regulations.

It was he who took me aside when I was turned down for the MI/M6 site and suggested: "Why don't you have a look at Donington Park? It could be ideal for what you've got in mind and I am told that it could soon be up for sale."

Return to Donington

O N A QUIET Sunday afternoon in early 1971, a few days after getting the tip-off that Donington might be coming up for sale, I drove up there with Lenchen to take a closer look around my old stamping ground.

It was an eerily nostalgic experience for someone whose most vivid memories were of huge, excited crowds lining the track to watch those sensational grands prix of 1937 and 1938 and the thrilling spectacle of the mighty Mercedes and Auto Unions as they thundered past at previously unimaginable speeds. All was now silent and an air of dereliction had fallen over the place. Nature had reclaimed parts of the cracked and crumbling track, there were Nissen huts where the paddock used to be and a large workshop had been erected at one end of Starkey's Straight, blocking off the Melbourne Loop.

The last race had been held at Donington Park in the summer of 1939. Once the war started, the whole of the 700-acre estate was then requisitioned by the War Office to become the country's biggest Army transport depot, with more than 50,000 vehicles parked there on hard standings hidden among the trees. It wasn't finally handed back to its owners, the Shields family, until 1955. In the meantime, attempts by Fred Craner and other local motorsport enthusiasts to get the circuit re-opened had all met with failure.

One of those involved in pushing for its revival in those early post-war years was motorcyclist 'Titch' Allen. Titch, who founded the Vintage Motor Cycle Club in 1946, had also been involved with motor racing in the pre-war years, mainly as a passenger for driver Bob Gerard, and his associations with motorsport generally at Donington Park go back further than anyone else's. He can even lay claim to the honour of being the first person ever to try out the track, having ridden his Francis Barnett Villiers motorcycle along the carriage drive from the Hairpin up towards Coppice Wood at a time in 1931 when the circuit was still little more than a twinkle in Fred Craner's eye.

Fred and Alderman John Gillies Shields had invited various local bigwigs and other interested parties to a lunchtime reception at Donington Hall at which they unveiled their plans for the circuit before leading everybody out to inspect the proposed route. As a 16-year-old cub reporter for the Nottingham Guardian and Evening Post, Titch had been sent to cover this event partly because he was the only person on the staff who knew anything at all about motorsport, but mainly because he was the only one who had his own transport to get him out to what was then a fairly remote location.

At this stage no real attempt had yet been made to connect the two main carriage drives that ran down to the Hall from Red Gate Lodge and Coppice Lodge, forming a wide V-shape that converged in front of the house at what was to become the Hairpin. At the top end, the drives were linked only by a rough farm track.

The reception took place on a rainy day in early spring and, with lunch awaiting them, nobody was too keen to spend any more time than was absolutely necessary walking the course. Michael McEvoy, the owner of a specialist garage in Derby where he tuned and prepared sports cars, had brought along a Star 'Planet' in which he whisked people back and forth from the Hairpin to McClean's Corner, which was then hidden deep in Coppice Wood. After that, everybody retired to the Hall for refreshments.

Rather than join them, Titch decided to take his Francis Barnett for a few spins up and down to Coppice Wood. As he recalls, all you wanted to do at the age he was then was to make as much noise as possible and, having carefully removed the silencer, he thoroughly enjoyed the sounds that reverberated off the trees once he got into the middle of what was then fairly dense woodland.

From the moment the circuit opened with that first, inaugural motorcycle meeting on Whit Monday, 1931, Titch, who by this time was working for the *Leicester Evening Mail*, covered just about every event held there up until late 1938, when he was moved to the paper's Rugby office. In those very early days the track consisted of a narrow central tarmac strip with an apron of compacted gravel either side. For a motorcyclist, the fully mature trees that lined the track through Holly Wood and Coppice Wood were a major hazard and accounted for some very nasty accidents, including three fatalities in the first year.

The most spectacular motorcycle accident witnessed by Titch involved Billy Wing, who ran the local Velocette dealership in Nottingham. Riding his own Velocette in a 1932 event, Billy had just come out of Holly Wood and down into Craner Curves when he lost control. As he skidded onto the grass at about 70 mph, he parted company with his machine and was sliding along on his back when his heels then dug in so that he was gradually brought upright into a standing position. At this point he was like a waterskier, still skimming across the grass, perfectly balanced, with his arms outstretched. At the same time, his bike carried on spinning round and round until it came to the original start/finish line down near the Hairpin, where it demolished the guy ropes and poles that held up the banner there, bringing it down onto the track. The marshals leapt forward and managed to hold it up while the other riders flashed through. Billy, meanwhile, had come to a graceful halt, completely unhurt.

At the same spot, shortly after the first car race was held at the circuit in 1933, Richard Turner had an almost equally dramatic mishap in his Austin Seven 'Ulster'. Having lost it on the bend, he barrel-rolled down the hill, finally coming to rest, upside down, against the paddock fence. To everyone's great relief, he was then seen to crawl out from underneath the dashboard, completely unscathed. And a few minutes later an announcement was made over the Tannoy, asking if anyone in the crowd with an Austin Seven might be able to lend him a set of wheels so that he could race again later in the afternoon.

The first fatal accident was recorded when motorcyclist Gordon Baxter died after hitting a tree in Coppice Wood; and when local hero Bob Vesey was also killed shortly afterwards, highlighting the dangers of the sport, there were calls for the circuit to be closed down. Mounting public concern was only headed off by assurances in the specialist press that neither the circuit nor the administration was to blame.

The first motoring fatality came during the third meeting, in August 1933, when P.J. Warren, driving a 1.5-litre Bugatti owned by the Junior Racing Drivers Club, went into a skid at the Hairpin, over-corrected and slid off into a tree. The car overturned, pinning him and his passenger, J. Gordon, underneath. Warren escaped uninjured, but Gordon died in the ambulance on the way to hospital.

A further historic fatality occurred during a twelve-hour race in 1937. At that time there were still four sets of five-barred farm gates at various points around the circuit, all of which had to be specially opened on race days. One of these gates, half way down what is now Craner Curves, had a wall on each side and, as there was room for only one car to get through, a no-overtaking rule was in place on that section of the track.

The two cars involved in the incident – a two-litre AC driven by Mr M.K. Bilney and a 1087cc Riley driven by Mr S.H. Robinson – were neck-and-neck as they raced towards the gate and it seems likely that there was confusion as to who should give way. The cars locked wheels and in the crash that followed both drivers were seriously injured. Mr Robinson survived, but Mr Bilney, whose co-driver in the race was Mrs Joan Richmond, died at the scene.

The race was stopped but then restarted – the only time, to my knowledge, that this has ever happened after a fatality – and the class for cars of over three litres was eventually won by B. Bira in a Delahaye, ahead of David Steele in a 4½-litre Bentley. In 2002, by then in his late eighties, Steele was re-united with the car, thanks largely to the efforts of motorsport enthusiast and unofficial Donington Park historian Alan Preston, and drove it for a couple of demonstration laps during a Vintage Sports-Car Club meeting at Donington, handling it very impressively given his age and the awkward configuration of the pedals compared to a modern road car.

Also in 1937, Freddie Dixon had a narrow escape when the brakes of his Riley failed completely as he came over the top of the rise on his way down to Melbourne Corner. When he hit the brake pedal nothing happened and the car went straight on, ploughing into the banking nose first. The tail flipped up and the car seemed to hang vertically in the air for a moment before crashing down to earth. Freddie suffered serious injuries, including several broken ribs, and although he was renowned for being as hard as nails, he never raced again after that.

Titch recorded all these dramas for his paper, phoning his reports over from a press box that he insists was actually nothing more than a large converted hen coop. Before filing his copy he would go up to Fred Craner's house at Coppice Farm – where the circuit's administrative offices are still located to this day – in order to check all the results, lap times and other statistics with the official timekeeper. There, he would invariably be offered a cup of tea and a slice of home-made fruit cake by Mrs Craner, a large, kindly woman whom I, too, got to know well when I went to watch the racing in those pre-war years.

As far as Fred Craner himself was concerned, appearances were deceptive. A short, burly figure with a red face that got redder and redder when he was angry, he was certainly a tough and determined character, forever strutting around and barking orders at all and sundry. But once you got to know him well, he was a kindly chap underneath all the bluster.

Typical of Fred in his more familiar mood of bristling aggression was a legendary confrontation in 1938 with Herr Major Korpsführer Adolf Huhnlein, the Nazi government official who was in overall charge of German motorsport. Arriving at the Coppice Gate in the back of a vast open Mercedes staff car, complete with armed guards in full Nazi uniform, Huhnlein arrogantly demanded immediate access to the circuit itself so that he could visit the Mercedes and Auto Union teams. Well, the only person who was allowed to give permission for that gate to be unlocked was Fred himself and he took exception to Huhnlein's highhanded manner. The brief argument that ensued ended with Fred, his face redder than ever, shouting: "I don't care if you're Adolf Hitler himself – you're not going through that gate until I say so!" And that was that.

Thanks to Adolf Hitler, of course, that gate was to remain closed to all motorsport fans for nearly forty years from 1939 and, as a result, Donington Park never did get the chance to consolidate its position as Britain's first and foremost road racing grand prix circuit.

Shortly after the war had started, Titch Allen found himself back at the circuit in his capacity as an Army dispatch rider when he was given the task of helping to deliver Army vehicles to the newly-established depot there from Ashford, in Kent, where he was based. He had carefully engineered this particular duty so that he could visit his wife in Loughborough. On arrival at the circuit he was horrified to find that the main R.E.M.E workshop had been built right across Starkey's Straight.

Returning to his job on the *Leicester Evening Mail* after the war, Titch added his weight to the campaign to get the circuit re-opened. Through the newspaper, he even arranged for Raymond Mays to come and address the local council about the importance of the circuit as part of the country's heritage, it being the only true road racing circuit in the UK at the time.

The councillors could hardly have failed to be impressed by Mays, a rather grand figure and one of the last of the great pre-war gentleman drivers, who went on to found BRM. However, they were not swayed by his arguments. It was, after all, a period of great hardship and not really the right time to be talking about luxuries like motor racing. With rationing still in force, you couldn't get the petrol to go and visit your sick grandmother, let along to go motor racing. Apart from that, the Army were in no hurry to move out and, with five hundred civilian staff employed at the depot, the local community had a vested interest in keeping them there.

When they did eventually leave in 1955 and the estate was handed back to the Shields family, Major John Gillies Shields almost immediately announced plans to re-open the circuit in 1957, keen to explore any means of paying off the heavy death duties that fell due when he inherited the estate from his grandfather. By this time, however, Fred Craner had died suddenly and unexpectedly while undergoing what should have been a fairly routine operation and without his drive, determination and know-how, the project foundered amid problems of planning and finance.

The Major, personally, had no great knowledge or experience of motor racing and, despite backing and advice from the RAC, he simply couldn't overcome the obstacles that were put in his way. He made a further attempt to get some sort of restoration venture off the ground in the sixties, but again it petered out in the face of mounting difficulties, mostly to do with the planning permission needed for an updated circuit and the costs involved in bringing it up to the required standards. At the same time, an attempt to turn Donington Hall itself into a hotel and country club also had to be abandoned. The house was later sold instead to British Midland Airways, becoming the administrative headquarters of the company that had started up operations from the fledgling East Midlands Airport next door.

This was the situation when I went to have a look around that Sunday in the spring of 1971. Just like Fred Craner when he did his original recce back in 1931, I found myself being accosted and warned off for trespassing. As I drove in I was waved to a halt by two women who were out walking their dogs. One of these ladies turned out to be the Major's wife. "You can't come in here without permission from my husband," she said, adding rather doubtfully: "Unless, of course, you want to buy the place."

She looked slightly taken aback when I replied: "Well as it happens, m'dear, I was thinking of doing just that."

I rang the agent first thing on Monday morning. "How did you know it was for sale?" he asked. "I only got the letter myself this morning!"

The Major had decided to sell just under half of the 700 acres, but he wanted to hedge it around with all sorts of conditions. He was also asking far too much money, so I said I wasn't interested. Two days later, I then got a call from the agent saying that they were prepared to waive the conditions and reduce the price. However, they were still asking more than I wanted to pay.

I told the agent: "Look, there's £25,000 between us – I'll toss you for it."

"I can't gamble with my client's money!" he spluttered, rather taken aback.

"All right," I said. "Leave it to me. I'll talk to the Major direct."

I drove straight up to Donington to see him. He received me with gentlemanly politeness, but you didn't need to be a genius to realise that, ideally, he would rather have been able to negotiate the sale of the family estate to somebody from his own officer class rather than to an ex-conscript from the other ranks!

In the years to come, the Major and I were to develop a rather abrasive relationship. On one occasion during the early days of my development of the site, when he came in search of me to protest about something he had seen that he didn't much like the look of, he actually rode his horse into the shell of what was to be the museum building and, without dismounting, bellowed at one of my startled workmen: "Where the hell is Wheatcroft!"

There was another difficult moment while I was clearing part of the site and he found my men about to cut down a large oak tree.

"You can't let them do that, Wheatcroft," he roared. "It's taken four hundred years for that tree to grow to that height!"

"That's right, Major," I replied above the buzz of the chainsaw. "And it's going to take about four minutes to fetch it down!"

I regret now that I didn't make more of an effort to get on with him, because in later years, towards the end of his life and when both of us had mellowed, I did come both to like and respect him.

Given the kind of man he was, I was quite surprised at that first meet-ing when he agreed to settle the price of the land on the toss of a coin. I guess he was probably fairly desperate for a sale and he must have realised that there were unlikely to be too many takers for a derelict racing circuit.

We flipped an old-fashioned two-shilling piece, I remember. I've always been lucky with anything like that, but on this occasion I lost, so I ended up paying the full, six-figure asking price. However, I was happy enough with the deal, which had taken just a week to complete from the moment I first went up to look at the place. Unfortunately, nothing from then on was to be quite such plain sailing.

In the face of concerted, relentless and often bitter local opposition from almost all sides, it was to take six years of expensive legal wrangling, including a full public inquiry and a series of expensive planning appeals, before I eventually won the right to realise my dream of re-opening Donington Park as a major motorsport venue. In the end, the whole lengthy process was to cost me over £2.5 million in legal fees alone.

Meanwhile, with this dispute rumbling away in the background, I got on with the construction of the building that was to house the Grand Prix Collection. At least there were no serious planning problems as far as that was concerned. The architect came up with a clever and neatly appropriate design that linked the five individual exhibition halls together in such a way as to resemble the overall shape of a crankshaft when viewed from above by passengers arriving at the airport next door. As the building started to go up on the chosen site, just inside the main entrance, I set about expanding and preparing my collection of cars for display.

The workshop at Aylestone Lane became a hive of activity as I rapidly acquired more and more cars for restoration. It is important to remember that the boom market in historic racing cars as investments had not yet taken off at this time. It was rare to pay more than a few thousand for a car, let alone the millions that some of the more sought-after collectors' items were fetching when prices reached their craziest peak in the mid-eighties.

In the late sixties and early seventies I was often paying around £1,500 or £2,000 for cars and spending perhaps twice that much on restoring them. A lot of these cars, although significant, were not generally considered to be worth the effort and expense of restoration at a time when obsolete racing cars were routinely either scrapped or chopped up and converted into something else, the parts ending up scattered all over the world. So, I like to think that I helped to save some important cars from extinction.

A good example would be the 1962 Brabham-Climax BT3. Sir Jack Brabham's first ever Formula One car after he left Cooper Cars and set up on his own, the prototype BT3 gave him his first Championship points in the US Grand Prix at Watkins Glen in 1962 and his first Formula One wins in a car bearing his own name in the non-Championship Austrian and Solitude Grands Prix in 1963. It later ended up in America, where it had a V8 Chevy engine shoved in it. By the time I acquired the car it had been chopped about and modified beyond recognition.

It arrived at Aylestone Lane as little more than a pile of bits and when we tried to put the proper engine in it we found out that it wouldn't even fit in the chassis. We then contacted Racing Frames, the Brabham-owned company who had built it in the first place, and although they weren't prepared to lend us the drawings, they offered instead to rebuild the chassis themselves. We then persevered and got the whole car back to its original condition. It hadn't been vastly expensive to buy and it is still not worth a huge amount in purely financial terms, but its association with one of the great names of motor racing and the fact that it is the only one of its kind in the world gives it great historical value. And it would have been scrapped years ago if we hadn't stepped in to rescue it for posterity.

Other cars that might also have disappeared include Jimmy Clark's 1961 Lotus-Climax 21 and the 1960 Lola Climax Mark 4 driven by John Surtees and Chris Amon.

The Lotus raced only once – at Monza in 1961, where it was involved in the fatal collision with von Trips' Ferrari that resulted in von Trips' death. As is the routine legal procedure in Italy after any fatal car crash, the wreckage was impounded by the police and for the next eight years or so it remained locked in a police compound at Monza, seemingly forgotten.

Quite by chance, I then happened to be having dinner with Colin Chapman at our hotel in Monza during the Italian Grand Prix weekend when a police officer arrived at our table, apologised for interrupting and then went on to inform Colin that he'd been sent over to tell him that the car was ready to be picked up whenever he wanted to collect it. When the policeman had gone, having handed over all the necessary documentation, I asked Colin what he was going to do with the car.

"Scrap it," he replied, without hesitation.

"Well, in that case, can I buy it from you?" I asked.

"No," said Colin. "You can't buy it. You can have it for nothing – as long as you're prepared to go and pick it up."

And that was that. After bringing it back to England, I kept it locked away in a garden shed at home for another three years before eventually rebuilding it in time for the opening of the museum in 1973.

Another very important car that I acquired at around this time was the 1966 McLaren M2B/2. The oldest surviving McLaren, driven by Bruce McLaren to sixth place in the British Grand Prix at Silverstone and fifth place in the US Grand Prix at Watkins Glen, it lay in the cellar of the museum at Donington for more than thirty years until quite recently, when we stumbled across the original 3-litre V8 Ford engine in Switzerland and decided to restore it fully and put it on display.

Throughout the sixties and seventies I was collecting cars at such a rate that I had them stuffed in sheds, at the back of garages, hanging off rafters – wherever I could find space to store them until such time as the mechanics could get round to working on them.

During this period I had a team of up to nine full-time mechanics and engineers working for me, including the legendary John Cole. Widely reputed to be the best panel beater in the country, John was a true artist, gifted in the most extraordinary way. Working from just a photograph and using nothing more than a manual wheeling machine, a set of nine hammers and a sandbag, he could knock out the most complicated body shapes with apparent ease and at phenomenal speed. People never believed me when I told them how little time it took him to do a car. I'd take him to a race meeting to show him a car that I wanted copying, he'd make a few quick sketches, jot down some measurements and the next thing you knew, you'd have the finished article there in front of you. And it was always perfect. Invariably, it would fit like a glove.

John himself had huge hands, with fingers like pork sausages, and he would sometimes simply punch metal into shape with his bare fist. As a result, the finished panel would often be smeared with blood but if you asked him about it he would just smile and say: "It's no good unless it's been christened."

Probably the two best examples of his work in the museum are the 1948 Cisitalia Porsche 360 and the 1959 BRM P25. He did the Cisitalia from photographs and, because it is not painted, the bare metal enables you to see quite clearly just how skilled he was. The P25 is one of three copies that we built from scratch and that were later raced very successfully by Neil Corner in historic events in the mid-seventies. Neil, a collector himself and an authority on historic cars, reckoned that the bodywork on those P25s was the best he had ever seen on any replica or restoration. The shut lines are what you have to look for, the places where the different sections of the bodywork meet. John's shut lines were always immaculate.

Another surprising thing about John was that he had trained originally as a cabinet-maker and used to make the most beautiful furniture in his spare time. As a panel beater he actually had no great passion for historic cars and was just as happy to work on the dented door of a Transit van as he was to make a body for a rare £1 million grand prix car. As far as he was concerned, it was all in a day's work – and, regardless of what he was doing, his day's work always finished at 5.00 pm on the dot. It was the same when he reached retirement age. That was it. He never did another job for us.

He could be an awkward bugger in that sort of way – very contrary and absolutely his own man. You had to handle him with kid gloves because he had a really short fuse and would throw things at people if they upset him. Like so many artists, I suppose, he was slightly eccentric. However, he and I always got on very well and in the thirty-odd years he worked for me we never had a cross word. He died in 2003 and I must say that both his craftsmanship and his personality are sorely missed.

John Cole was by no means the only eccentric I got involved with while expanding the Grand Prix Collection in readiness for the opening of the museum. In fact, John was relatively conventional compared with Denis Jenkinson. A former World Sidecar Champion passenger, riding in the chair alongside Eric Oliver, 'Jenks' also navigated Stirling Moss to a famous victory in the 1955 Mille Miglia, pioneering the use of incredibly detailed navigation notes which he wrote out on an 18ft-long roll of paper and then scrolled through a prototype metal roller box that he and Moss had had made especially for the event. But it was as one of the world's most respected motorsport journalists that he made his name. Working mostly for *Motor Sport* magazine, his success stemmed mainly from the fact that he absolutely lived for the sport and knew everybody that mattered, from the team bosses and the drivers to the mechanics in the workshops where he spent much of his time, often lending an expert hand. As a result, his reports always contained the sort of inside information that nobody else could get hold of.

At the same time, he was an extremely odd character. He had a huge bushy beard and never wore socks or a shirt, just the same grubby turtleneck sweater. A bachelor, he lived on his own like a gypsy, 'squatting' in a derelict lodge house on an estate down in Hampshire, without the benefit of running water or electricity. He had a dynamo rigged up to an old Fiat 500 engine to give him a bit of light and apart from that he just made do with candles. He never seemed to have any money, often preferring to be paid in kind for his articles with groceries and petrol and anything else he happened to need.

A fanatical motorcycle racing enthusiast, he rode a motorbike most of the time, but he also had an old Jaguar XK150 and a couple of other wrecks round the back of his house that he was always threatening to do up. And rather like me with Stirling Moss's Lotus, he once drove an F1 car on the public highway – but with a bit more style than I had managed. He had worked out that on Christmas Day there would be no traffic cops on duty and arranged to borrow a Lotus from his friend Colin Chapman, running it round a 20-mile circuit of roads near where he was living. Unfortunately, he ended up putting it in a ditch, which caused a bit of a panic. Colin had to rush out with a low loader to collect the evidence before anyone else got there and started asking awkward questions.

When it came to his passion for cars, Jenks was a man after my own heart. I must say, I liked the bloke – and there was no doubt he knew more about the history of old racing cars than anybody else in the country. He had an encyclopaedic knowledge about the specifications of certain rare models – exactly how many bolts they had on the sump and all that sort of thing. So, when I was setting up the museum I got him to come and live at Donington for about six months so that he could advise me on what cars I should go after, where I might find them and whether they were the genuine article or not. I gave him a deserted cottage on the estate to live in, so in some ways it must have been like a home from home!

By the time the museum opened in 1973 I had a total of nearly seventy cars to put on display, mostly my own but some of them on loan from various private owners, companies and museums. Alan Clark, the late Tory MP, Cabinet Minister and diarist, let us have his 1949 French Grand Prix-winning Talbot-Lago; there was an Alfa Romeo Monoposto – the first ever successful single seater – from Neil Corner; and Jackie Stewart loaned us the Tyrrell Ford that he drove to a record eight grand prix victories in 1971 and 1972 and that was then presented to him by Ken Tyrrell and Ford on his retirement in 1973. Also included were several cars that I was looking after on a permanent basis for my old friend John 'Jumbo' Goddard.

Jumbo was a larger-than-life personality in every way, a six-foot-four-inch giant of a man, with enormous hands and feet – hence the nickname. The black sheep of an extremely wealthy banking family, he had been apprenticed as an engineer at Thorneycroft after leaving college, but all he really wanted to do was to live, quite literally, in the fast lane. He was fascinated by anything to do with speed, especially racing cars, and in the thirties he emigrated to Australia where he spent most of his time collecting historic cars and racing them.

He returned to Britain during the war to work for Vosper Thorneycroft and actually received a special civilian decoration for his part in designing and developing a revolutionary fast-attack patrol boat. Fitted with a Merlin Spitfire engine, this thing flew across water like Bluebird and the theory was that it would skim over the anti-submarine nets that protected German battleships when they were in harbour before dropping down into the water to fire torpedoes and then making a lightning escape.

It seems that when it came to testing this craft no regular naval crew could be found with the skill and nerve to pilot it on full power, so Jumbo volunteered to do it himself. Once he had proved that it would work, he then took it on an actual mission and it was for this that he was decorated.

Having inherited a fortune shortly after the war, he went back to

Australia, where he was able to indulge his passion for cars to the full, and it was there that I first met him during one of my early visits Down Under in the sixties. We bumped into each other in the paddock at a race meeting in Sydney and my initial impression was that he must be a bit of a nutter, because it was bucketing down with rain at the time and there was this great bear of a man wearing a sou'wester back to front, apparently oblivious to the fact that the water was simply being channelled down the back of his neck. But once we started chatting we got on like a house on fire. As I was preparing to leave at the end of the afternoon he asked me which hotel I was in and when I told him he said: "Oh, you can't possibly stay there – it's far too bloody expensive! Come back to my place. I'll put you up."

I wasn't too sure about this, having only just met him, but he wouldn't take no for an answer. I knew hardly anything about him at this stage and my jaw dropped in amazement when we drove up to his spectacular house on the top of a hill. We were both like drowned rats after being caught in the downpour and as we got inside he threw me a towel, provided me with a set of dry clothes and boomed: "Have a shower and get dressed, dinner's in half an hour."

We then had a superb meal, complete with the finest vintage wines, and I was generally treated like a king. And there was another very pleasant surprise in store after dinner when he led me out to what he referred to, in true Edwardian style, as his 'motor house', to look at his collection of cars. The place was stuffed with Bugattis and Bentleys and a whole lot of other rare and highly desirable items, including a single-seater Frazer Nash, a Q-Type MG, a 30/98 Vauxhall and OKV1, the works D-Type Jaguar, plus a selection of historic motorcycles.

He also possessed a wonderful library, made up entirely of books covering every aspect of motorised transport. Apart from that, every room in the house was full of all manner of unusual and fascinating items – everything from clocks to antique firearms and from old farm implements and model ships to a fantastic array of antique tools. Overall, it made a deep impression on me and from then on my own collecting style was much influenced by Jumbo and what I saw there at his home.

We went on to become great friends over the years. I would always go to stay with him whenever I was in Australia and we also travelled all over Europe together to various race meetings. He was wonderful company, a man who loved his sport and was always on the lookout for a bit of fun. Genuinely eccentric, he was sixty-nine before he eventually decided to settle down and get married!

Towards the end of his life he got a bit strapped for cash and we did a deal whereby I bought a load of his cars on the understanding that he would retain possession and could go on using them for as long as he lived. This was a private gentlemen's agreement between the two of us, something that he didn't want anyone else to know about – not even his wife Katy – so my claim to many of these cars was disputed after his death from cancer in the early eighties and I never did manage to take possession of all of them. However, I was able to keep the ones that were already on display in the museum at Donington.

These included the Frazer Nash in which A.F.P. Fane became the first man to break the 40-second barrier in the 1937 Shelsley Walsh hill climb near Worcester – a very important pre-war event. I also had his 1931 Bugatti Type 51 once owned by Richard Shuttleworth, winner of the 1935 Donington Grand Prix. Best of all was the twin turbo-charged, 8-litre 1923 Bentley 'Special' in which Jumbo himself, at the age of sixty-two, recorded an average speed of 158.2 mph on the Kennedy-Laan Highway near Ghent in 1972, making it the fastest W.O Bentley of all time – W.O denoting that it was built during the lifetime of Mr Bentley himself.

I once had the pleasure of driving this same car at well over 140 mph on the M42 – with Gavin Strang, the Minister of Transport at the time, sitting beside me in the passenger seat! This came about when he officiated at the formal opening of a new section of the motorway. I got a call beforehand asking if I could supply a really fast car to take him for a spin as a bit of a publicity stunt.

"I've got just the thing," I told them. "The fastest W.O. Bentley in the world!"

They sealed off a stretch of motorway between junctions especially for the occasion and I counted nineteen police cars lining the route. I warned the Minister before we set off that he would have a lot of trouble breathing once we got over 130 mph because of the force of the air rushing around the small windshield, but he wasn't in the least bit bothered. He couldn't wait to get going. I still had two gears to go when I looked across to see his cheeks literally flapping in the wind!

We got on like nobody's business. He was supposed to have lunch with various Council officials afterwards, but was clearly looking for an excuse to get out of it and when I suggested that I could take him for a few laps round the circuit at Donington instead, followed by a tour of the museum, he jumped at the opportunity. As I was showing him around I told him about all the planning problems we'd been having.

"Well, you seem now to have got everything you wanted," he said.

I explained that, as it happened, my request for brown tourist information motorway signs, directing people to the circuit, had just been refused. He said he would look into that for me and, the very next day, I got a call from an official at the Highways Authority, informing me that the signs would be up within six weeks.

Jumbo's Bentley continued to occupy a prominent spot in the main hall of the Grand Prix Collection until very recently, a splendid reminder of a wonderful character and a great friend. In the end, I rather reluctantly decided that the time had come to sell it on. I am not usually at all sentimental about the cars in my collection, but because of the association with Jumbo this one was a bit special. What eventually persuaded me to part with it was the fact that I no longer seemed to have much opportunity to take it out and actually drive it – and I do believe that this sort of car should be used and not just confined to a museum. So, I agreed to sell it to an enthusiast in Yorkshire who was keen to get it back on the road and the race track and I am sure that Jumbo would have approved of that.

The Donington Grand Prix Collection was formally opened in March 1973 by Swedish grand prix star Ronnie Peterson, with Raymond Mays as guest of honour. I'd become very friendly with Ronnie in the days when he and Derek Bell were in Formula Two together and Derek was driving for me.

Raymond Mays' presence was arranged by leading motorsport journalist Eoin Young, an old friend whom I had brought in to help promote the occasion.

Eoin came up with the bright idea of exploiting Mays' historic 50-year link with Mumm's champagne through his two famous 1923 Brescia Bugattis Cordon Rouge and Cordon Bleu, one of the first-ever motorsport sponsorship deals, and used this to persuade the importers of Cordon Rouge to make it the official champagne of the opening. With ITV covering the event, they got some fantastic publicity. Among the cars on prominent display in the museum was a Yardley BRM and Eoin got Raymond to sit on the front wheel for his TV interview, saying: "Don't you think these modern cars look awful with all this advertising on them?" before adding with a grin: "Mind you, it was me that started it all back in 1923 with the Bugatti and Cordon Rouge." The Cordon Rouge people were so impressed that they subsequently got Eoin to organise a whole series of promotions for them with the Bugatti Owners' Club.

Also present at the museum opening were Graham Hill and Sir Jackie Stewart, both of whom I had got to know quite well by this time as a result of my increasing involvement in motor racing, not just as a spectator but also as a sponsor and a private entrant.

The whole atmosphere surrounding Formula One was much more relaxed back in the fifties, sixties and early seventies. It is impossible nowadays to imagine even the most regular and well-connected outsiders being able to socialise freely with the likes of Michael Schumacher, David Coulthard, Jenson Button and the rest. But in the days before their lives were governed by fearsome fitness regimes, intense security and all the demands of modern celebrity status, the drivers were much more accessible and approachable. If you mixed in motor racing circles and happened to be staying in the same hotel, you were quite likely to end up chatting to them in the dining room over breakfast or in the bar before dinner. Sometimes you might even find yourself getting involved in the pranks and practical jokes that were part of the general camaraderie that existed.

Many of the more outrageous escapades seemed to revolve around

Innes Ireland. Innes was a tremendous character, but you always had to watch out for yourself when he was around. In fact, if you went out on the town with Innes, there was always a 50/50 chance that you'd finish up having to spend the night in the local nick!

Nobody was safe. There was an occasion once at Monza when Dan Gurney had to catch a very early flight to Indianapolis on the Monday morning. He was planning to drive himself to the airport in a little Fiat hire car that he'd got for the weekend. Everybody had been taking the mickey out of him because of this Fiat. Outside our hotel was a big inter-section and right in the middle of it was a little podium where a police-man would stand to direct the traffic. On the Sunday evening, after everybody had had a few drinks, Innes got the rest of us together and persuaded us to help him lift the car up bodily and stick it on this podium, which was where Dan found it the next morning when he went to drive to the airport. He was not amused.

Graham Hill was equally unimpressed when, in Austria, Innes got up on the table towards the end of a fairly lively dinner party at the hotel where we were all staying and launched into an impromptu Scottish dance, wearing nothing but his racing boots and a kilt that he'd managed to borrow from someone. One or two people, including Graham, had their wives with them and Innes kept hitching up the kilt to give them a bit of a flash. Graham wasn't too happy about that, so he grabbed a small potted cactus plant and next time Innes came down his end of the table he shoved it right up under his kilt. That wasn't at all funny for Innes, who ended up with an arse full of cactus thorns that were extremely difficult to get out since he couldn't quite see what he was doing back there and certainly didn't want anybody else giving him a hand! The thorns that were left embedded in his backside then turned septic and Innes couldn't sit in a racing car for some time afterwards.

And then there was the time he organised a peeing contest off the upper deck of the Queen Mary! This was in 1976, on the occasion of the inaugural US Grand Prix meeting at Long Beach, California. I had taken over a couple of cars from the Donington Collection – the 1955 BRM P25 and the 1959 2.5-litre Cooper Climax – to take part in a Historic race that was run as a curtain raiser to the main event. We came 1st and 2nd, and one of the most remarkable things about that was the fact that the cars put in times that were only a second or so behind those recorded by the modern grand prix cars.

Another interesting aspect of that meeting was the unexpected driving skills displayed by the actor James Garner, best remembered as the star of The Rockford Files. He was one of the celebrities making guest appearances in the historic event and he drove our P25 as quick as anybody out there that day. He had to rush off immediately afterwards to a backstage party in Las Vegas following a concert by Elvis Presley and asked casually if Kevin and I fancied going with him. I wasn't that interested but Kevin jumped at the opportunity and came back in a high state of excitement, having actually got to meet the great man face to face. He said that Elvis had been charming and had also come across as being very intelligent, talking knowledgeably about motorsport.

Back at Long Beach, everybody was staying aboard the Queen Mary, already converted by then into a floating hotel. It was one evening after we'd all had a few drinks that Innes came up with the bright idea of a contest to see who could pee furthest over the side from the top deck. He volunteered to lead the way but made the mistake of going over the seaward side – straight into the breeze! Needless to say, he was not very popular with those down below who got caught in the shower, but Innes himself thought it was a huge joke and was giggling like a naughty schoolboy.

Because of this sort of thing, the other drivers were always looking for ways to get back at him. Once, when we were all flying out to Germany for an event, Innes was seen to be busy chatting up one of the air hostesses and when he didn't come down for dinner at the hotel that evening word soon went round that he must be otherwise engaged in his bedroom. A raiding party then rushed upstairs, having somehow managed to get hold of a master key, invaded the room and, sure enough, found Innes in bed with the hostess.

The unfortunate couple, both stark naked, were then bundled up together in a sheet and carried downstairs to the dining room where a table was cleared and they were ceremoniously rolled out in front of the assembled throng, amid much jeering and clapping. Innes, as usual, managed to carry it off with a flourish, but the poor girl, of course, was mortified.

While Innes was an irrepressible Jack-the-Lad, forever playing the fool, Jim Clark, another driver whom I got to know quite well, was the perfect gentleman – although he, too, would occasionally join in with the fun and games. I remember once watching him perform an impromptu party trick that gave an insight into what made him such a brilliant driver. I have often heard it said that a superior sense of balance is one of the key qualities that separate the very best drivers from all the rest, instinctively allowing them to brake that split second later going into a corner, for instance. To my mind, this was borne out one evening at a party where a pogo stick was suddenly produced. Everyone, including all the drivers present, had a go and most people managed just one or two hops before falling off. When it came to Jimmy's turn, however, he not only hopped all round the room but out into the hall and up a flight of stairs! And afterwards he swore blind that he'd never been on a pogo stick before!

During this period I travelled the world on a regular basis to watch all the major motor racing events and gradually got to know many more of my greatest heroes, including Fangio, Stirling Moss, Mike Hawthorn, Jack Brabham, Bruce McLaren and Jackie Stewart. At the same time, I was also making contact with a lot of other key figures in motorsport, such as Bernie Ecclestone, Max Mosley, who was then running March Engineering, Colin Chapman, Tony Vandervell, Ken Tyrrell, BRM's Louis Stanley and Rob Walker. Rob, a member of the Johnny Walker whisky family, was a wonderful character whose passport gave his official occupation as 'Gentleman', but who also happened to be one of motor racing's most successful private entrants.

As I got caught up more and more in the fun and excitement of it all I began to fancy the idea of becoming a bit more actively involved as a private entrant myself. It was at this point that the idea of Wheatcroft Racing began to take shape in the back of my mind.

Triumph and Tragedy

WHEATCROFT RACING would almost certainly have made a glorious European F2 Championship-winning debut with driver Derek Bell in 1970 had it not been for film star Steve McQueen. Far-fetched? Well, it may be a little unfair to blame McQueen personally for our failure to clinch the title at the first attempt, but the late Hollywood hard man certainly played a part in knocking us out of the running when we were on the very brink of victory.

As with quite a few of my racing stories, it all began Down Under, this time in New Zealand. Having made his name with regular wins in F3 in 1966 and 1967, Derek Bell had been given his first grand prix drive with the Ferrari works team in 1968 and was still under contract to them when I first met him during the Tasman Series in January 1969. He and Chris Amon were racing a couple of 246 Dino Ferraris and I was there purely as a spectator. Up until then a lot of Derek's racing had been sponsored by his stepfather Bernard Hender, known to one and all as 'the Colonel', and from the moment we bumped into each other in the paddock and started chatting, he and I got on really well. From then on I followed them around from race to race and the Colonel and I had a great time, downing a fair amount of booze together.

Out on the track things were not going quite so brilliantly and, sensing that Derek's relationship with Ferrari was heading for the rocks,

I mentioned casually that if he ever needed help with anything in the future he should give me a call. Sure enough, Ferrari and he parted company midway through the following F1 season and, finding himself suddenly left high and dry, he was soon on the phone, wondering if I'd meant what I said about giving him some help.

"Aye, of course, lad," I told him. "What would you like to do?"

We first considered putting him into the Tasman Series in a Formula 5000 car like the one in which Peter Gethin had won the previous year's F5000 Championship with the Church Farm Racing team that the Colonel ran from the family farm in Pagham, Sussex. However, it was near Christmas by this time and we found that we couldn't get a new car built in time. Instead, we contacted Jack Brabham and bought the Brabham BT26A in which Jacky Ickx had won the 1969 German and Canadian Grands Prix. The idea was to run it in the Tasman Series with a 2.5-litre Cosworth engine rather than the original 3-litre F1 engine in order to comply with the regulations there.

It is quite unusual to reduce an engine rather than stretching it, but our feeling was that this might actually make it stronger. Unfortunately, it turned out we were wrong about that. We got off to a good start in the first race of the series at Levin and were lying in 2nd place after twenty-five laps when a brush with a Lola damaged the front spoiler and put us out of the running. We bounced back in the New Zealand Grand Prix at Pukekohe the following week, coming 2nd to Australian Frank Matich, but in the Lady Wigram Trophy at Christchurch the engine blew up during the thirty-fourth lap when we were again going well in second place. It was sent back to Cosworth for a re-build but got lost somewhere along the way and turned up a year later in Bombay! Meanwhile, we had a replacement flown out, which arrived just in time for the fourth race at Teretonga.

It is a mark of Derek's skill as a driver that he had been able to put himself in contention in the first three races despite the fact that the car was not handling at all well, possibly because we were running it on Dunlop tyres rather than the Goodyears for which it had originally been designed. During practice at Teretonga, Derek's friend and former Ferrari team-mate Chris Amon, who had a reputation as one of the best set-up drivers in the world at the time, offered to help us sort it out – only for the replacement engine to blow up before he'd even got out of the pit lane!

With no spare available our series was now over and arrangements were duly made to fly the car back home, while at the same time I flew on to Australia, as originally planned, to watch the rest of the series as a mere spectator. As I got off the plane in Sydney I heard an announcement on the Tannoy requesting me to go to the airport information desk, where I was given a message to ring a certain number urgently.

Whenever that happens you immediately think it is bad news, instead of which it turned out to be the Repco engine people in Australia with a very generous and totally unexpected offer. They reckoned we could still win the championship in the BT26 and were eager to give us some of their engines so that we could carry on. I had to tell them that, unfortunately, the car had been flown home that very morning. Repco were top of the tree at the time, so who knows what might have been had we been able to take them up on their offer.

One way and another, the BT26 turned out to be a rather unlucky car for us. Later that year we decided to run it in the Belgian Grand Prix at Spa, with the engine converted back to the 3-litre original and with Goodyear tyres fitted. Things started to look very promising when Derek recorded the second-fastest lap during practice, only for disaster to strike during the warm-up lap. Going flat out through a dip in the circuit, the car bottomed out, ripping the rivets out of the gear change housing in the monocoque.

It was then that I was guilty of the only dishonourable thing I've ever done in motor racing. In those days you got £2,500 appearance money as long as you completed at least one full lap in the race. So, I got the mechanics to jam it in second gear for the start. We were actually leading into the first corner, at which point everybody overtook us and Derek just cruised round for the rest of the lap before retiring. That car has never run since and is now confined to the museum – although we did bring it out specially for a nostalgic re-union with Derek at the 2005 Historic Motorsport Show at Stoneleigh.

Back in 1970, we were having much better luck with the orange Brabham BT30 that we had entered for that season's European F2 Championship – until, that is, Steve McQueen came on the scene. Derek had been chalking up a string of consistently good results – 3rd at Thruxton, 4th at Pau, 3rd at Hockeheim, 2nd at the Nurburgring, 2nd at Zolder and, most impressive of all, an emphatic win at Barcelona.

Derek has always said that Barcelona gave him his finest hour in a single-seater. The circuit there was made for his style of driving and he romped home in some style ahead of Emerson Fittipaldi and François Cévert, setting a new lap record along the way. It was a fantastic achievement all-round, especially for a small private team that was up against the might of the factory-backed opposition and some of the world's best drivers.

At that stage in the season we were a long way ahead of our nearest challenger and seemed odds-on to take the championship. However, our smooth progress towards the title was interrupted when Derek accepted a lucrative offer to double for one of the actors in the film 'Le Mans', starring Steve McQueen. This meant missing a couple of events, which wouldn't have been so bad had it not been for an unfortunate incident during filming at Le Mans itself.

Derek, in a Ferrari 512, and Steve McQueen, in a Porsche 917, were shooting a scene that involved storming up the Mulsanne Straight from the Arnage to the Ford chicane. As he changed down at the end of the run, Derek noticed that something was not quite right with his clutch so, as they turned to go back the way they had come, he called out to McQueen to go on ahead. No mean driver himself by all accounts, Steve went everywhere flat out and he immediately took off like a scalded cat. Following behind, Derek was just coming out of Indianapolis in second when he heard what sounded like a minor explosion and the car suddenly went up in flames.

The fire was so fierce that the car – later bought and restored by Pink Floyd drummer Nick Mason – burned to the ground before the firemen could get to it and Derek was very lucky to get out relatively unscathed. As it was, he did suffer some quite severe burns to his face. To make matters worse, the French ambulance crew who came to pick him up didn't secure the stretcher properly and as the ambulance moved forward he shot out the back and cracked his head.

As well as missing two races, Derek also seemed to lose momentum. He retired at the Nurburgring and again in Sicily, where an oil pipe burst and spewed hot oil down his back. As he himself commented: "What with having a burnt face to start with and then getting my arse burned as well, I wasn't exactly over the moon!"

By now, Clay Regazzoni had caught right up and in the end it all came down to the final race. All we needed to do to win the championship was to finish somewhere ahead of Regazzoni, instead of which he just pipped us, to win by a couple of points.

It was very frustrating and, even more so than when we had had to turn down the Repco engine offer at the end of our ill-fated Tasman Series, I couldn't help thinking about what might have been. If Derek hadn't done that film, I reckon he would have won the championship. And if he'd won the championship, I'm sure one of the F1 teams would have picked him up and who knows what might have happened? As for me, my future as a team sponsor might also have been very different.

As it was, my relationship with Derek started to splutter and fizzle out after that. At the end of 1970 I did a deal with John Surtees for Derek to drive the TS7 in the US Grand Prix at Watkins Glen, but when we arrived there Surtees suddenly announced that the deal only covered the car itself and that he hadn't got an engine for it. We had a few words about that – some of them quite serious! In the end, I went down the pit lane and managed to borrow a spare engine from Ken Tyrrell. The fact that Ken was prepared to help me out of a hole in such circumstances was a measure of the man he was, one of the most straightforward and trustworthy individuals I ever encountered during my time in motorsport. There wasn't much I wouldn't have done for him as a result.

Despite clutch problems that forced him to back off in the last stages of the race, Derek managed to nurse the car to sixth place at Watkins Glen, scoring the only F1 point of his career. The following year we put him in the Argentine Grand Prix with the March 701-1 in which Chris Amon had won his first F1 race at Silverstone and which I had then added to my collection. Derek was running 3rd in Buenos Aires when the camshaft broke. Driving the same car, he also came 15th in the Questor Grand Prix in California. And that was that as far as he and I were concerned.

He went on, of course, to have tremendous success as a sports car driver, winning two World Sports Car titles and five Le Mans 24-hour victories between 1975 and 1987. As for his lack of success in Formula One, Enzo Ferrari always said that family life and F1 don't mix and in Derek's case I think that was probably right. I had the greatest admiration for his driving skills – on the road he was undoubtedly the fastest and most precise driver I have ever had the experience of being driven by – but once he'd got the children to worry about in the back of his mind he no longer seemed to have quite the edge that you need to succeed at the highest level.

Unfortunately, we parted company on rather a sour note after he sold the BT30 that I'd bought for him, under the impression that the proceeds should count as part of the sponsorship money. That did cause a bit of a row and I even threatened to sue him over it at one point, but I'm pleased to say that we did eventually manage to get things sorted out fairly amicably, with no hard feelings on either side. As well as being a great driver, who deserved to have a lot more success than he did at the highest F1 level, he is a very nice chap and wonderful company and apart from that final disagreement I always got on very well indeed with him and his family, including his wife, Pam, and the Colonel. I was therefore delighted when he agreed to make a guest appearance on the Donington Grand Prix Collection stand at the 2005 Historic Motorsport Show, where he was re-united with the BT26. We spent a very enjoyable day together, remembering the many good times we'd had together and reflecting on some of the might-have-beens.

Donington Park kept me fully occupied in the weeks immediately after I bought it in the spring of 1971 and I was in no particular hurry to get actively involved with another driver. However, that soon changed when I made my annual visit to Monte Carlo for the 1971 Monaco Grand Prix and first met the young man who was to become like another son to me.

I had been reading snippets about Roger Williamson in the motorsport

Press for some time before that and because he was a Leicester lad I took a special interest, noting his impressive progress through karting, Mini and then Ford Anglia racing. At eighteen, he set a new kart speed record of 114 mph and shortly after graduating to Ford Anglia racing he came top of his 1-litre class in the Hepolite Glacier Championship, famously winning some races outright over the 2-litre boys, which was unheard of. It was at Mallory Park that I first saw him win a race and afterwards I went round to the paddock to say hello, but by the time I got to him he was already surrounded by quite a crowd of people, all trying to get his autograph, and because I didn't want to spoil the moment for him I held back from approaching him on that occasion. Shortly after that he moved into F3 with a March 713M.

As usual, I had gone down to Monaco with the family, booking into my regular room at the Metropole Hotel with its balcony overlooking part of the circuit. Watching from there as the final of the F3 event was being run, I kept a close eye on Roger and was very impressed by what I saw. Having started near the back of the grid, he stormed through the field from 18th at the end of the first lap to finish in 7th place. However, I couldn't help noticing that although he was going very well, he was putting out more and more smoke as the race progressed. I said to the family when it was over: "If you'll excuse me, I'm going to leave you for a while to go and find that lad."

It was quite a walk down to the railway station, where they'd got the paddock set up, and by the time I got there and found Roger he'd already got the engine out on the pavement and was busy taking the sump off. I introduced myself, explained that I was also from Leicester and got chatting to him. "You drove a great race there, but to be honest I didn't think you were going to finish," I told him.

"I know – I've got major problems with the engine," he agreed. "I've got to put new piston rings in before the next race in Montlhéry."

I said: "You can't do that with a racing engine, lad. It's too dangerous. Say you break a con rod – it's odds-on the others will all crash into you! Tell you what – don't put that engine back in. I'll treat you to a new one. Who did you get this one off?"

"We bought it on HP from Holbay," he said. Pointing to a van on the other side of the paddock, he added: "That's them over there. But I daren't show my face. We're already behind with the payments. In fact, we haven't paid them anything at all so far."

Well, you had to know Roger's father, Herbert, to appreciate that this came as no great surprise. Not for nothing was he known universally as 'Dodge'. A Leicester garage owner and former speedway rider, he was definitely the sort of bloke who would go into a revolving door behind you and come out in front. And although he was only about five-foot-four, he was punchy and aggressive and was quite liable to thump anybody who upset him.

The extraordinary thing about this, as I was to find out once we all got to know each other well, was that Roger was the complete opposite. The lad was so honourable in every way – he would never dream of doing anything that wasn't perfectly honest and above board. In all the time I knew him, he never once lied to me and he never asked me for anything. It was almost as if he were trying to make up for his dad.

"Don't worry," I told him, heading towards the Holbay van. "I'll talk to them."

Holbay Engineering had been started by brothers Roger and John Dunnell and specialised in F3 engines. Roger was the engineer and John was the businessman of the outfit and, although I didn't know it at the time, it was Roger who was there at Monte Carlo.

"I'd like to buy this lad an engine," I told him. "Have you got a spare one with you?"

"Yes, I have," he replied, adding suspiciously: "But how do we get the money?"

I told him who I was and explained that I was going to be in Monte Carlo until the following Wednesday, but that I would make sure that he was paid as soon as I got back to England. That wasn't good enough for him. Even when I spotted my good friend Rob Walker across the paddock and offered to get him to stand guarantor for me, he still didn't want to know. Things then got a bit heated. In the end, I agreed to pay for both the engines and to have the first one rebuilt – but even then he wasn't sure. I almost had to drag him to a phone to call his brother back in England before he finally agreed to hand over the new engine.

I went back to Roger and said: "That was the hardest thing I've ever had to do, lad! But here's your engine – and the best of luck to you. You were brilliant today."

I was delighted for him, but thought no more about it until a week or so later when there was a knock on the front door very late on a Friday night. I was asleep in an armchair so Lenchen went to answer it and came back saying that there was "a black lad" on the doorstep wanting to see me. That's funny, I thought – I don't know any black lads.

I went to see who it was and there stood Roger, wearing a pair of overalls made for a man four-stone heavier and covered from head to foot in oil and grease. He apologised for his appearance, explaining that he'd had to work late changing a back axle on one of the clapped out old school buses that Dodge was running at the time.

"I'm sorry to bother you at this time of night, Mr Wheatcroft, but I've brought you a ticket for Silverstone because I'm racing there this weekend with your engines and I thought you might like to come and watch me."

"That's really good of you, lad," I said. "Unfortunately, I don't know that I'll be able to make it this time. I've got rather a lot on over the weekend. But thanks very much for the offer – and good luck."

It got to midday the next morning and I began to feel really uncomfortable. I thought to myself, if that lad had the decency to drop me a ticket at twelve o'clock at night, I ought to have the decency to go. So, I had a piece of cake and a cup of tea, jumped in the car and drove straight over to Silverstone.

I arrived just in time to see the car come in, smashed to buggery. In the pits, Roger was unhurt but in despair. "That's my career finished," he wailed. "Have you seen the state of the car?"

I had a close look at it and it was a real mess. I was also horrified to see that the tyres weren't really fit to be on the track, especially the way he was driving. Even at that stage he was blindingly quick, with lightning reactions. He was extraordinarily gifted, so much so that he used to sort himself out in the middle of a corner, waiting until the very last moment before deciding exactly what line to take out of it. But you couldn't do that sort of thing with dodgy tyres. It would be suicidal.

I told him: "It's nothing to do with me, lad, but you shouldn't be out on those tyres. Why don't you let me see if I can get you some new ones and at the same time I might be able to get the car fixed up for you."

I first went off to see Max Mosley, who had founded March Engineering a couple of years earlier in partnership with Alan Rees, Graham Coaker and Robin Herd. I asked Max if there was any chance that we might be able to get the car to the factory so that we could put on new corners, wheels and a nose and get it generally straightened up in time for the race on Sunday. His first reaction was to explain that, quite understandably, there could be a slight internal security problem with the idea of outside mechanics going into the workshops where his people had all their valuable tools.

"Well, what if I were to pay your men double time – do you think they might agree to sort if out for us themselves?" I suggested.

He thought about this for a moment and then told me to hang on while he made a call from the phone box in the paddock. After a quick conversation he came back and said: "OK. Get the car to the factory straightaway and your own men can work on it overnight."

I offered to sign an indemnity for anything that might go wrong or go missing while we were there, but he waved me aside. "No, don't worry," he said. "I trust you completely." As far as I was concerned, Max was a friend for life after that, a man I have always admired and respected.

I next went to see Dick Jeffries of Dunlop, whom I already knew quite well.

"Any chance of you giving this lad a helping hand? " I asked.

"What had you got in mind, Tom?" he inquired.

"Well, how about giving him some tyres and £5,000 worth of sponsorship?" I suggested.

"Ooh!" says Dick. "That's rather a lot."

"Look, you can take it from me, this lad's going to be something special," I assured him. "He's really got what it takes."

There was a short pause while he mulled this over and then he said: "OK. It's a deal. And I tell you what, I'll give you a technician for every race as well."

Finally, I went off in search of BP's Harry Downing. Again, I knew him well because my cars had always run on his petrol. I gave him the same spiel.

"Harry, I've found a lad who's ever so good. I ain't saying we're going to pick up the championship this year, but it's a dead cert for next year."

"I've heard all that a million times before," replied Harry with a sigh.

"Well, it's up to you," I said. "All I'm asking you for is petrol and £5,000. And oil, of course."

Again, there was only a moment's hesitation before he nodded and said: "Alright."

And that was how it all began, casually and almost by chance, during the course of that one weekend at Silverstone. There was never any formal arrangement between Roger and me. He was free to go at any time if he was offered a better drive elsewhere. All I wanted to do was to give him a helping hand up the ladder. As his outstanding talent became blindingly obvious to everybody over the next two years a lot of people came after him, but he turned them all down to stick with me, purely out of loyalty. He was, in every way, a remarkable young man.

There were three separate F3 championships in those days. I'd read a magazine article somewhere suggesting that it would not be possible for one driver to win all three, but when I put it to Roger that we should have a go he was all for it. It was largely a matter of planning his schedule very carefully, choosing races that wouldn't clash in any way and building up a lead in one championship so that he could then afford to miss a few races there while he concentrated on the other two. And he very nearly pulled it off, two years running.

In 1971, driving the March 713-Ford, he won the Lombard North Central Championship and came 2nd in both the Shell Super Oil and the Forward Trust. The following year, alternating between a March 723-Ford and a GRD 372-Ford, he won both the Shell and the Forward Trust and came 4th in the Lombard.

While plenty of people were now starting to sit up and take notice of Roger, I also found myself under siege from other ambitious young drivers. I could hardly go for a Jimmy Riddle without them following me into the gents' to give me an ear bashing. "I could be just as good as your man Williamson if you would back me," they would plead.

"I guess you could," I would reply. "But I only want one driver."

As it happens, it would probably have paid me to run two cars. After all, I had the transporters and everything else I needed. However, I didn't want a situation where my attention was divided.

While all this was going on, I had not been quite so single-minded as far as my own family life was concerned and my marriage was suffering badly as a result. My increasing involvement in motor racing meant that I was hardly ever at home at weekends and the business kept me fully occupied for the rest of the time. One way and another, Lenchen and I were seeing less and less of each other.

The situation wasn't helped by the fact that she had never been one for going away. I would have been only too delighted to take her with me when I went to the more glamorous grand prix events abroad, but she was never keen on that sort of high life. She was quite shy, with very simple tastes, and much preferred to stay at home with the children. And while I was enjoying myself on the grand prix circuit, her idea of a good time was to take the kids off for a caravan holiday at Skegness. I have to say that she was the most wonderful wife and mother, whereas I was not always the greatest husband and father. I was too busy indulging my passion for motorsport.

I must also admit that I was no angel. However, when it came to the incident that eventually prompted Lenchen to walk out on me, I was completely innocent. I had a secretary, Anita, who used to look after all the day-to-day office administration involved in running Wheatcroft Racing – sorting out the travel arrangements for the team, booking flights and accommodation and all that kind of thing. She was always dropping hints about how much she would love to go along to one of the events herself, so in the end I gave in and said she could come with us to Monte Carlo for the Monaco Grand Prix.

Well, of course, the classic thing then happened. Lenchen was sitting at home with the kids, watching the race on television, when the camera zoomed in on the pits. "Look, mummy, there's daddy," piped up one of the girls. "Ooh! And look! There's Anita, too!"

In fact, there was nothing going on between the two of us, but I guess it didn't look too clever. Anyway, by the time I got home, Lenchen had already packed her bags. There was no talking her out of it. As far as she was concerned, this was the last straw.

She eventually moved into a house I'd built in Market Harborough, taking Kevin and our two youngest daughters with her. The older girls had already married and moved away and David, Kevin's elder brother, had also flown the nest, so I found myself on my own. I sold The Firs and built another house nearby in Wigston before then moving into the converted windmill at Arnesby that has been my home ever since.

There was never any question of divorce. My feelings for Lenchen never changed and, as far as I am concerned, marriage is for life. We continued to see each other on a regular basis. I was a frequent visitor to the house in Market Harborough and would often drop in on Sunday evenings on the way back from race meetings with Roger. The separation lasted nearly eight years and then, just as I had always hoped she might, Lenchen eventually agreed to move back in with me at The Mill.

At the time of the split, Roger and I were going from strength to strength. In 1971 he won a Grovewood Award as the most promising young driver of the year as well as being named BP 'Superman of the Year' and also 'Driver Of The Year' by the British Racing and Sports Car Club. The following year he picked up the John Cobb Award for Best British Driver, presented by the British Racing Drivers Club, while I myself was awarded the BRDC's Nigel Moores Trophy as Best Private Entrant in International Motorsport. In those two years Roger had notched up over thirty wins and with his name now on everyone's lips, we decided it was time to think about moving up into Formula One. Our plan was to start off by running a full F2 programme in 1973 with just a few selected F1 events before moving fully into F1 in 1974.

In 1972 we spent six weeks at the Kyalami track in South Africa, testing

Goodyear tyres for March in an F2 car. The end of our spell there coincided with the South African Grand Prix and Roger's lap times were so fast that we seriously considered putting an F1 engine into the car and entering him in the race. I got signatures from all the other teams agreeing to let him run with them in practice and his performance was so phenomenal that people were soon climbing all over the pit wall to watch him.

The next day everybody was swarming around us, accidentally on purpose finding an excuse to stop by at our pit. The excitement that Roger had created was unbelievable. People kept sidling up to ask me: "What are you going to do with your lad next year, Tom? Would you be interested in selling him?"

"Ooh, would you have that sort of money, then?" I'd reply teasingly.

It was such fun – and, of course, I loved every minute of it. Those few days at Kyalami were among the happiest of my life. Unfortunately, the powers that be decided at the last moment that they could not allow Roger to take part in the Grand Prix. "We can't afford to have an F2 car winning an F1 race," they told me. But by then Roger's reputation was spreading fast.

In the run up to the 1973 season I received an urgent telephone call very early one morning from Tim Parnell, the team manager at BRM. I was still in bed at the time.

"Tom, I'm in trouble and I wonder if you could help me out," he said.

"I shouldn't think so, Tim, not at this time of the bloody morning!" I replied. "What's the problem?"

He explained that Clay Regazzoni, who had switched from Ferrari to BRM for the 1973 F1 season, was supposed to be testing for them at Silverstone that day, but was fogbound in Europe and couldn't make it. Would Roger be prepared to stand in for him?

I was non-committal, but agreed to speak to Roger, adding that I would leave the decision entirely up to him. Roger, typically, was all for it. "I'd love to do it, Tom," he said excitedly.

We arrived at Silverstone later that morning to find Tim Parnell, wrapped in a big overcoat to protect him from the February chill, along with an army of mechanics and two cars – a P180 and a P160. Once the introductions had been made and everything had been got ready, Roger first went out in the P180 and almost immediately equalled the lap record that had previously been set by Regazzoni in the slightly faster 160.

He went on to repeat this performance over several consecutive laps, proving that it was no fluke. And then the front upright broke as he was going down the straight at about 180 mph. One wheel came right off and we were very fortunate to avoid a serious accident because as the underside of the car scraped along the tarmac it wore away the bottom of the aluminium tub around the petrol tanks, leaving the rubber tank itself exposed.

I insisted on putting him into the 160 quick, so that he didn't have time to brood on things. It's like falling off a horse – you have to get straight back on or you might lose your confidence. No fear of that with Roger, though. He went out and immediately knocked two tenths of a second off Regazzoni's record.

They ran him all day, going through about twenty sets of tyres, and he kept recording exactly the same time over and over again. If there hadn't been all these witnesses, nobody would have believed the sheets. When you consistently get exactly the same time, lap after lap, it means you are flat out, that you can't squeeze anything more out of the car. In the circumstances, that was quite extraordinary.

It got to about four o'clock in the afternoon, by which time Roger had done the equivalent of more than two grands prix. Watching from the pit wall, I could see the look of exhaustion in his eyes. I jumped off and went to see how he felt.

"Are you tired, Roger?" I asked.

"I'm just beginning to feel it," he replied. "I didn't while I was out there, but I do now."

"Right, jump out," I ordered. "We've had enough."

Tim Parnell wanted him to carry on through two more sets of tyres, but I wouldn't have it. Tim then excused himself and went off to make a phone call, returning a few minutes later to inform me that Louis

Stanley, the boss of BRM, wanted to meet me at the Dorchester for lunch the next day.

"What for?" I asked.

"He wants to talk to you about something that is going to be worth a lot of money to you," he said.

Louis Stanley had taken control of BRM after marrying into the family of industrialist Sir Alfred Owen, the chairman of Rubery Owen, who had owned and sponsored the team for many years. He was a notoriously arrogant, pompous man, who insisted on always being addressed as 'Mr Stanley' or 'Sir' by his staff. And when it came to business meetings, he liked to impress people by summoning them to his regular table at the Dorchester for lunch.

He waited until the dessert was served before coming to the point.

"I want to sign your driver for next year," he said with a flourish. "And I want him here at three o'clock tomorrow to finalise the arrangement." He then got out a little chequebook. "Here's £8,000 for you now. I'll get Marlboro to send you a further £8,000 tomorrow, as soon as everything has been agreed."

"No, Louis," I told him. "You can't have Roger. Apart from anything else, it's already been decided that when he goes into Formula One he'll be going with the DFV engine." The Cosworth DFV was winning everything at the time.

It was as if he hadn't heard me. "Just-tell-me-how-much-you-want," he insisted with a sigh, speaking very slowly and emphasising each single word.

"It isn't money, Louis," I said. "I'm not in this game to make money out of selling a driver, I'm in it for the love of it."

Still he wouldn't give up. He even offered to give me a BRM V16, but, as it happened, I already knew that the valuable V16s weren't his to give away. They were Rubery Owen property and had been carefully stored away in a private house with a special label on them to that effect, forbidding their sale in the event that BRM went bankrupt, a possibility that had been the subject of much speculation at around that time.

In the end, things became rather heated. I got up and left before we'd

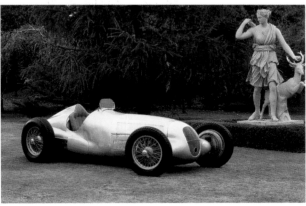

Outside The Mill with the 1958 Vanwall and Winston, who cocked a leg in appreciation of some fine restoration workmanship, and (left), also in The Mill gardens, the Mercedes W125 loaned to the Grand Prix Collection in 2003 by the Musée Nationale de l'Automobile Schlumpfs.

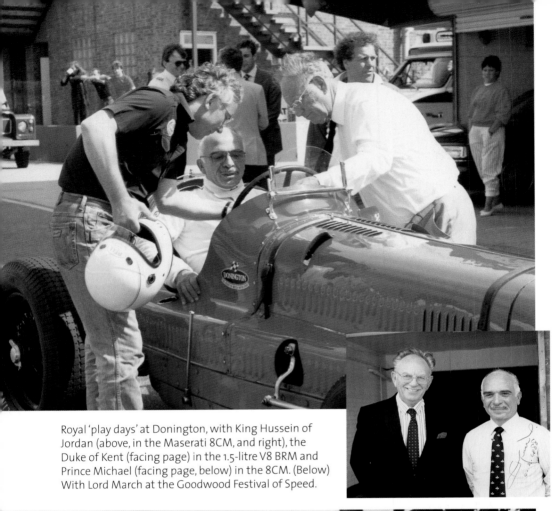

Royal 'play days' at Donington, with King Hussein of Jordan (above, in the Maserati 8CM, and right), the Duke of Kent (facing page) in the 1.5-litre V8 BRM and Prince Michael (facing page, below) in the 8CM. (Below) With Lord March at the Goodwood Festival of Speed.

At Donington during the making of a television film about the history of BRM, with Froilan Gonzales at the wheel of the V16 Mk II and (l to r) Froilan's son Pedro Gonzales, BRM designer Tony Rudd, Sir Stirling Moss, BRM driver Richie Ginther, Bette Hill, me and BRM aficianado Alec Rivers-Fletcher.

(Below, left) Rick Hall with the V16 Mk II engine exposed and (right) me in an Austin 7 twin-cam racer.

Rob Hall (above), dressed in Nuvolari colours, at speed on the Melbourne Rise in the beautifully restored Auto Union that was loaned to us for the 65th anniversary of Nuvolari's 1938 victory.

Nuvolari himself on the Melbourne Rise (right) and (below) Rob Hall's father Rick on the same spot with the Bimotore.

Mike Hailwood (above), still cheerful despite having broken his collar bone in practice at Donington and (below) Barry Sheene after yet another win.

(Left) Beatle George Harrison (under the helmet) trying out Stirling Moss's 1961 Monaco-winning Lotus for size. On the left is Rick Hall.

Two of the biggest crowd-pullers at Donington – the British Motorcycle Grand Prix and (below) the Monsters of Rock heavy metal rock festivals.

With Kevin and one of the tanks from his collection, a Panzer III of the sort I was up against during my time in North Africa and Italy during World War II.

(Below) The McLaren Hall at the Donington Grand Prix Collection.

finished the meal, telling him: "You've spoilt a nice day for me, Louis. You can have my dessert."

As I walked away he called after me: "In future, by the way, my name is Mr Stanley."

"I'll do my best to remember that, Louis," I said. And that was the end of that.

Louis Stanley was not the only one who tried to buy Roger off me. Ken Tyrrell also wanted him.

"Well, he ain't for sale, Ken," I said when he made his approach. "But if it's alright with Roger, and as long as you've got the right car, you can have him for nothing. All I want to do is get him into Formula One in the best possible way."

I got on well with Ken and had a lot of respect for him. He could be as stubborn as a mule, but he had a reputation as one of the straightest men in Formula One at a time when there was not a lot of honesty about. He had done a lot to help quite a few drivers and I also liked his small, family set-up, so I would have been more than happy for Roger to go with him. In fact, it had all been pretty much agreed in principle and we had even got as far as starting to discuss the terms of the contract when Roger came to see me with something on his mind.

I already knew this before he arrived because his mother had phoned me while he was on his way over to tell me: "Don't let Dodge or Roger know that I've told you this, but Roger's been restless for days now. There's something he needs to talk to you about. I won't say any more – I just thought I'd better warn you."

I wondered what it could be. It was obvious as soon as he turned up that something was bothering him – I would have known that even if his mother hadn't called me. I could see it in his eyes. By this time we had become so close that each of us could tell what the other was thinking almost before we opened our mouths.

I waited patiently for him to raise whatever subject it was he wanted to talk to me about – but he said nothing. We met in the office to get a few routine things sorted out, had lunch and visited the workshops. He then came back with me to have a meal at home. We had got into the habit of ringing each other every evening for a chat just after the nine o'clock news and, sure enough, it was as the news finished that he suddenly turned to me and said: "Tom, there's something I've got to ask you."

"What's that then, lad?" I asked, wondering what was coming next.

Looking rather anxious, he went on: "Well, I've been thinking about it a lot and I want to ask if I can stay with you rather than going to Ken Tyrrell. I've got nothing against Ken, but my motor racing won't be the same without you."

"But Ken's forgotten more about motor racing than you and I together know about the sport," I pointed out.

"Yes, but we've won everything we've done so far," he argued. "Why shouldn't we be able to go on and win at the next level? I'd be much happier staying with you. I don't want any wages and you can have all the prize money. I just want to drive – and I don't really want to drive for anyone except you."

It didn't take much to persuade me. By this time there was absolutely no doubt in my mind that Roger was blessed with a natural talent that made him, potentially, another Fangio, Jimmy Clark or Stirling Moss. Apart from that, I had come to love him like a son. He was such a great lad in every way and in the relatively short time we had been together we had developed a perfect understanding.

Finally, there was my own long-term ambition to get involved in F1, possibly even as a constructor. In this respect, I had held back as far as Roger was concerned because I wanted him to have the best possible opportunity and, obviously, my experience at that level was limited. However, if he was that keen to stick with me, then I was more than happy to give it a go.

My first move was to get in touch with Pat McLaren to talk about the possibility of ordering two McLaren M23s, but Pat, who had been running the company following her husband's death in 1970, told me that for various reasons these could not be delivered before the start of the 1974 season.

At this point I made up my mind that I would definitely take the plunge and get involved as a constructor myself. The idea was to start off with an

F2 car that we could also run with an F1 engine. Roger and I sat down and spent hours trying to decide who we should bring in as our designer, settling in the end on Harvey Postlethwaite, the man who had designed the winning Hesketh car. Fired with enthusiasm, I then had a workshop built from scratch in seventeen days and ordered all the latest equipment needed to build the car, including the spot welders to make our own tubs. Sadly, that kit was destined never to come out of the boxes.

The project was put on hold when the opportunity arose for Roger to make a much earlier Formula One debut in a works March 731G – a hybrid F1/F2 car that had rather conveniently been vacated by the sudden defection of French driver Jean-Pierre Jarier. Max Mosley was one of those who had been hugely impressed by Roger's performance at Kyalami and he was only too happy to have him take Jarier's place, starting with the British Grand Prix at Silverstone.

Meanwhile, we had started the 1973 season in fairly low-key fashion with a few F3 races before moving into F2 with a GRD 273. This turned out to be a real swine of a car, so we switched to a March 732-BMW and after blowing up at Rouen owing to a faulty oil pump – by which time Roger had already secured pole position with a lap time twelve seconds ahead of his nearest challenger – we then totally obliterated the opposition in the Monza Lotteria, winning by more than sixteen seconds.

As a result, we arrived for our big day at Silverstone on July 14th in a buoyant mood. For any British driver there is obviously something very special about the British Grand Prix. And Roger was in a relaxed mood, because although he was aware that everybody would be watching him with interest as a possible star of the future, he also knew that he was under no great pressure to perform miracles, it being his first Formula One appearance.

He qualified 22nd, and was looking forward to improving on that in the race itself. Out on the grid, we went through our usual routine. I never actually strapped him into the car – that was done by his mechanic – but I always used to stay with him until the five-minute signal before tapping him on the shoulder and leaving him to get his thoughts together and his mind in focus, ready for the off.

These are always tense moments, but as the noise of the revving engines then rises to a screaming crescendo, the flag drops and the cars lurch away towards the first corner, pure excitement takes over. Unfortunately, on this occasion, it was to be short-lived, the whole race being brought to a sudden and dramatic halt after just one lap by a spectacular crash involving Jody Scheckter in a McLaren.

The South African was in the lead when he suffered a catastrophic blow-out as he was coming around Woodcote. Having lost control, he bounced off the barrier and spun back across the track into the path of the cars behind, several of which ploughed into him and each other. At the back of the field, Roger managed to avoid most of the debris before eventually hitting a car that had turned right around. Because of the angle and the shape of the nose this was almost like a ramp and Roger's car just took off. It went so high that when you watch the video of the incident it is right out of the frame for a moment. When it landed, all the wheels and the suspension collapsed.

Describing the accident later, Roger told reporters: "It all happened so fast. I turned into Woodcote, saw all the dust flying about and got straight on the brakes but everything was cold because it was only the first lap. I started to slide towards the dust and I was aiming for the pit wall, thinking that there wouldn't be any cars there. But I had to swerve to miss the back of one car, then there was another one and now I took off, hit Jody Scheckter's car, then the pit wall and ended up under the bridge. All the drivers were just glad there was no fire because, of course, we all had full tanks."

The race, which had been stopped immediately after the accident, was re-started as soon as the wreckage had been cleared away, but Roger's car was so badly damaged that he was unable to take any further part. His grand prix debut had lasted less than two minutes. It was a terrible disappointment, but I was just thankful that he had somehow managed to emerge unscathed from such a terrifying multiple pile-up. Any fears that his confidence might have been undermined were removed the following weekend when he led the Misano Adriatico F2 event convincingly up until the moment when an electrical fault forced his retirement.

Meanwhile, back at March, the engineers and mechanics were working overtime to get the 731G back in shape in time for the Dutch Grand Prix at Zandvoort on July 29th.

All these years later, I can still hardly bring myself to recall the dreadful events of that day. It had started on such a positive note. The day before I flew out to Holland I had confirmed the order of a pair of the latest McLaren M23s for the following season, at a cost of £40,000 each. That may sound ridiculously cheap compared with today's prices – a two-year-old Schumacher car recently changed hands for £2 million and there's no way you would ever be allowed to buy a current works grand prix car – but it was a great deal of money at the time. And the fact that an M23 went on to win the World Championship for Emerson Fittipaldi in 1974 and James Hunt in 1976 showed that I'd made the right choice. Ironically, as things turned out, one of my other main considerations in choosing a McLaren was their reputation for being safe cars.

At this stage, everything seemed to be falling perfectly into place. On the day of the race itself I was offered the biggest sponsorship deal there had ever been up to that point. It came from Marlboro via a third party, who took me out to lunch and asked if Roger would race under their colours in 1974. The figure mentioned was much bigger than anything I had been thinking of – and I had been thinking big!

One way and another I was in high spirits as we prepared for the start of the race. The first hint that perhaps not everything was going our way came in the pit lane when the car wouldn't initially fire up. The three-minute signal was up by the time we did get it going, so Roger had to go to the back of the grid. However, he more than made up for this during the first few laps, rapidly moving up through a field led by Jackie Stewart, Ronnie Peterson, François Cévert, Denny Hulme and James Hunt. He was going so well at this stage that Max Mosley turned to me in the pits and shouted excitedly: "We could win this, Tom!"

Roger was lying 13th when, on Lap 8, disaster struck. As he was coming through the fast Hondenvlak right-hander at 140 mph, the offside front tyre simply disintegrated, part of it peeling off and wrapping itself around the suspension, interfering with the steering. The car immediately slid out of control, slammed into the safety barrier at an awkward angle and was catapulted back across the track, flying through the air for 275ft before landing and skidding a further 100ft, finally coming to rest, upside down, against the Armco. The fuel tank had ruptured and it now burst into flames.

This was the first event that I had been to at which there were closed circuit TV screens in the pits. The mechanic came over and grabbed my arm as the pictures of the crash came up on screen. By then the car was enveloped in smoke and flames.

"My God, it ain't ours, is it?" I asked.

"Yes, it is," he replied. "And I didn't see Roger get out!"

What happened during the next few minutes must rank as one of the most disgraceful and tragic episodes in the annals of motor racing history.

David Purley, following immediately behind in his similar, privately-run, March 731G, had screeched to a halt and sprinted across the track to Roger's assistance. Far from already being dead at this stage, as the circuit officials later tried to suggest, Roger was fully conscious and had managed to activate the on-board fire extinguisher, temporarily dousing the flames. David could hear him screaming: "Get me out! Get me out!" But as he fought heroically and single-handedly for nearly three minutes to right the car – straining so desperately hard that he burst blood vessels in both his arms – the marshals, who were standing nearby, refused to lift a finger to help him. At the same time, the race officials did not see fit to stop the race so that the fire trucks could get to the scene. One of those trucks was actually stationed within sight of the accident, but was not allowed to go against the flow of the race traffic.

As the fire once again took hold, David rushed across to a dithering marshal and forcibly grabbed an extinguisher off him, only to find when he hit the activating button that it was a dud. He ran back to get a second one – and that, too, was not working. Eventually, beaten back by the heat of the flames and realising that Roger was beyond help, he was dragged away in tears. At the same time, hundreds of horrified spectators at the side of the track, appalled by the inactivity of the marshals, were trying to climb the fences to go and help David's lone rescue operation, only to be held back by police and marshals. And all the while the race continued, with the live TV cameras intermittently recording the tragic sequence of events each time the cars passed that point. Ayrton Senna is probably the only other driver ever to have suffered quite such a public death.

Back in the pits, I was frantic. Dodge was there with Roger's girlfriend and, as well as everything else, I was doing my best to look after them. At that stage, I felt as if I was trying to be three men in one. But when I eventually got to the scene of the accident at the end of the race, I realised I was only one tenth of a man.

The other drivers were horrified when they were made aware of exactly what had been happening. As race winner Jackie Stewart levered himself out of his car Ken Tyrrell stopped him from removing his helmet, so that nobody would be able to see his face or read his lips, before breaking the news to him. On the podium, Jackie refused the champagne, wouldn't touch the trophy and showed absolutely no elation. And he later revealed that it was at that moment that he finally made up his mind that he was going to retire, that the sport had become too dangerous. At the same time, the shock waves resulting from what he described as "a horrible tragedy" prompted an urgent review of safety and emergency procedures at grand prix circuits around the world, with particular regard to fire-fighting facilities.

Back at my hotel, I was formally arrested by the police and spent the night in a cell. The law in Holland is the same as it is in Italy, where, as the owner of a racing car in which a driver has been killed, you are theoretically liable to a charge of manslaughter. David Purley's manager was the first person who came to see me at the police station, sent by David with orders to help me in any way we could. He got hold of the local British consul, who was brilliant. He not only got me out of jail, but also helped me with the task of finding an undertaker and making arrangements to fly Roger's body home.

The day that Roger died was the saddest of my life. What made it worse was that his death was so needless. Today, with the vastly improved safety regulations that Bernie Ecclestone and the FIA now enforce so rigorously, he would not only have survived, but might well have escaped unscathed. As it was, even with the less effective measures in place in 1973, he should never have died.

I tortured myself with the thoughts of what might have been, if only certain things had been different. If only, if only…

I worried that maybe I was to blame in some way, that I had perhaps pushed him too far, too soon. For years afterwards I had a recurring nightmare in which judges in wigs would accuse me, pointing their fingers at me and saying: "You killed him! You killed him!"

Looking back now, my conscience is clear in that respect. He was such a brilliant talent and, at twenty-five, was more than ready to compete at the highest level. Jackie Stewart later revealed that it was after watching Roger test for Ken Tyrrell that he first started thinking about retiring, simply because Roger was so quick. Everybody could see that he was gifted in a very special way. Fangio was the best I'd ever seen and yet I could imagine Roger matching his record. There is certainly no doubt in my mind that he would have gone on to become World Champion – and that he would probably have done so sooner rather than later.

I think almost everybody agrees that it was the officials at Zandvoort who were totally responsible for his tragic death. The Dutch Grand Prix had been taken out of the calendar the previous year after the drivers had questioned the safety of the circuit following the 1971 event there. And although improvements had been made in the interim, the Armco posts were still simply set in sand and the marshals were not equipped with fireproof clothing, both of which factors had a bearing on the accident and its immediate aftermath. Even more unforgivable was the utter failure to recognise the severity of the incident and the urgent need to stop the race immediately so as to get the emergency services to the scene as quickly as possible. In the end, it was at least eight minutes before they eventually arrived.

I was advised to sue the circuit owners and the race organisers, but decided against it in the end. What good would it do? Suing wouldn't bring Roger back – and he himself was not the type who ever would have sued.

There was, however, a rather poignant and revealing postscript to the whole sad story. On July 29th, 2003, exactly thirty years to the day after the accident, we unveiled a special memorial to Roger in the memorial garden in front of the museum at Donington Park. Anyone who had known him, either as a driver or a friend, was invited to attend. A large number of people turned up to watch the unveiling of a bronze statue of Roger by his sister, Barbara Upton. But it wasn't until afterwards that I was told about one man whose presence at the ceremony had not been expected.

He had been noticed standing slightly apart from everybody else and hanging back, but nobody recognised him. John Bailie, the public relations and design consultant responsible for marketing, communications and events at the Grand Prix Collection, eventually went up and introduced himself, asking him politely who he was and what had brought him there.

"I've come here for one purpose only – and that is to lay a ghost to rest," he replied rather mysteriously. He wasn't very talkative at first, but when John gently persisted and asked him if he had had a good day he was silent for a moment or two before replying: "No. This is probably the second worst day of my life."

He then went on to reveal that he had been one of the leading officials at Zandvoort back in 1973 and that, ultimately, it had been his decision not to stop the race. "We simply did not appreciate the gravity of the situation until it was too late and that has haunted me ever since," he said. "It is to try and make some amends to my conscience that I have come here from Holland today."

John Bailie wisely decided not to tell me about this conversation until later, after everyone had left and gone home. It had been a highly emotional day and even after all those years I don't think I could have found forgiveness in my heart.

Back on Track

THE SHOCK of Roger's death knocked all the wind out of my sails. At his funeral I was hardly aware of who else was present or what was going on around me. People I didn't even recall seeing there told me later that we had actually had lengthy conversations. And for days afterwards I could barely summon the energy to get out of bed in the morning, let alone go to the office. Life seemed suddenly empty, the future blank. I have never been an emotional man, but for a while I was completely overwhelmed with grief and for the first time ever in my adult life I found myself in tears.

Even now, all these years later, scarcely a day goes by when I don't think about Roger. At the time, I couldn't get him out of my mind for a moment. In particular, I kept going over and over the events of that fateful day. I am not normally at all superstitious, but it seemed that the number thirteen had come into everything. Although the car ran under the number 14, we were actually 13th in the list of entries, sandwiched in between Graham Hill and Emerson Fittipaldi; the race started thirteen minutes late and Roger was in 13th place at the time of the crash. For months afterwards I was obsessed with the number 13.

It was nearly a fortnight before I felt able to leave the house and face the world again. In an effort to take my mind off everything else, I then plunged myself back into work with a vengeance. There was certainly more than enough going on there to keep me fully occupied. While the building business was starting to feel the effects of the world recession brought on by the OPEC oil price hike, my ambitious plans for the revival of Donington Park as a top motorsport venue were in danger of being scuppered by the local planning authorities.

I thought this was pretty rich, given that it was their people who had actually suggested Donington to me in the first place, knowing full well what I had in mind. I had been told that planning consents for the re-introduction of motor racing had already been granted in 1957 and again in 1967, when the previous owner, Major John Gillies Shields, had been contemplating the resurrection of the circuit, and I was led to understand that this meant I would have no problems in getting the go-ahead, especially as Donington fell within an area set aside for leisure and recreation. However, when I submitted a detailed planning application in December 1971, eight months after buying Donington and three months after being given the green light to build the museum, it was turned down.

That signalled the beginning of a bitter five-and-a-half-year battle that was to cost me well over £1 million in legal fees and other expenses associated with a series of appeals, culminating in the lengthy, six-week public inquiry that eventually cleared the way for me to realise my dream of re-opening the circuit. The need to fight further planning restrictions at almost every stage of development over the years since then has pushed that figure up to around £2.5 million altogether.

It has been said that anyone less determined than me would have given up very early on in the face of such escalating expense, not to mention the relentless opposition of various local pressure groups. These included powerful vested interests such as the East Midlands Airport next door and Rolls Royce, who had moved into some of the offices and workshops vacated by the Army after the war. However, surrender was never really an option as far as I was concerned. I have always had an awkward, stubborn streak when it comes to being told I can't do something. In particular, I have never been one to let planning officials get the better of me.

I could fill an entire chapter with stories of my run-ins with planners over the years, but that would probably not be of much interest to the general reader. Suffice it to say that they are an occupational hazard for any builder. My main objection is that all too often their attitude is totally negative. Bad planners – and, in my experience, there are an awful lot of them – seem to take great delight in imposing petty and often nonsensical restrictions that don't benefit anyone in the long run.

I have also come across a fair bit of corruption in my time. I've always had a liking for old windmills and the one at Arnesby that is now my home was by no means the first that I had restored and converted over the years. On a previous occasion, my conversion plans having been turned down for what seemed to me like no good reason, I decided to go ahead anyway and argue about it later. I'd already moved in when the phone rang and a certain local planning official came on the line.

"I hear you're converting a windmill into a house without the proper planning permission," he said.

"You're wrong there," I replied. "The job's already been done!"

He immediately threatened to throw the book at me and started quoting various regulations. I listened in silence and waited for him to finish before warning him: "Listen. If you're going to fight me, I'll fight you. And when we're done, I rather doubt whether you'll still be working for the Council." I then went on to reveal certain information that had come my way regarding his wife's car and his son's car, who it was who had actually bought them and was paying to maintain them. By some strange coincidence, this generous benefactor happened to be a building contractor who, shortly afterwards, had been allowed to go ahead with a particular new development in the area in rather irregular circumstances.

At this point it all went very quiet at the other end of the line and, next thing I knew, a bloke on a racing bike turned up on my doorstep with the plans for my mill conversion, all wrapped up and with 'Approved' stamped on them. Not that this made an awful lot of difference as I'd actually changed my mind and built the place to a completely different plan than that originally submitted!

Occasionally, a builder's frustration with unnecessarily negative and obstructive planning regulations will boil over in spectacular fashion.

Some years ago a developer I knew was denied permission to build houses on a plot he owned near the Leicestershire County Council offices, on the grounds that it was designated as agricultural land. His response was to build some sties there and move in a load of pigs instead. On warm summer days when the breeze was in the wrong direction the council had to keep their windows closed because of the stink. I did like that man's style!

The nearest I got to doing anything quite as imaginative as that was when I was ordered to knock down the last house on a small estate I'd built after it was found to be a matter of inches too close to the boundary fence. The local council backed down when I reminded them that there was an acute housing shortage at the time and that the Press would undoubtedly be very interested in the story of such a wasteful demolition. If they had persisted, I was quite prepared to donate the house to Shelter rather than pull it down!

As it happens, the leading planning official involved in the Donington Park saga, Maurice Pettifor, was among the better ones I have ever had to deal with. I have no doubt that when he originally pointed me in the direction of Donington, after I had been turned down at other sites for various reasons, he did so in good faith, genuinely believing that I would have no difficulty in getting permission to restore the existing circuit. And I happen to know that he was personally in favour of a development that he felt would be of great benefit to the area generally. Unfortunately, of course, it was not to be that straightforward.

The first major complication centred on the interpretation of what, in planning terms, constituted the "existing use" supposedly established by the 1957 and 1967 consents. It soon became clear that we couldn't simply restore the original circuit exactly as it had been before because it would no longer come anywhere near meeting the routine safety regulations laid down by the RAC, still the governing body for motor racing in this country at that time. Among other things, the track itself would have to be widened overall and slightly re-routed in certain sections, most notably where it passed through the narrow fourteen-foot stone arch of Starkey's Bridge, which lies between the Hairpin and McLean's Corner. The pits and paddock would also have to be rebuilt and modern grandstands erected.

Leicestershire County Council's Planning Committee not only turned down planning applications for all such improvements, but also announced that having taken further legal advice, they had decided that the 1957 and 1967 consents had lapsed and were no longer valid. So, in July 1972, lengthy consultations and meetings with council officials having got us nowhere, I submitted a fresh planning application.

At the same time, the management of East Midlands Airport lodged a formal objection to the re-opening of the circuit on the grounds of public safety. They argued that the close proximity of the main runway meant that there would be the risk of a major disaster, with thousands of casualties on the ground, if a plane were to crash on landing or take-off while a race meeting was in progress.

This was later to be officially dismissed as such a remote possibility that it shouldn't be seriously considered as a valid reason for stopping the redevelopment of the circuit. In the meantime, however, airport director Eric Dyer led a delegation to the Minister of Aerospace that resulted in the Department of Trade and Industry convening a special meeting between the County Council, the Airport and the Civil Aviation Authority in October 1972. Although it was conceded at this meeting that the element of risk was very slight, it was left to the local planning authority to weigh that risk against the advantages of allowing the circuit to develop.

The County Council duly came down on the side of the airport and once again rejected our application. To my cynical mind, this did not come as a great surprise. What had originally been the Diseworth RAF base had become a civil airport only in 1965 and, although it was concerned mainly with freight traffic in those early days before the era of mass air travel, there is no doubt that its owners were already looking forward to the time when it would become the fastest-growing airport in the country. Foreseeing the likely need for all sorts of expansion in the future, the last thing they wanted was any sort of development right on their doorstep. Better to have unused land there, ready to be taken over by themselves as and when they needed it. And, considering the commercial value of such an important regional facility as a flourishing regional airport, one can well understand why they might have more clout with the local authority than an individual who had been a thorn in the side of the planning department for years!

So, it was undoubtedly self-interest rather than concern for the safety of motorsport fans at Donington that motivated the airport's objections to what we were planning, a fact that was underlined in the most ironic fashion some time later when the boot was on the other foot and they wanted to extend their runway to accommodate bigger aircraft. At that point they changed their tune completely, producing evidence to show that this posed absolutely no significant threat to the safety of competitors and spectators at the circuit.

The County Council's December 1972 decision against us was probably made easier by the rather unfortunate timing of one of the first events of any kind to take place at Donington following my takeover. Earlier that same month it had served as a checkpoint for the RAC Rally, with the 150 drivers then going on to complete a special stage on sections of the old existing track. Huge crowds turned out to watch this event, causing massive traffic jams on all roads leading to the circuit. This seemed to confirm the fears of local residents, who had been objecting to our plans mainly on the grounds of noise and congestion. As we tried to point out, the event had been organised not by us but by the RAC, and they had simply underestimated just how many spectators would turn up. But the damage had been done.

Although we had faced predictable and very vocal opposition from an action group that included members of Castle Donington Parish Council, the long since defunct Rural District Council and an organisation called the Civic Society, the vast majority of Castle Donington residents were actually in favour of what we were trying to do. This was confirmed after butcher Syd Bates and housewife Mrs Muriel Tomlinson organised a petition in favour of bringing back racing and collected 4,000 signatures from people living in the area. Mr Bates explained that they were fed up with all the noise created by councillors campaigning against the project and pointed out there was already constant noise from aircraft landing at the airport whereas the circuit would only be in use for a few hours each week. Dismissing the risk of a plane crashing onto the circuit during a meeting as "a million-to-one chance", he also called for a sensibly balanced attitude towards the prospect of occasional congestion. "Thousands of people will be provided with entertainment, so we must be prepared to make do with some small inconvenience once a week," he said.

At around the same time, the Donington Park Racing Association was formed by a group of local racing enthusiasts in support of our bid. Claiming a membership of over 1,000, the Association challenged some of the more alarmist statements made by the Action Group, including assertions that the return of racing would mean an increase in the rates and that the park itself would be "ravaged". Such comments were wild and irresponsible, they said, and made without knowledge of the true facts. They stressed the fact that any extra services connected with the racing, such as policing and traffic control, would be paid for by the organisers, just as at any other sporting event. As for the park being ravaged, they pointed out that although areas of woodland had been cleared – with the full approval of the Forestry Commission – to make way for the proposed new circuit, more than seven hundred trees had been replanted, including cedars, oak, maple, weeping willow, mountain ash and sycamore.

In the face of all this mounting controversy, the Parish Council organised a referendum among Castle Donington residents, who proceeded to vote overwhelmingly in our favour – by 949 to 599. Despite this, the County Council planning authorities persisted in refusing any application we put forward in relation to the development of the circuit. I appealed and in this deadlocked situation the Department of the Environment eventually decided to hold a Public Inquiry.

This involved a time-consuming and extremely expensive process. It takes at least a year to set up a Public Inquiry once it has been called and a further year before it finally announces its decision. By the time I had engaged a leading QC to represent me, I found myself facing costs of around £10,000-a-day for the Inquiry itself, which, I was warned, could go on for weeks.

In fact, it lasted for thirty-one days. Presided over by a lady Inspector, Gillian Pain, it was held in early 1975 at the offices of the North West Leicestershire District Council in Coalville. I sat through every minute of the proceedings, listening intently to every word while unintentionally driving everybody else mad by constantly jingling the loose change in my pocket. This is a nervous habit I've got into whenever I'm trying to concentrate hard. The trouble was that in the stillness of the council chamber the sound was amplified and I had to be warned repeatedly by the Inspector to stop doing it.

The same thing was to happen a year or two later when a dispute with Tarmac over the resurfacing of the track at Donington ended up in court. On that occasion the judge eventually threatened, after several warnings, to hold me in contempt of court if I did it once more! We ended up losing that case, which everybody thought we should have won, and I reckon my jingling coins may have been at least partly to blame.

Back at Coalville, it seemed to me that there were two or three key turning points in the Inquiry, one of them quite dramatic. While preparing our case, our legal team had stumbled across information relating to the background of one key objector appearing on behalf of the East Midlands Airport, information of a sort that would clearly undermine his personal credibility in such a way as to cast doubt on the reliability of the claims he was putting forward.

My QC asked me if I wanted to make use of this information and I replied that I felt we should only do so as a last resort, but that I would leave it up to his discretion. In the event, he decided that it was too significant to be ignored. While conducting his cross-examination, he waved a piece of paper and announced that certain facts had come to light regarding this individual's personal and career background and also his professional qualifications that didn't quite square with what he had told the Inquiry. Could he explain that? It wasn't necessary to go any further because, on hearing this, the chap immediately turned deathly white and passed out.

Rolls Royce's argument that the noise of racing car engines would make it impossible to work collapsed in almost comical fashion when the

Inspector decided to visit the site to see the exact set-up for herself. The manager had produced decibel readings for a DFV Cosworth engine at full throttle and had claimed that this meant his men wouldn't be able to hear each other talk. Happily for us, however, a jet came in to land just as the Inspector was being shown round. It passed right overhead and was so low that, even with my poor eyesight, I reckoned I could just about see every rivet! The noise was deafening and we all rushed to take refuge inside the building.

"We're so used to them here that we hardly notice when they go over," said the manager. He must have regretted that casual admission as soon as the words were out of his mouth because the Inspector asked immediately: "Well, if that noise doesn't bother you then how is it that the cars are going to be such a problem?"

One of my other favourite moments came when a local resident objected on the grounds that it would be very dangerous to have heavy race-day traffic coming out of Donington Park and onto a main road that went down a hill in one direction and into a long straight with a concealed dip in the other.

"And how long have you been driving, sir?", inquired the Inspector.

"Oh, I don't drive at all," he replied indignantly. "It's far too dangerous!"

Some of the rubbish I had to sit and listen to during that Inquiry was quite unbelievable and it seems that the Inspector must have felt the same way, because when she eventually announced her decision exactly a year later in 1976 it was almost entirely in our favour. With regard to the objections raised by the East Midlands Airport, she concluded that the development of the circuit would not result in any unacceptable risk to public safety and would have no detrimental effect whatsoever on the operation, efficiency or foreseeable development of the airport itself. On the subject of traffic congestion, she said that problems were only likely to occur when major international meetings were held and that she did not consider that this should override the general benefit of a well-located site. As for noise, she was satisfied that there would not be any serious disturbance to the majority of residents in neighbouring areas and, once again, she stressed that she did not consider that these objections should override the natural advantages of the site.

I couldn't have hoped for a better result if I'd written it myself – except in one tiny but vital respect. Although I had won on virtually every issue that had been contested, my appeal was still dismissed on a minor technicality. This concerned the splay line at the Wilson Lodge access, which was deemed to be too narrow to provide proper visibility. Widening it would be more than a mere formality because I did not own the land on either side. Fortunately, I was able to buy this from the Shields family and carry out the necessary work, but although the family were decent enough not to hold me to ransom over the land, this all added further expense and delay.

After formally re-applying for planning permission yet again I was finally given the go-ahead in 1976. The battle had lasted almost as long as World War II and, at times, had seemed to me to be just as much of a struggle against the odds.

To celebrate our hard-won victory we decided to throw a party in one of the halls of the museum and among those who turned up was a local councillor who had been at the forefront of the campaign against us. The champagne had been flowing freely when, towards the end of the evening, he approached me in an expansive mood. With a big smile on his face he stuck out his hand and said something to the effect that it had been a no-holds-barred fight, but that now I'd won he'd like to offer his congratulations and hoped there would be no hard feelings. I guess he was trying to make a conciliatory gesture, but I didn't quite see it that way at the time. We'd all had a good drink and in my slightly befuddled state the only thing that came to mind was all the trouble and strife and aggravation that he and his fellow objectors had caused me. It hadn't cost them a penny to throw spanners in my works at every possible opportunity whereas I had incurred expenses of well over £1 million. Five years of repressed anger and frustration welled up inside me and instead of shaking his outstretched hand I threw a punch at him.

Ben Warr, my wartime Army pal, would have been proud of me if he had seen it. As it was, everyone around us froze in horror for a moment before jumping forward to usher me away, warning me to behave myself.

"He's on our side now, Tom," somebody hissed in my ear. "That's why he came along tonight. Now look what you've gone and done!"

It was all a bit awkward and embarrassing for a while, but we somehow managed to patch things up. A few months later, however, it turned out that the fighting over Donington was still not entirely finished.

We had originally hoped to hold the first official race meetings in the late summer of 1976, but had been forced to put the date back to the following season because of the extra planning delays. In the meantime, in July 1976, we hosted a special stage of the Texaco Tour of Britain Rally. This was a fun day with lots of family entertainment, including a fairground attraction, a parachute display and a concert appearance by Chris Barber's All Stars jazz band, while Dave Lee Travis presented the Radio 1 Road Show live from the site. The drivers, among them Roger Clark, Timo Makinen, Ari Vatanen, Walter Rohrl and Tony Pond, started the special section on the rough twisting tracks in the middle of the Park before doing a lap of the new circuit, which was ready by this time, apart from the top surface. Also taking part in the event were Prince Michael, who was driving with Nigel Clarkson in a Ford Escort RS 2000, and Noel Edmonds – then at the height of his fame as a Radio 1 DJ and children's television presenter – who partnered James Hunt.

I read later that Edmonds, a great motorsport enthusiast in those days, had not enjoyed the experience at all, finding Hunt to be less than totally congenial company. Knowing James Hunt as well as I did, that came as no great surprise to me. He was not always the easiest man to get along with. I first met him when I was involved in F3 with Roger Williamson and actually helped him quite a bit when he was starting out, but as soon as he made a name for himself it seemed he didn't want to know me any more.

One of my earliest memories of him was when he got himself disqualified at Brands Hatch after it was found that a hole had been drilled in the manifold of his car to increase the air intake illicitly. He was a very emotional lad and when this happened he broke down in tears, crying: "That's me finished!"

I immediately took him round the back of the pits, out of sight of the spectators, and told him: "Look, lad, don't let the public see you like that. You must try not to let your feelings show."

Later on, I loaned him a new engine on one occasion – and even helped to save his career after Max Mosley had sacked him from the March Formula 3 team. It was me who then introduced him to Lord Hesketh, with whom he famously went on to win his first World Championship race. And yet once he had made a name for himself his attitude towards me changed completely and it was as if our friendship had never existed. I would see him in the paddock and he would look straight through me. I didn't have a lot to do with him from then on.

Following the Tour of Britain Rally we set to work on getting the circuit completed in time for the inaugural road race event, a motorcycle meeting to be staged on May 14th, 1977 by the Pathfinders and Derby Motorcycle Club. As well as laying down the tarmac surface on the track, extending the run-off areas and building pits, grandstands and various public facilities, the work also involved constructing a ten-foot-high concrete wall around the entire perimeter of the circuit. As I mentioned earlier, I didn't want anyone sneaking in for free as I had done when I was a lad!

Our efforts to get everything done on time were hampered by atrocious weather conditions during the winter months, not to mention one or two of the mishaps that are always likely to occur when you are working against the clock with heavy plant. I was sitting in the offices at Donington one day when there was a huge explosion and a blinding flash of light. For a moment I thought that there really had been a plane crash at the East Midlands Airport. However, when we rushed out to see what had happened we found that a crane, which someone had unwisely decided to move with its jib still raised, had hit an overhead power line, with spectacular results. Amazingly, the crane driver remained completely unharmed, thanks, presumably, to the rubber tyres on the crane.

Later, there was another incident in which a digger cut through a 50,000-volt underground cable, causing an explosion that set the surrounding grassland on fire. On this occasion, it wasn't our fault. We knew exactly where the cable was and had carefully marked its position. What nobody had told us was that the Electricity Board, in laying the cable, had found that it was longer than it needed to be and instead of shortening it they had simply looped it to one side. Our driver, digging a parallel trench, went straight through it. Once again, he somehow avoided injury

Even luckier was the driver involved in a third incident. This time we were putting a drain across a stream at another site and the digger was actually standing in the water when it struck a 30,000-volt underground cable. The resulting shockwave tore the front off the digger and melted the tow-chain connecting it to the bulldozer that had pulled it into position. It also left the nearby brickyard and dye works without power. They were intent on suing us for a considerable amount of damages as a result, but two days before the case was due to be heard we were able to prove that the Electricity Board had made a mistake on the plans they had given us that purported to show exactly where the power line was located.

These things happen on big building sites – and even elsewhere. We once inadvertently brought mainline rail services between Leicester and St Pancras to a halt after we hit a bridge at Market Harborough while moving a large digger on a low-loader. That was partly my fault. Because the only chap available to drive the low loader didn't actually have a licence for such a vehicle, he had to be accompanied by somebody who was qualified. I'd come out of the Army with a licence to drive anything so it was me that went with him. We then got chatting and forgot all about the bridge until it was too late. We hit it with such force that it knocked all the rivets out and if you look underneath you can still see the dent we put in it.

The police and the fire brigade were called and the line was temporarily closed while engineers inspected the damage, but, fortunately, it turned out that it had not been structurally weakened in any way. Even so, it's a mystery how we got away without being summonsed. All it cost us in the end was the price of a new bike for the cyclist who had been following closely behind us and who ran straight into the back of us. He himself wasn't hurt too badly, but his bike was a complete write-off.

Given such a chapter of fairly dramatic accidents, it is extraordinary that in well over forty years in the building business, no one working for us was ever seriously injured. The nearest anyone came to real disaster was poor old Mick Higgins. It happened shortly after I had bought some very smart aluminium ex-USAF radio caravans to serve as mashing huts. Mick, who always had a pipe on the go, went in one morning as usual to put the kettle on, only for the whole place to blow up in his face.

It seemed someone had left the gas on all night and when Mick went in with his pipe it sparked a massive explosion. They found the window frame 100 yards away! Mick was blown through the door, catching the side of his face on the frame and causing damage to a nerve that resulted in him losing his ear some time later. It didn't seem to bother him that much. We went to see him in hospital and he was as chirpy as ever, still clutching his pipe.

Despite the difficult conditions up at Donington we did eventually manage to get everything done in time for the grand re-opening. The big day arrived and veteran motorcyclist 'Squib' Burton opened the proceedings by riding an exhibition lap on the very same 350cc Raleigh on which he had won the first ever race at Donington back in 1931. He was followed by fellow veterans Arthur Wellsted, Freddie Frith and Peter Goodman, all of them doing laps on their old-time machines. Clerk of the Course for the day was Arthur Taylor, a former secretary of the Pathfinders and Derby Club and a paddock marshal at Donington when the last meeting had been held there thirty-eight years previously on August 26th, 1939 – just eight days before the outbreak of war. The honour of being the first winner on the new circuit went to 'Rocket' Ron Haslam, who clocked an average lap speed of 88.52 mph on his 750cc Pharaoh Yamaha. Ron went on to become a Donington favourite over the next few years before retiring to run a professional riding school based at the circuit.

Motor racing was due to return to Donington a fortnight after the motorcycle event, on May 28th. This was the moment I had been looking forward to ever since the day, six years earlier, when I finalised the deal to buy the circuit. As we made final preparations everything seemed set fair – including, for once, the weather. A full programme of ten races, including both Formula Ford and Formula Libre events, had been organised by the Nottingham Sports Car Club with sponsorship from the local Else Motor Group. A heatwave had been forecast for the weekend and crowds of up to 40,000 were confidently expected. Then, late on the Thursday night, we suddenly got a call from the RAC informing us that they had decided to withdraw our racing licence on legal advice. Without it, racing could not go ahead.

It emerged that a few members of the Castle Donington Civic Society, unhappy with the outcome of the Public Inquiry and still determined to find some way of preventing the return of racing to Donington Park, had discovered a minor technical irregularity relating to the diversion of a footpath, something that they thought could be exploited and used against us. The path had originally crossed the circuit via Starkey's Bridge, which was actually more like a miniature viaduct than a bridge. When we were then forced to divert the circuit so as to bypass the narrow arch through which it had previously run, we had had no option but to cut away the banking on one side of the bridge, so that it now ended abruptly with a sheer twenty-foot drop.

The footpath had been virtually unused for years and was almost totally overgrown with brambles in parts. What's more, we had taken great care to divert it so that it took walkers on what was actually a much more scenic route. But this counted for nothing with the members of the Civic Society who seized on the issue in triumph as an opportunity to thwart our plans all over again. Their argument was based on the technicality that we had not quite followed the correct procedure in giving formal notice of the diversion. Strictly speaking, this has to be done with an announcement both in the local press and in the *London Gazette*. We hadn't been able to put a notice in the *Gazette* in time because its publication had been halted for some weeks by a strike. And we had only placed the announcement in the *Derby Evening Telegraph* on May 9, which meant that people had until June 9th to register any objections before the diversion could be formally approved.

This was nitpicking of the most bloody-minded kind, but the RAC, having been tipped off about the dispute by the Civic Society, then got cold feet and withdrew their licence on the advice of their lawyers, who told them that it would be a criminal offence to obstruct the footpath until the situation had been fully sorted out.

Having announced that the meeting would go ahead "come what may", we drove to London and spent the whole of the Friday locked in talks with the RAC and their lawyers, trying to work out some kind of compromise. A lot of the debate centred on another minor technicality, which was all to do with whether we had permission to block the footpath temporarily during full race meetings or only during testing.

It was what the Press described as 'a cliff-hanger' and by quite late on the Friday evening there was still no agreement. Competitors who had arrived at Donington during the day expecting to practice were unable to do so and, when they heard what was going on, many of them turned straight round and went home. Up in London the first sign of a breakthrough finally came after the RAC's lawyers hinted that things might be different if the bridge over which the original path had been routed were actually deemed to be unsafe. I thought to myself: "Well, I can soon make the bridge unsafe – that'll only take five minutes with the help of a bulldozer!" I quickly left the room to make a discreet telephone call, arranging for one of our workmen to take a bulldozer out there and give the bridge a bit of a shake-up – accidentally on purpose, as it were! We then got the local RAC man out of bed to go and inspect it and he duly confirmed that it was indeed unstable. On this basis we were granted a licence for the eight production car races in the programme, but not the Formula Ford and Formula Libre racing car events. The reason for this differentiation was never made entirely clear.

My solicitor, who was with me for many years, always used to maintain that the pen is mightier than the sword – or, in my case, the bulldozer – but this was not the only occasion on which I was able to prove him wrong.

The first time was shortly after I had bought Donington and found myself facing the problem of what to do about the fourteen or so small companies that were 'squatting' in the Nissen huts that had been left behind by the Army. They had no legal right to be there, but repeated efforts by the County Council to get them out had failed. They simply claimed squatter's rights and sat tight. I had been anticipating a long drawn-out dispute, but as things turned out they all gave up without a fight after an early skirmish that took place after I invited respected motorsport journalist Philip Turner to take one of my cars for a spin on what remained of the original circuit.

Philip and I knew each other well. We had got chatting one day about our favourite grand prix cars and he happened to mention that he would love to be able to drive an 8CM Maserati before he got too old.

"Well, I've got one and you're very welcome to have a go in it," I told him. "Just let me know which circuit you want to go to and I'll set it all up for you, with a couple of my mechanics."

"Oh, I'm not that good," he said. "I would just like to take it for a short run, to get a feel of what it's like to drive. Why not at Donington?"

I was quite taken aback because no official announcement had been made at that stage that I had bought the place and I didn't think anybody knew about it. "Ah well, being a journalist you have to keep your ear to the ground," he explained with a smile.

I warned him that the track was rough and overgrown in parts and that the surface was very loose, but he wasn't bothered about that. "At the speed I'm going to be driving, that won't matter," he insisted.

We duly arranged his trial run for a few days later. However, as soon as we arrived and got the 8CM fired up we were confronted by a chap who was running a business from one of the Nissen huts. Clearly unaware that I was the new owner of the circuit, he complained furiously about the noise and ordered us off the premises. After an angry exchange, during which I made it clear that I had more right to be there than he did, he then stormed off, only to re-appear a few minutes later at the wheel of a farm tractor. On the front was a forklift and sticking out of it was one of those big spikes they use for picking up hay bales.

"If you don't get that car out of here I'll ram it with this," he yelled.

"I'm not bad at ramming things, either," I shouted back. And once we'd moved the 8CM out of harm's way I went down the road to the nearest phone box and called up the bulldozer. When it arrived, I pointed to the Nissen hut and ordered the driver to flatten it.

"But there's some machinery in there," he said hesitantly.

"I don't care," I replied. "The whole lot's got to go."

He shrugged his shoulders, climbed aboard the bulldozer and proceeded to demolish the entire building in a matter of minutes. He just went through it from one end to the other, shoving all the machinery out in front of him. One chap came running out with his trousers round his ankles – he'd been sitting on the toilet when the building began to collapse around him.

While all this was going on, our friend with the tractor was left jumping up and down with rage, screaming blue murder and threatening to call the police. But because he had no legal right to be there in the first place there was absolutely nothing he could do about it. As the police informed him when they did eventually arrive, he hadn't got a leg to stand on.

Strangely enough, the occupants of all the other Nissen huts became amazingly co-operative after that! One after the other they volunteered to go quietly if I would just give them time to find alternative premises and move their stuff out. Everything was sorted out quite amicably and the way was left clear for me to get on with my restoration plans.

The only company with a legal right to be there was Rolls Royce, who had a leasehold arrangement. The main problem here, as far as we were concerned, was the proximity to the actual circuit of some of the buildings they were occupying and to which they demanded uninterrupted access at all times, even on race days. They were very awkward about this for years, refusing to negotiate any sort of compromise – until another unfortunate little mishap involving a digger and some underground power lines brought their operations to a complete standstill!

At that point they decided to be a bit more reasonable. One of their top executives came along from head office to see me and, as luck would have it, he turned out to be a motorsport enthusiast. He and I got on famously, did a bit of horse-dealing over a drink and came to an agreement that kept both sides happy until they eventually moved out altogether some years later. But, once again, it was the bulldozer that had helped to break the deadlock.

The fact that we only got the go-ahead for that first meeting at the eleventh hour meant that the attendance fell far short of the 40,000 we had hoped for, many fans having cancelled plans to come because of uncertainty as to whether the event was going to be on or off.

Those who did come along enjoyed a great day's racing in blistering heat. Alistair Lyall, a local 22-year-old Leicestershire driver, secured a footnote in motor racing history when he became the first man to win at Donington on four wheels since 1939, steering his Ford Escort to victory in the opening event for Special Saloon Cars. Willie Green won the Historic Sports Car event in a GT40, while the Clubman's £500 first prize, donated by the Else Motor Group, went to Richard de la Rue in a Mallock U2. By this time it was so hot that umbrellas were taken out onto the grid in an effort to prevent cars and drivers from overheating.

In the Frazer Nash Handicap, Guy Smith recorded the fastest lap of 70mph, but was beaten on handicap by M.T. Joseland in a Fast Tourer. Nick Whiting won the Super Saloons event in his 3400cc Escort, Roger Friend easily won the Historic Lotuses race in an Elite and in the final event of the day, open to MG 'A' and modified sports cars, Roy Standley's E-Type Jaguar was followed in by Mike Donovan's MG Midget and a Sprite driven by Ian Knowles.

In terms of thrills and spills it was the Formula 1300 race that provided the most excitement, Graham Kay winning by less than a car's length from Paul Webb after Phil Williams' Hibbit Mk 1 had blown up in a cloud of smoke right in front of the pits and Peter Child had been involved in a dramatic prang at Redgate Corner. Happily, Peter emerged unscathed from the wreckage after misjudging the bend in spectacular fashion and making a nasty mess of his Sceptre 2PC. I took this as evidence of the effectiveness of the innovative safety measures that we had designed into the run-off areas, which were wider than normal and featured a combination of grass, sand traps and low concrete barriers.

In this respect, there was further encouragement from Lotus Grand Prix driver Gunnar Nilsson, who entertained the crowd with a few demonstration laps in a JPS Special. It was to be one of the popular Swedish star's last public appearances behind the wheel of a Formula One car before his tragic death from cancer the following year.

He was already quite ill at this stage and yet still put on a great show. He even enjoyed a little joke at my expense. I had known Gunnar ever since his Formula Atlantic days and liked him very much indeed. He was a lovely man with a great sense of humour and we had developed an easy-going, jokey relationship, always exchanging banter and taking the mickey out of each other. When he first got the drive with Lotus I ribbed him unmercifully, telling him: "You can't be serious! You're such a plonker – you'll never make a decent F1 driver!" He, of course, had never forgotten this and now, when somebody persuaded me to ride down the straight on the side pod of the car for the benefit of the photographers, he got his revenge. We were already going at quite a lick when he lifted his vizor, looked up at me with a wicked grin on his face and, blipping the throttle menacingly, asked: "Before we go any further, Tom, just remind me – what was it you said about me when I first signed up with Lotus?"

"I think I said you were the most talented driver I'd ever set eyes on," I replied nervously, hanging on to the side pod for dear life.

Later, after averaging just over 100 mph on his demonstration laps, Gunnar pronounced the circuit to be ideal for F1 racing, combining a demanding drive with first class safety arrangements.

Given all the fuss that had been made during the planning stages by local residents worried about the possibility of excessive noise, it was interesting to note that a report of the meeting in the *Derby Evening Telegraph* included the minor criticism that announcements over the public address system were regular drowned out by the sound of aircraft taking off from East Midlands airport!

Apart from that, and a brief power cut midway through the afternoon, everything went fairly smoothly and, despite the disappointment of the small crowd and the consequent financial loss, we had good reason to feel satisfied with the return of motor racing to Donington, especially in view of all the potentially ruinous last-minute problems we had faced. However, if I ever imagined for one moment that it was going to be plain sailing from then on I was soon to be disillusioned when it became clear that it wasn't just a few disgruntled locals who were intent on trying to ensure that Donington Park never recaptured its former glory as Britain's first and foremost grand prix road racing circuit.

Circuit of Dreams

I TRULY BELIEVED that my interest in backing a driver and any ambition I might have had to run a successful Formula One racing team had gone forever with Roger Williamson. Quite apart from the shock and anguish I had suffered as a result of his death, I was convinced that nobody else could ever take his place. It seemed to me that any other driver would only be second best and that there was therefore no point in getting involved again. However, although the deep emotional scars left by the events of that terrible day at Zandvoort will never fade completely, the raw grief did gradually begin to heal as the months went by and I came to accept, as we all must try to do in such situations, that life has to go on. I also came to realise that there was no point in denying the fact that motorsport was in my blood.

It was through Neil Corner that I first began to get actively involved again in a small way. Although he did actually get to drive one Formula One event in his time, standing in for Vic Elford in the Spanish Grand Prix in a Cooper Maserati owned by his friend Colin Crabbe, Neil was always best known for racing the historic cars of which he was also an enthusiastic collector. We got to know each other quite well through this shared interest and he was kind enough to loan me his Alfa Romeo P3 for the opening of the museum at Donington. Also in my collection at that time were three BRM P25s that my mechanics had rebuilt, using original bits that I had bought from BRM along with the drawings. Neil had admired these cars and in 1974 I asked him if he would be interested in racing one of them for me in historic events.

The P25s had been driven at various times during the late fifties by Jean Behra, Jo Bonnier, Hans Herrmann and Stirling Moss, enjoying rather mixed fortunes. With big four-cylinder engines, featuring massive inlet valves and large ports and carburettors, they developed an impressive 248bhp at 9,000 rpm and, like all BRMs, made a wonderful and very distinctive noise. But although blindingly fast they were also notoriously unreliable. In part this was due to the sheer power of the engine, which initially caused the cars to vibrate so much that they almost literally shook to pieces. Modified several times between their debut in 1955 and their replacement in 1960 by the rear-engine P48, their overall record shows just one Championship grand prix win – Jo Bonnier driving one to victory at Zandvoort in 1959 – while Stirling Moss finished 2nd in the French and British events of the same year.

When Stirling heard that Neil was going to race one for me he told him: "Boy, you'll enjoy that! (Stirling tends to address everyone as either 'Boy' or 'Old Boy'). "It's a beautiful little car and handles really well." But he added the warning: "The problem is getting it to go the distance. It was never very reliable over a 250-mile race."

Neil had a very good mechanic at the time, a chap called Arthur Birchall who had worked for Team Lotus and for Jim Clark, personally. We also had access to a marvellous man, Cyril Embrey, who had worked for both BRM and Rolls Royce, and these two, with help from my own team of mechanics, completely rebuilt the engine, making it just about bullet proof. As a result, the car amazed everyone by going on to win nineteen of the twenty-two Historic races it started over the next few seasons. It finished 2nd in two of the other three and only had to retire once.

The opposition were caught completely by surprise – they hadn't really expected the dear old P25 to win a single race, let alone almost every one it entered! A lot of the credit for this success must go to Cyril Embrey, but, at the same time, Neil Corner drove it brilliantly. It was still a fragile car in many ways and wouldn't have reacted too well to anyone who was in the least bit ham-fisted. Neil was justifiably proud of the fact that far from breaking it, he never so much as even spun it – despite pushing it close to the limits of its phenomenal power. Vibration remained a problem and in this respect the Achilles heel of the car was the throttle linkage, which was liable to shake until it disintegrated. At Silverstone it gave out on the final lap, and yet Neil – by far the best vintage car racer of his time in my opinion – still managed to coast around the last corner to victory.

Encouraged by this success, I decided to venture into Formula Atlantic – the 4-cylinder, 1600cc class for single seaters that is somewhere between F3 and F2. Having started with a Chevron B30 driven by Richard Morgan, I hired ex-BRM designer Mike Pilbeam to design our own Wheatcroft R18. This was a very pretty car – at least it was until driver Brian Henton took it out at Oulton Park for its shakedown run. He didn't even get as far as completing one full lap. He roared off and the next thing we knew he came walking back along the pit lane with his head down. "Sorry, Tom," he said. "I don't know how to tell you this, mate, but it's bent like a banana."

The car was a complete write-off and I wasn't too pleased with Brian, whom I suspected of having given it too much welly, much too soon. However, we built a second one and this became a great success, chalking up a string of victories that led to an order for about thirty of the cars from Alex Blignaut, a circuit operator in South Africa, who was keen to set up a regular one-make series. We ended up making five for him and then sold him the kit and all the rights so that he could build the rest himself. By then I was once again itching to move on to bigger and better things.

Lord Hesketh's success with James Hunt had helped to re-awaken my own Formula One ambitions and the success of the R18 persuaded me to design and build my own F2 car – the Wheatcroft R26 – for the 1976 season, with a view to moving up into F1 the following year. Despite his initial mishap with the R18, I offered the R26 drive to Brian Henton.

A native of Castle Donington, where he owned a garage and ran a Ford dealership, Brian was a very different character from Roger Williamson.

While Roger had been a typical boy-next-door type, quiet, modest and easy-going, Brian had deliberately developed an image as a loud-mouthed self-publicist from the moment he recorded his first win in Formula Vee at Thruxton in 1970, immediately announcing to the world that he expected to be driving F1 for Lotus within five years. He had apparently decided to model himself on Muhammad Ali and the famous boast: "I am the greatest!" He claims now that this was just part of a ploy to get himself noticed, dreamed up with a young friend of his who was a journalist on *Motoring News*, but it has to be said that Brian, by nature, was no shrinking violet.

Anyway, his plan worked insofar as he certainly did get plenty of publicity – even if most of it was along the lines of: "Who does this big-headed little so-and-so think he is?" At the same time, he was undoubtedly a talented driver and by 1975, having won a couple of F3 championships with March, he did indeed manage to get himself signed up by Lotus for his F1 debut, filling the vacancy left when a disillusioned Jacky Ickx walked out on the team in mid-season. Unfortunately, Lotus were already having all sorts of problems by then and the cars were not remotely competitive, which was why Jacky had jumped ship. At the end of the season, having competed only in the British, Austrian and American Grands Prix, everything went pear-shaped and Brian found himself left high and dry, without a drive of any kind.

Once again, I had commissioned Mike Pilbeam to design the R26, with a power unit developed by my old friends at Holbay from an existing Fiat Abarth engine.

Running at a maximum 13,000 rpm and producing 308bhp, the six-cylinder, 2-litre engine they came up with was certainly more powerful than anything else around in F2 at the time. It performed fantastically on the dyno and sounded absolutely incredible. The problem, in very simple terms, was that it couldn't be made to fit happily into an F2 chassis. This was because it had been designed originally by Ferrari as a flat twelve, before then being converted to an in-line six for sports car racing. That would have worked OK, because sports cars are bigger and heavier and things aren't quite so critical. But the only way to get it into an F2 was to incline it at an angle of 30° and that produced all sorts of problems relating to configuration and weight distribution.

On paper, the idea of a straight six was fantastic and, later on, the V6s proved that six cylinders was the way to go for the 2-litre engine. We were just a bit too far ahead of our time. We had this state-of-the-art car that was bloody quick when it was going, but the Abarth engine was completely unreliable. It just kept blowing up for one reason or another, to such an extent that we never got to finish a race.

I had great respect for Brian as a driver and thoroughly enjoyed our time together. But he didn't seem to have much luck in our cars. We couldn't even get him to the church on time for his wedding! I had offered to chauffeur him there in a 1930s Austin 'Big Twelve' Tourer, one of the cars in the British Leyland Heritage Collection that is now housed at the Heritage Centre at Gaydon but which first went on public display in the museum at Donington. Before that, the sixty or so cars – including everything from Austin grand prix cars and MG land speed record cars to the first Mini, the first E-Type and the entire Jaguar collection – had been languishing in storage at Longbridge and various other locations all over the country, incomplete and unrestored. By doing a deal whereby I agreed to restore and rebuild them in return for having them on display in the museum for five years, I like to think that I helped to save this important collection for posterity.

The Tourer is a very pretty car, ideal for a wedding, but, unfortunately, the gradient of the hill leading up to the church at Castle Donington was a bit too steep for it. After a couple of failed attempts, and with Brian's bride, Sue, already circling the church, anxious not to break with tradition by arriving before the groom, we decided that there was nothing for it but to reverse up the hill. And so it was that Brian arrived for his wedding going backwards. He reckoned it was a bad omen, but the marriage did last twenty-seven years – and Brian and I have remained the best of friends.

As for the ill-fated R26, it wasn't until we put a Brian Hart 420R engine in it that it started to perform a little better, and by then it was too late. Brian had decided to move back into Formula One with his own March

761, which he ran briefly from the garage next to his home in Castle Donington before going on later to enjoy great success in Formula 2 with Toleman, winning the European Championship in 1980, having been runner-up the previous year. His place in our car was then taken by ex-BRM driver Bob Evans, but having already shelled out hundreds of thousands of pounds without any tangible success, and with Donington requiring more of my attention and a great deal of investment in the months running up to its official re-opening, I decided to put the whole R26 project onto the back burner, where it eventually just fizzled out. The car itself remains on permanent display in the Donington Grand Prix Collection – preserved exactly as it was on the day Bob Evans stepped out of it for the last time, complete with dead flies and stone chips on the bodywork. We simply took the battery off, emptied the fuel tanks and wheeled it into position.

That really did mark the end of my ambitions in Formula One. By this time, the writing was on the wall for privateers like me, the sport already starting to become so prohibitively expensive and so fiercely competitive at grand prix level that it was almost impossible for any team to survive without hefty financial backing and full technological support from a manufacturer. Hesketh Racing's sensational victory with James Hunt at Zandvoort in 1975 seems likely to remain in the record books forever as the last grand prix win by a private team. When you consider that in 1973 I was able to order a pair of McLaren M23s for Roger Williamson at £40,000 each and you compare that with the situation that exists today, whereby the leading teams pour tens of millions of pounds into the development of each new season's grand prix car, it helps to put things into perspective.

Apart from the escalating cost of going racing at Formula One level, I was becoming disillusioned with the way the sport was developing. Disappearing fast were the good old days of pit lane camaraderie and easy-going paddock sociability, when a lot of people were still in it purely for the sport and when even the fiercest rivals would help each other out in a crisis. I am not afraid to admit that in my heart of hearts I am one of those old-fashioned types who still tend to think that motorsport should be all about big engines, small tyres and seat-of-the-pants driving – hanging the tail out, opposite lock, lots of tyre smoke and all that kind of thing. That's what I grew up with and I have to say I think it was far more exciting to watch than today's high-speed processions. I have been right behind the recent moves made by Bernie Ecclestone and Max Mosley to change the rules drastically in an effort to reduce the part played by advanced computer technology and other artificial driving aids and to put the drivers themselves back in control.

It was my own desire to turn the clock back and re-create some of the excitement of an earlier era for both drivers and spectators alike that lay behind my final venture at the sharp end of motorsport in the 1990s with the short-lived Formula Classic venture. This was a one-make series for pre-war style racing cars, with the engine at the front, the gearbox located in between the driver's legs and tyres that looked old fashioned but were actually made to modern specifications. Our idea was to start off by making twenty or thirty of these cars, which would be available to amateur drivers on a drive-and-go basis – in other words, you would pay a fixed amount for a season's racing and would then simply turn up, do the race and go home, leaving us to maintain the car and set it up for the next event.

There was a great deal of interest in the project at the time – I'd even managed to get Sky television on board. Unfortunately, it never really got off the ground in the end because of problems with the development of the car. Once again, the engines were to be supplied by Holbay. What I hadn't realised was that the company was already in financial trouble before we started the project – in fact, I think they probably saw it as a way out of their difficulties. These eventually came to a head in tragic circumstances when John Dunnell, one of the two brothers who had founded the company and a man for whom, despite everything, I had a lot of respect, was killed in a light aircraft accident. Holbay finally went bust very shortly afterwards.

By then I had already had to write off the whole Formula Classic project, along with a personal investment of more than £1.6 million We did actually get as far as running a couple of events, but experienced so many little teething troubles with the cars that people soon lost interest. It was a big disappointment all round, especially as I am still convinced that if we could have got the cars running properly right from the start it would have been a sure-fire winner.

The concept was a good one and, on the evidence of the events we did run, the racing was fun to take part in as well as being very spectacular to watch. I hate to admit to failure and I still haven't entirely given up on the idea. Secretly, I carried on developing the cars until all the bugs were ironed out and they ran perfectly. We have got twenty-six of them stored in the cellar of the museum at Donington and I hope to revive the whole project at some time in the future.

During the seventeen years that had elapsed between the R26 and the Formula Classic ventures, my motorsport ambitions had been focused almost exclusively on Donington.

In the mystical Hollywood film 'Field of Dreams', the Kevin Costner character hears voices urging him to create a baseball diamond in the middle of nowhere at his mid-Western farm in order to help free the spirits of 'Shoeless Joe' Jackson and other disgraced players caught up in the Boston Black Sox match-throwing corruption scandal of the 1930s. He is encouraged in his obsession with the assurance: "Build it and they will come." Well, I certainly didn't hear voices, but if I ever dreamed that all I had to do was to rebuild Donington and a grateful motorsport fraternity would come flocking to the gates, then I soon got a rude awakening.

The local resident NIMBYs (NIMBY standing for Not In My Back Yard) were far from being the only people opposed to the return of racing to the circuit. Rival circuit owners and managers at Silverstone, Thruxton, Brands Hatch and elsewhere were also against us for the obvious reason that they didn't want the added competition of another major venue in their midst. From the moment that we eventually got the planning go-ahead following the public inquiry they started a dirty tricks campaign of disinformation aimed at undermining our professional credibility.

In this respect, the succession of last minute postponements of the official re-opening of the circuit that were forced upon us played into their hands. At the time you had to give the RAC two years notice of any event, but, having applied in anticipation of having everything ready by the autumn of 1976, we had to put back the date of the first meeting several times as the planning complications dragged on. Atrocious weather in the winter of 1976/77 then put us further behind schedule with our final construction work.

The other circuits took full advantage of this by surreptitiously floating all sorts of negative stories and rumours to the effect that I was having major business, financial and even health problems – all totally untrue. When word started going around that I was terminally ill with cancer we decided that it was time to hit back with a little trick of our own. Ian Phillips, a former editor of *Autosport* who had become our first circuit manager and who is now Director of Business Affairs at Jordan, sent out a spoof letter on headed notepaper to Jimmy Brown at Silverstone, Sidney Offord at Thruxton and John Webb, who was involved in the running of Brands Hatch, Cadwell Park, Mallory Park, Oulton Park and Snetterton, inviting them all to my funeral. Jimmy Brown and John Webb knew me well enough to get the joke straightaway, but Sidney Offord actually sent some flowers!

Although this caused a few smiles all round, it did nothing to help us prise open the doors to what was effectively a closed shop run by the RAC, the British Racing Drivers Club and the British Racing and Sports Car Club in close co-operation with the existing circuits. Silverstone, Brands Hatch and the rest had got all the premier British championships at every level nicely carved up between them and the last thing they wanted was somebody new coming to the table and trying to grab a slice of the cake. In some instances, the only way we could get a look-in was to 'buy' events from them, something that didn't make any financial sense at all. It was a complete stitch-up.

The only answer, we decided, was to take the initiative by going out and finding our own events elsewhere. We formed our own organising club for this purpose and Robert Fearnall, another former *Autosport* journalist who had come from Silverstone to be managing director of Donington

Park Racing Ltd in mid-1977, started combing Europe for races that could be imported.

Robert, who continued to run the circuit until quite recently, succeeded in attracting all manner of events – the German Touring Car Championship, the Belgian this, the French that and so on. These people were only too happy to have rounds of their championships in territories other than their own and although it is quite commonplace these days it was quite a novel idea at the time and we were pioneers in bringing overseas motorsport to this country in that way. Later, we were also to lead the way in staging everything from truck racing to heavy metal rock concerts.

Among the earliest imports was American motorcycle racing. This was an immediate hit with the public, not only drawing the crowds that helped us to survive those difficult first few years, but also laying the foundations of our long-term future success. More than anything else, it was motorcycling that put Donington right back on the map. The circuit is particularly well suited to motorcycle racing, its undulating terrain and fast corners providing the momentum that flows perfectly for two wheels. In the heyday of superstar riders such as Barry Sheene, Mike Hailwood, Kenny Roberts, Phil Read, Randy Mamola and Ron Haslam we stole a march on everybody else by staging some of the greatest motorcycle races ever seen in this country.

The World Cup, the Nations Cup, the World Sidecar Championship and, in particular, some thrilling Trans-Atlantic Trophy races provided many memorable occasions in the first ten years between 1977-87. The highlights, certainly as far as I was concerned, revolved around the two greatest names in modern British motorcycling – Barry Sheene and Mike Hailwood. Murray Walker, paying tribute to Barry after his tragically early death from cancer at the age of fifty-two, said simply: "He was not only one of the most brilliant motorcyclists who has ever lived, he was also a lovely man." The same could be said of the even more legendary and yet equally likeable Mike Hailwood.

Barry Sheene's close association with Donington started in September 1977 when he swept the board at one of the first major events we staged there after the re-opening, winning both the individual legs of the Donington Road Race on his 750cc Suzuki, taking the overall prize and also smashing the lap record. One of the most colourful and popular characters ever to have graced any sport, he arrived that day in typical style, driving a lemon yellow Rolls Royce, customised with flared wheel arches and Wolf Race alloy wheels, and accompanied by an entourage that included not only his stunning model girlfriend Stephanie MacLean – who later became his wife – but also Beatle George Harrison.

I was never very well up on pop music and didn't recognise George at first, although it was fairly obvious from his appearance and the fact that he had arrived in a Ferrari that he must be a celebrity of some sort.

"Hello, mate," I said, nodding in his direction as I walked into my private suite to find him sitting there amid a whole crowd of people, quite a few of whom I didn't know. I should explain that in those days what I rather grandly refer to as my private suite was actually a large caravan, parked permanently near the start/finish line, exactly where the grandstand is now. I had brought it down from the east coast, where it had served for many years as a holiday home for Lenchen and the kids when they were younger.

Everybody who was anybody seemed to end up in that caravan on race days and the place would be so packed at times that the windows would get all steamed up. We had some wonderful sessions in there in the days before we built the current Goddard suites, especially when the likes of legendary saloon car racer Gerry Marshall were around. A great twenty-stone bear of a man, Gerry was a larger-than-life character in every way. He could often be found in the caravan sinking a pint immediately before going straight out to win yet another race, notching up an extraordinary total of 620 victories in his colourful forty-year career. He died in April 2005, aged sixty-three, after suffering a massive heart attack while driving a V8 Chevrolet Camaro during the annual Historic Grand Prix Cars Association test day at Silverstone – which was exactly the way he would probably have wanted to go out. Always the life and soul of any party, he is sadly missed by all those who knew him well and who loved his spectacular style of driving.

George Harrison was even younger when he died and is just as sorely missed by pop fans the world over. Seeing him in the caravan for the first time that day and realising that he was probably somebody I should know, I took Kevin on one side and whispered: "Who's that long-haired bloke over there?"

"It's George Harrison," replied Kevin.

I paused. "Ah, right. So who's he, then?"

"He's a Beatle."

Another pause. "A Beatle?"

"Yeah, you know The Beatles. The pop group."

"Ooh, ah. From Liverpool! Now I've got you!"

Kevin loves to tell that story to show just how out of touch I am with things like that. As it happens, George and I really hit it off once I got to know him a bit better and he became a regular visitor to Donington. A classic car collector himself, he was particularly interested in Ferraris and I invited him along to drive my cars at one or two of the 'play days' I organised at the circuit for special friends. On those occasions he impressed everybody with his driving skills.

It was at Donington, five years after that initial visit with George, that Barry Sheene made his first public come-back appearance following the terrible 160 mph accident at Silverstone in 1982 that broke almost every bone in his body and left him requiring so many nuts and bolts to pin them together that he was dubbed 'the bionic man'. Absolutely fearless, he was given a fantastic reception by the crowd who loved his extrovert nature and his reckless, devil-may-care style of riding.

It was at Donington, too, that he rode his last race as a professional before retiring to live on Australia's Gold Coast in the hope that the dry heat there might help to ease the pain in joints that had become increasingly wracked by arthritis, the legacy of all those fractures. And on a much sadder note, it was at Donington, in 2002, that he rode his very last competitive race of all. It was a Classic event and despite his deteriorating health and aching limbs, he signed off with a final victory on his Manx Norton. Shortly afterwards he was diagnosed with the cancer that finally overcame his seemingly unquenchable spirit in March 2003.

Away from the track itself, I have one particular memory of Barry Sheene that tells you all you need to know about what he was really like as a personality. It concerns an incident that took place during a meeting at Donington towards the end of his professional career. At some point in the afternoon Donington Park's publicity manager, David Fern, was approached by one of the executive suite holders seeking a special favour. This gentleman explained that his guests for the day included a young girl who had been permanently paralysed following a motorbike accident. She had come specially to see Barry race and was distraught because the people she was with had been caught in heavy traffic on the way up and she had missed his race. By way of consolation, he wondered if there was any way that David could possibly get Barry to sign a photograph for her.

David agreed to see what he could do, but was not hopeful because he knew that Barry was not in a very good mood. In fact, he was in a pretty foul temper and understandably so. He was at a low point in his career, he was having all sorts of problems with the bike and he had generally had a pretty bad day. One way and another it was not a tactful moment at which to ask him to sign autographs. As soon as he saw David approaching, knowing that he did all the local newspaper reports and suspecting that he was probably after an interview, he didn't even wait to hear what he had to say before telling him, in no uncertain terms, to **** off! Even at the best of times, Barry's language tended to be just as forthright and colourful as the rest of his personality.

Unfazed, David persisted and Barry eventually calmed down enough to hear him out. Having listened to the whole story, he then asked if the girl was in a wheelchair. When told that she was he said: "OK. Go and get her and bring her over."

David went off to collect her and Barry put her wheelchair on the tail lift of his truck so that she could be gently hoisted into it. He then sat and chatted to her for half-an-hour, signed her photograph and even gave her one of his official team jackets as a souvenir. From being in tears, the girl was suddenly all smiles.

At the end of it all, Barry turned to David and said: "Nobody else is going to know about this – right? It stays between us."

He was fully aware that it would make a great public relations story as far as he was concerned, but he didn't want to be seen in any way to make any publicity capital out of it. When David thanked him for his kindness in giving her so much attention and for helping to make her day, he simply shrugged it off. "It was the least I could do," he said. "Apart from anything else, it helped me to appreciate just how fortunate I am. I walked away from my accident – but she'll never walk again."

It was that sort of attitude, allied to his bravery on the track and the daredevil talent that brought him more international 750cc and 500cc titles between 1975 and 1982 than any other rider, that helped to make Barry so universally popular. "A guy who put a smile on a lot of people's faces," was how he was described in another of the many tributes that flooded in after his death.

In some ways, Mike Hailwood was cast in an even more heroic mould – and was just as nice a guy. An iconic figure, generally acknowledged by experts worldwide to have been the best motorcycle racer of all time, he won no less than ten World Championships, seventy-six grands prix and an incredible fourteen TT races on the Isle of Man, a course so notoriously dangerous that Barry Sheene, a man who normally knew no fear, refused to take part in it.

Having won everything there was to win on two wheels, Mike then proved his versatility by switching to four wheels with considerable success, finishing third in the Formula 5000 Championship and also coming third in the Le Mans 24-hour race before going on to win the Formula 2 European Championship with the Surtees team. He then moved into Formula One with McLaren and was lying 4th in the World Championship when leg injuries sustained in a crash at the Nurburgring ended his driving career prematurely in 1974. The previous year he had been awarded the George Medal, Britain's highest civilian bravery award, after single-handedly rescuing Clay Regazzoni from his blazing car in the 1973 South African Grand Prix.

In 1978, eleven years after retiring from motorcycle racing, he made an astonishing comeback at the age of thirty-seven, winning the Isle of Man

TT on a Ducati V-Twin and completely blowing away reigning World Champion Phil Read and the rest of the all-powerful works Hondas. To prove it wasn't a fluke, he repeated the performance against the same opposition at Mallory Park a few days later.

His appearance in an international event at Donington the following year drew one of the biggest crowds ever seen there or at any other motorcycle event anywhere in the world, with more than 120,000 fans flocking to watch the great man in action. The police started to get concerned about the sheer volume of traffic and we had to contact local farmers to arrange extra parking space in surrounding fields, just so that we could fit everybody in. After all that, there was a bit of an anti-climax when Mike crashed and broke his collarbone during practice on the Saturday so that he couldn't take part in the race on Sunday. Characteristically, he then felt awkward about accepting his appearance money. I suggested that if he was worried about not actually making an appearance then perhaps he might like to let me drive him on a lap of honour in Jumbo Goddard's record-breaking 8-litre Bentley so that he could wave to the crowd from the open car. He thought that was a great idea and was given a huge standing ovation all the way round.

His death in a road accident in 1981, in which his young daughter, Michelle, also died, was one of those tragedies made even worse by a sense of futility. It seems cruelly ironic that a man who had survived twenty years of putting his life on the line in the most dangerous of all sporting arenas should die in a road accident just a few miles from his home while doing something as mundane as driving to the local fish and chip shop to pick up a take-away supper for the family. By another terrible twist of fate, he only went out because his wife, Pauline, had been helping to decorate their new home and hadn't had time to cook a meal. He was only forty-one years old. Michelle was just four.

I was proud to count Mike among my friends. Like Barry Sheene, he was a hugely charismatic figure, but at the same time he was also very unassuming. He was almost boyish in some ways, with a great sense of humour, and we got on ever so well. He even loaned me his entire collection of World Championship bikes, including the works Hondas – the four-cylinder 350, the four-cylinder 500 and the 500 with the Reynolds frame.

Along with his trophies, his helmets and various other memorabilia, these remained on display at Donington for some years before going back to his widow, Pauline. However, the most famous of all his bikes, the legendary six-cylinder Honda 250, was sold to a Dutch collector within days of Mike's death in 1981 by his business partner, whose legal right to dispose of it was disputed. Throughout the twenty-three years since then, true ownership of the bike has been the subject of what has become the longest-running court action in Dutch legal history. I have been fighting the case on Pauline's behalf and will continue to do so until the issue is finally resolved. I never got the chance to thank Mike properly as much as I would like to have done for all the things he did for me and this is my way of making up for that.

In the ten years following the re-opening of the circuit in 1977, Donington steadily built a reputation as the leading motorcycle racing venue in the country, a reputation that was sealed in 1987 when we took over the British Motorcycle Grand Prix from Silverstone.

The event had been dying a death there, partly because the wide, flat circuit makes it very much a car venue, not nearly so well suited to motorcycle racing. Although it continued to have the support of motor cycling's official governing body, the ACU, there was a growing feeling among the fans that not only was it not a proper bike circuit, but also that the people running it didn't really care for bikers or their interests.

This general air of dissatisfaction was blamed for growing public order problems at the event, police coming in with riot shields on one occasion to deal with a mass brawl on the campsite, and this had contributed to a further decline in crowd figures to the point where it was losing money. Knowing this, I went behind the back of the ACU, who had stubbornly refused to consider my bids to take it over, and did a deal direct with the Silverstone board, buying out the last two years of their existing five-year contract. The ACU rather grudgingly accepted this fait accompli and we have run the event with increasing success ever since.

Everybody immediately seemed much more at home at Donington.

The attendance for that first 1987 event was 55,000 – it has since risen as high as 120,000 – and the police reported afterwards that there had been only eight arrests during the entire weekend, making complete nonsense of the fears voiced in advance by some locals that the whole area was going to be overrun by gangs of Hell's Angels intent on raping, pillaging and foraging their way through the surrounding countryside.

It had been much the same when we held the first Monsters of Rock concert in 1980, only that time it was marauding, drug-crazed heavy metal fans that had been perceived as the potential threat. The parish council tried to get an injunction to stop the event, but although 50,000 people did indeed descend on the area for the weekend, attracted by a bill that featured seven top bands, including Judas Priest, Saxon and Rainbow, it all went off so well that even the councillor who had been leading the local opposition had to admit afterwards: "It was a lot better than we thought it was going to be."

The following year, 80,000 people came to hear Whitesnake, Slade and AC/DC and this time there was again so little trouble that the superintendent in charge of the police operation was able to report: "The young people who have been here have been very, very well-behaved and there has been a good relationship between them and the police. I have not heard any complaints from the residents. I don't think they have any grounds for complaint."

From then on it became a regular annual event until 1993, by which time the local shopkeepers, publicans, restaurant and café owners and tradesmen had actually started looking forward to it as a particularly lucrative source of extra business. Even some of the more entrepreneurial homeowners were cashing in, setting up impromptu roadside refreshment stalls to cater for an audience that reached a peak of 127,500 one year. A lot of the people who had initially been rather anti were actually quite disappointed when the event then moved to the Milton Keynes Bowl, big name American bands like Bon Jovi and Guns 'n' Roses preferring to be nearer London.

Meanwhile, in 1989, two years after securing the British Motorcycle Grand Prix, we were voted the Best Organised Grand Prix of the Year by the riders, teams, officials and the Press. Right from the start, we had never been out of the Top Three in the annual end-of-season poll and in 1991 we achieved the highest ever rating, as well as winning four other top awards, setting a standard that we have maintained consistently ever since.

However, the motor racing establishment generally and the RAC Motorsports Association in particular were proving much more difficult to impress. By the early eighties we had successfully forced our way into the FIA calendar and were actually running more international events than any other circuit in the country, thanks to the efforts of Robert Fearnall and his team. But I was no nearer realising my ultimate ambition of bringing grand prix racing back to Donington.

I had first sounded out the RAC about the possibility of being considered as a future venue for the British Grand Prix as early as 1973, four years before the circuit actually re-opened, but at that stage the idea was pretty much dismissed out of hand by the Motorsports Division. A formal application in 1978 then led to a meeting with Dean Delamont, head of the RAC Motorsports Council at the time, at which he revealed that the long-standing arrangement whereby the event alternated between Silverstone and Brands Hatch was contracted until at least 1985, adding that there was every reason to suppose that this agreement would be extended indefinitely after that, as long as the two circuits continued to do a satisfactory job. "It would be wishful thinking on the part of anyone to expect otherwise," he said, with an air of finality.

The fact that we had already invested over £2 million on developments aimed at bringing the circuit up to the required F1 standard and that we were in the process of spending a lot more on further improvements, including extra grandstands and other spectator facilities, apparently counted for nothing. It seemed clear to me from their tone that the RAC had closed their minds to the idea of adding a third venue to the grand prix roster, no matter how worthy its credentials, and I believe this was borne out by subsequent events.

If they thought I was just going to give up and forget my dream that easily, they were mistaken. Maybe nobody had warned them about just how obstinate and determined I can be when I've got my heart set on something. It was to take another fifteen years, around £10 million, a paper mountain of solicitors' letters and the repeated threat of court action before I eventually got my way. It cost me a fortune and put me under so much stress that I almost didn't live to see the day, but it ended with Donington staging what is generally acknowledged to have been one of the most memorable grands prix of all time.

On the podium with Ayrton Senna after his sensational European Grand Prix victory at Donington in 1993 and (below, right) Princess Diana watching the race from the enclosure in front of my private suite at Donington.

(Below left) On-course doctor Lyn Jarrett leads Princess Anne on a tour of the medical centre at Donington, where I myself ended up on the day.

(Top) My curtain-raising lap in the Mercedes W154 before the start of the European Grand Prix in 1993, the car showing signs of damage sustained when I spun off into the gravel, and (above) getting a send-off moments earlier from Denis Jenkinson.

(Left) Kevin and me with Ayrton's McLaren at the Senna Fangio Memorial.

(Above) With Eddie Jordan, who celebrated Jordan Grand Prix's tenth anniversary with a party at the Donington Grand Prix Collection in 2000, and (left) with Ian Phillips, our first circuit manager at Donington who went on to work with Eddie at Jordan Grand Prix.

(Below) At the wheel of the Bugatti Royale, one of my most ambitious re-creation projects.

At the opening of a special heritage motorcycle section at the Grand Prix Collection with veterans 'Titch' Allen and Alf Briggs, 'Rocket' Ron Haslam and the 350cc Raleigh on which 'Squib' Burton won the first ever race at Donington in 1931.
(Right) Tom Delaney who raced his Lea Francis (VC 5461) at Donington in 1933 and again (main picture) in 2003 at the age of 92, by far the oldest driver in the world ever to have held a current racing licence. In the other Lea Francis, being chauffeured by Willie Green, is Max Turner, three years younger than Tom, who drove an Austin in the first car meeting at Donington in 1933.

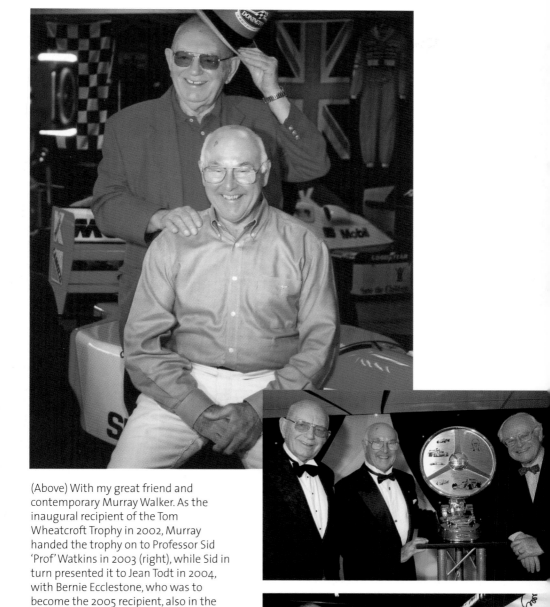

(Above) With my great friend and contemporary Murray Walker. As the inaugural recipient of the Tom Wheatcroft Trophy in 2002, Murray handed the trophy on to Professor Sid 'Prof' Watkins in 2003 (right), while Sid in turn presented it to Jean Todt in 2004, with Bernie Ecclestone, who was to become the 2005 recipient, also in the frame (below).

With Bernie Ecclestone and Chris Aylett, CEO of the Motorsport Industry Association, on the terace of the House of Lords (above) after Peter Hain had presented me with the 2003 MIA Award for the Most Outstanding Contribution to UK Motorsport.

(Left) With Murray Walker after he had presented me with the Chrysler Lifetime Achievement Award and (below) at Donington with some of my other awards, including (centre) the award to Donington Park for the European Grand Prix as the best organised grand prix of the 1993 season.

With Sheila on our wedding day, when the guests included some of the younger grandchildren – (l to r) Kevin's daughters Madison Leigh and Tayah Georgia with Craig, James, Reuben and Ross, sons of Sheila's daughter Debbie.

(Below) With the rest of the family at the dinner party we continue to hold each year on Lenchen's birthday. (l to r: Jill, Sue, Kevin, Tina, Joy, David and Mandy.)

In my robes after receiving an Honorary Doctorate from the University of Derby. Not bad for someone who left school at 13! The rest of the lads in my unit during the war would certainly never have believed it if you had told them then that this was how I'd end up one day.

(Left) Wearing my medals for the first time ever at the war memorial in Haugesund in Norway on VE Day 2005 after cutting the ribbon to mark the 10th anniversary of the opening of the Arquebus Krigshistorisk war museum, which is twinned with Kevin's own planned military vehicle museum.

Lap of the Century

WE ACTUALLY staged our first Formula One event as early as 1979. "Donington's First Grand Prix For Over 40 Years" was how *Motor Sport* magazine described the Gunnar Nilsson Memorial Trophy meeting of June 3rd that year. Unfortunately, although the occasion turned out to be historically interesting for several different reasons, it could not, by any stretch of the imagination, qualify as a grand prix.

Organised in aid of the Cancer Fund that Gunnar had launched only months before his death the previous year, it was originally intended to be a full non-Championship 'Race of Champions' event. However, the FIA refused to sanction it as such because we didn't yet have a full F1 licence and, as a result, most of the teams withdrew. Left with just five cars and drivers, we re-organised it as a glorified speed trial, with the cars going out for timed practice in the morning to decide the order in which they would run in the afternoon.

Guest appearances by Dan Gurney, Denny Hulme, Jackie Stewart and Fangio, each of them driving demonstration laps in cars with which they had been famously associated, provided an added attraction during the interval, helping to boost the crowd to a respectable 20,000. A non-championship F3 event and a BMW saloon car race completed the programme for the day.

The five drivers taking part in the speed trial included James Hunt, who had been instrumental in setting up the Cancer Fund, Mario Andretti, Nelson Piquet, Rupert Keegan and Alan Jones. The eventual winner was Alan Jones whose time of 1'01.37" in a Williams FW07 equated to an average speed of 144.82mph. James Hunt, in a Wolf WR8, was second in 1'02.54", followed by Mario Andretti in a Lotus 79 (1'02.67") and Nelson Piquet in a Brabham BT46B (1'03.61"). Rupert Keegan, in an Arrows A1B, was the only one who failed to break the existing lap record of 1'04.91", set by Brian Henton in a March F2 car in 1978.

Despite the disappointingly reduced status of the event, it did provide an interesting footnote to Formula One history for two reasons, marking the final competitive appearances by both James Hunt and the outlawed Brabham BT46B 'fan' car. The fan car had been banned after its one and only previous outing in the Swedish Grand Prix the year before, but, because F1 rules did not apply to our event, it was free to run. As for James Hunt, he announced his retirement almost immediately afterwards and never raced a Formula One car again. At the time, I don't think anyone in the crowd can have realised that they were watching his farewell performance.

For me, personally, the most thrilling part of the day was the sight of my hero, Fangio, in action behind the wheel of a Mercedes W125. He was sixty-eight by then, but soon showed that he had lost none of his natural skill and panache. The W125, one of the half-dozen or so still in existence and the only one in private hands, had been found behind the Iron Curtain by Colin Crabbe, but was owned at this time by Neil Corner. Having brought it along especially for the occasion, Neil then had some anxious moments during the morning when it absolutely refused to fire up. He eventually traced the problem to the fact that the needle had dropped out of the bottom of the carburettor and we all gave a sigh of relief when the mighty engine sprang to life with that distinctive roar.

Neil himself took it out for a lap to warm it up before handing it over to Fangio, with the request not to take it above 5500 rpm. Sitting in the cockpit in his shirtsleeves and his helmet, Juan-Manuel beamed and nodded and, in that famously squeaky voice of his, said: "OK, fine." And then off he went.

Well, he came through the chicane at the end of his first lap and he gave it a bit too much welly. The moment was captured for posterity in a marvellous picture that was used on the cover of *Autosport*. The back end stepped right out of line and for a fraction of a second we all held our breath. But because he was the great driver that he was – and despite the fact that he had been retired for many years by then – he simply wound the opposite lock on and carried on as if nothing untoward had happened, totally in control. On every lap after that he just played to the crowd, with Hunt, Piquet, Andretti, Martin Brundle and all the other drivers leaning over the rails to watch him. When he came in, he looked up at Neil, half closed that lazy eye of his, patted the side of the car and said with a grin: "Mucho potencial!" What a man.

The excitement of that day simply whetted my appetite, making me more determined than ever to see full-scale grand prix racing back at Donington. At the same time, I began to become increasingly angry and frustrated with the RAC and the 'blazer brigade' of the British motor-sport establishment, who seemed equally determined to make sure that it would never happen. It was their blind refusal even to consider Doning-ton as a possible venue for the British Grand Prix that most incensed me. Their attitude was that it would be awkward and inconvenient for them to alter the arrangement whereby the event was shared exclusively between Silverstone and Brands Hatch and it soon became obvious that they had closed their minds to the very idea of a third alternative, regard-less of whether we could provide equally good or maybe even superior facilities.

As the dispute deepened and we started communicating via our respective solicitors, they became secretive about the exact nature of their agreement with the other two circuits, didn't even bother to acknowledge some of our grand prix applications and were generally unhelpful and obstructive. I responded by suggesting that they were fail-ing in their duty to play the honest broker. By this I meant that the RAC Motorsports Association, the body having exclusive control over motor-sport in the UK, was not honouring the commitment required from any sporting Association to maintain a fair and impartial balance between those professionally involved in that sport. In effect, they seemed to be giving Silverstone and Brands Hatch permanent protection from any competition over the right to host the British Grand Prix.

Our suspicions about how our rivals in the motorsport establishment were ganging up against us seemed to have been confirmed when, in 1981, the Donington Racing Club, our race organising arm, gained representation for the first time on the RAC MSA Race Committee. The committee, which made the regulations governing British motorsport, was packed with all our main rivals and to our dismay they proceeded to push through a couple of proposals that were quite blatantly aimed at undermining our whole hard-won race programme.

Firstly, they decided to restrict the amount of prize money that could be offered for an international race run in Britain, demanding that it should not exceed that offered for a national race. As I have already mentioned, the other circuits had effectively got the National Championships sewn up and, because we couldn't get a look-in, our only means of survival in these early years was by staging International races, mostly by way of importing rounds of championships from other countries, including the Euroseries Formula Ford 2000, Formula Ford 1600 and Sports 2000, the Belgian Group 1 Touring Car and the German Group 5 Championships.

One of the main reasons why we had been able to attract these events was that we paid decent prize money. If we were to offer only the maximum £225 available for national races it would not be nearly such an attractive proposition and people probably wouldn't want to come. Just in case that might not be enough to do the trick, a second proposal put forward by the Race Committee was that rounds of foreign championships should only be allowed to run in the UK with the official approval of the committee and, once again, it was quite clear that this would be used specifically to spike our programme.

Far from putting me off, such manoeuvring simply hardened my resolve to see things through at any cost. At the same time, I had also been encouraged by developments elsewhere involving Bernie Ecclestone and his increasingly influential Formula One Constructors Association

(FOCA). Having taken over as chief executive of the Association in 1978, with Max Mosley as his legal advisor, Bernie had started to flex his muscles in a series of power struggles with the FIA and its sporting arm, FISA. These came to a head in the winter of 1980/1 when FOCA set up the World Federation of Motorsport and put together their own rival calendar of events, a move that forced the FIA to negotiate the first Concorde Agreement. This gave FOCA the right to negotiate the worldwide TV contracts for F1, a key step towards full commercial control of the sport. In the meantime, their contract with the RAC MSA, whereby they basically agreed to supply the cars for the British Grand Prix, was about to come up for renewal at the end of 1981.

I had got to know Bernie quite well over the years and I liked him. We first made contact in the early seventies when he bought Brabham from Ron Tauranac and rang me to ask if there were any bits and pieces out of the factory I might be interested in buying. He's a hard man to do business with, no doubt about that, but, in my experience, he's also dead straight. You always know exactly where you stand with Bernie.

A good example of his rather abrupt bargaining technique came when he decided he wanted to buy one of my Thinwall Specials for his collection. It started with a phone call and the negotiation process went something like this:

Bernie: "Hello, Tom – I hear you've got a couple of Thinwall Specials?

Me: "Yes, Bernie, although one is in bits. Big bits, mind you. The chassis, the engine and the body are all there."

Bernie: "What do you want for it, then?"

Me: "I don't want to sell it, Bernie."

Bernie: "I'd like to buy it."

Me: "I told you, Bernie, it ain't for sale."

Bernie: "Go on, sell it to me."

Me: "Oh, alright, Bernie. £350,000.

Bernie: "£350,000! For a load of rust?!

Me: "It's not bad rust, Bernie. It's been kept inside. Steel goes that colour over time."

Bernie: "Tell you what – I'll give you £250,000."

Me: "No, Bernie. Definitely not."

Bernie: "Oh, you're in one of those moods, are you? Well, let's split the difference."

Me: "No, Bernie. I don't know as I really want to sell it."

Bernie: "I see. OK. Who do I make the cheque out to, then?"

It arrived in the post the next day.

Right from the start, I had backed Bernie and FOCA against the FIA and when they were trying to set up their alternative calendar of events I was one of the few circuit owners around the world who immediately agreed to take their races. The likes of Silverstone, Brands Hatch and Snetterton had been wary of upsetting the FIA, on whom they were heavily dependent for their race programmes, but as I had no racing anyway I had nothing to lose and so I had been happy to throw in my lot with Bernie. As a result, he and I had established a good working relationship. He now indicated verbally that he would not renew FOCA's agreement with the RAC MSA for the British Grand Prix unless Donington was included in some way in the future. He also promised me that Donington would get a new non-Championship Formula One race he was planning to add to the annual calendar in 1982.

I don't know if Bernie's influence had any effect or whether it simply had to do with the fact that we had been putting the RAC under constant pressure, even threatening court action in order to establish our legal right to be given equal consideration as a candidate to host the British Grand Prix, but the first sign of a breakthrough came shortly afterwards when the RAC MSA announced at the end of 1981 that they had given Silverstone and Brands Hatch the required four years' notice that their rolling contracts were to be terminated as from December 31st 1985.

The announcement came just as we were on the very point of serving a writ on them, seeking to establish a legal requirement for them to do precisely that. The writ would also have sought an undertaking that our application to host the British Grand Prix would then be considered under the same criteria as would be applied to Silverstone and Brands Hatch, along with the need for them to specify exactly what those criteria would be. Following their announcement, we agreed to delay court proceedings pending an acceptable outcome of the new arrangement.

We had to wait until June 1983 before the MSA finally announced their decision that the British Grand Prix was to be awarded to Brands Hatch in 1986, Silverstone in 1987 and Donington Park in 1988. Although delighted to have been given a place in the queue, we were still not very happy about being last in line. And we felt even more aggrieved when we discovered the circumstances in which the order of precedence had been decided.

It emerged that the Ad Hoc Committee appointed to review the situation had recommended that the event should be awarded to Donington in 1987 rather than 1988, with Silverstone taking the last spot. However, the board of the MSA had then taken it upon themselves to overturn this recommendation. The fact that the board of the MSA included Jack Sears, who also just happened to be chairman of Silverstone Circuits, added to the suspicion that we had been stitched up yet again.

We were also upset by the further stipulation that we would only get the event in 1988 on condition that we were able to show that the circuit had been brought up to full FISA Formula One spec by April 1st, 1986. This merely rubbed salt in the wounds. As it happened, we had always contemplated having the circuit ready well before 1986, but it seemed unreasonable for the MSA to dictate that we should incur the enormous expense involved so far in advance, having relegated us to the 1988 slot. If we had to have the circuit ready by 1986, why could we not have the grand prix that year?

Meanwhile, our hopes of staging the non-championship F1 event promised by Bernie Ecclestone for late 1982 had been thwarted when problems arose over dates. The teams couldn't get back from the previous event in Las Vegas in time for the originally projected date of October 10th and we reluctantly decided that to hold it any later in the year would not be commercially viable. Instead, we agreed to postpone it until 1983. However, it then emerged that the RAC had, instead, supported an application from Brands Hatch for a Grand Prix of Europe in 1983 as part of an arrangement whereby this event would then alternate annually between Brands Hatch and the Nurburgring in Germany. For some reason, the RAC had conveniently omitted to mention during their negotiations with FOCA and FISA that we, too, had applied to host a European Grand Prix.

Increasingly desperate and frustrated, we even went so far as to inquire about the possibility of staging either an official Irish or Swiss Grand Prix, but these ideas were rejected out of hand by the RAC on the grounds that there was not room in the UK calendar for any further grand prix events.

All in all, it was very hard for me to escape the conclusion that the RAC, Brands Hatch and Silverstone between them were conspiring to make things as difficult as possible for us. But at least I now had the consolation of knowing that my great dream of bringing the British Grand Prix to Donington, although still five years distant, was within sight of fulfilment, with a firm date in the diary. Or so I thought. As it turned out, the cup was to be dashed from my lips yet again in a manner that hinted at even greater skulduggery in certain quarters.

The first sign that all was not going to plan came in early 1986 with a letter from the RAC MSA's chief executive, Peter Cooper, in which he said that it would not be "appropriate" to settle contractual arrangements for the staging of the British Grand Prix beyond 1986 "for the time being" in view of comments made by FOCA in a letter from Bernie Ecclestone to MSA chairman Michael Southcombe. In this letter, a copy of which was enclosed, Bernie made it clear that FOCA were strongly opposed to the idea of a third British Grand Prix circuit. In fact, they favoured the idea of having just one single 'Grade A' circuit in each country to host the national grand prix and other significant events. He added that the existing Concorde Agreement with FISA was likely to be extended until 1991 and that as far as the British Grand Prix was concerned, he saw no reason why FOCA should not enter into a contract with the chosen circuit to cover that period.

Apart from the despair I felt at this ominous indication that we were not going to get the British Grand Prix in 1988 after all, I was infuriated to see that Bernie's letter, dated November 8th, 1985, was almost four months old. During that time there had been not the slightest suggestion from the MSA that their arrangement with us was in serious doubt and yet, as I pointed out in my reply to Peter Cooper, I had gone ahead meanwhile and spent an extra £800,000 on getting the track ready by April 1st, as they had demanded.

In his letter, Peter Cooper had said that he was in the process of arranging a joint meeting between the MSA, FOCA, Brands Hatch, Silverstone and Donington to clarify the situation. That meeting was eventually fixed for the first week of June 1986, but in the last week of May we read in the Sunday newspapers that FOCA had in fact already signed a deal with Silverstone, giving them the exclusive right to run "the British round of the Formula One World Championship" – as distinct from the British Grand Prix, a title owned by the RAC – for the next five years, starting in 1987.

By the time we all sat down around a table at the RAC Club, it was pretty much cut and dried. According to Bernie, it had been FISA who had decided against allowing the rotation of grand prix venues, one of the main reasons being that the financial investment required to fund the installation and maintenance of increasingly sophisticated and costly modern safety features meant that a circuit running a grand prix needed the security of a long-term agreement, so that all the profits could be ploughed back into continual improvements. Although FISA did later agree to make an exception, in principle, for the UK, conceding that it was a special case because of the long tradition of sharing between Brands Hatch and Silverstone, they absolutely refused to consider a third alternative and specifically ruled out Donington.

We were right back where we started and, once again, I was far from convinced that the RAC had been fully committed to pressing our case with FISA. In fact, formal discussions I had later with Bernie Ecclestone, Max Mosley and others gave me good reason to suspect that they did little more than go through the motions on our behalf while arguing much more enthusiastically for Brands Hatch. As it happens, it probably would not have made much difference in practice because FOCA had done the deal with Silverstone and were not about to go back on it before 1991, if then.

Shortly after FISA's final decision regarding the rotation of circuits in the UK killed off any lingering last hope that we might still get the 1988 British Grand Prix, I launched a £1.4 million suit for damages against the RAC, alleging breach of contract, breach of duty and negligence. At the same time, I issued a statement explaining that I had embarked on a massive programme of capital expenditure at Donington on the strength of their assurance that I would be getting the Grand Prix in 1988.

The claim for damages related to work carried out at the circuit between June 1983, when the RAC formally awarded the event to Donington on condition that certain improvements were carried out, and September 1987 when they wrote to me saying that in view of the FISA decision, it appeared unrealistic to suppose that a grand prix could be held at Donington "in the foreseeable future".

As I said in my statement: "It now transpires that, throughout that period, the RAC was in possession of facts and engaged in discussions which it knew would create major obstacles for the staging of the 1988 British Grand Prix at Donington. For reasons best known to itself the RAC largely withheld the existence of these facts and discussions which made the expenditure on obtaining a Formula One track licence pointless."

And still the saga of crushing disappointment went on and on. At the meeting held at the RAC Club in June 1986 to discuss the future of grands prix in the UK following FOCA's deal with Silverstone for the British Grand Prix, Bernie Ecclestone had made a point of expressing support for the idea of staging the proposed European Grand Prix at Donington and had even remarked that it would be nice if this could be arranged in 1987 – the year of my 65th birthday – as a way of repaying me for what I had contributed to the sport. We were therefore stunned to hear rumours a few months later that the RAC were in the process of tying up an agreement with FISA whereby the event would alternate annually between Germany and the UK, with Brands Hatch as the preferred British venue. This was confirmed shortly afterwards, with the news that the Nurburgring was getting it in 1987 and Brands Hatch in 1988.

When I confronted the RAC, one of the reasons they gave for failing to push our claim was that FOCA had told them they would not support

Donington for any grand prix. When challenged over this and reminded of what Bernie Ecclestone had said at the June meeting, they dismissed his comments as a mere puff of wind, without any substance, made purely to pacify me for the loss of the 1988 British Grand Prix. In fact, I later had a meeting with Bernie and Max Mosley at which Bernie insisted that the support he expressed at that meeting had been genuine. He strongly denied that FOCA had ever ruled us out of contention – as was to be proved later in the most emphatic circumstances.

The real truth of the matter, as far as Bernie and Max could recollect, was that the RAC had made it abundantly clear right from the start that they would be pressing heavily in favour of Brands Hatch. We also had reason to believe that at the Plenary Conference of FISA in October 1986, when the decision to nominate Brands Hatch was endorsed, no mention was made of Donington's interest in staging the event or of the support voiced at the June meeting. Nor was there any attempt to make FISA fully aware of the huge programme of improvements that we had carried out. This all seemed to confirm what I had already suspected – that our effective exclusion from the selection process was yet another example of flagrant bias against Donington on the part of the RAC MSA.

By this time I was becoming resigned to the likelihood that I never would get my grand prix. It seemed that everything and everyone was against me. Since buying Donington in 1971, I had invested precisely £5,904,086 in providing some of the best facilities in the country, including £1,325,920 spent since 1983 on improvements demanded by the RAC MSA track inspectors as a condition of getting the 1988 British Grand Prix. And still I was no nearer breaking into the magic circle.

Partly as a result of this continuing frustration and partly because of the need to devote more time to my other business commitments, I had meanwhile decided to lease out the day-to-day management of the circuit to our former managing director, Robert Fearnall, and his business partner Maurice Jones, the concert promoter who had been responsible for bringing the enormously successful Monsters of Rock shows to Donington. Together they now formed Two Four Sports to run all the events at Donington on a yearly lease.

At the same time, I continued to maintain a very keen proprietorial interest and still went through the motions of lobbying for a slot in the F1 calendar, albeit without entertaining any real hope of getting very far. And then, quite out of the blue, towards the end of 1992, Bernie Ecclestone suddenly came up trumps. I had yet again been bending his ear about how much it would mean to me to have a grand prix at Donington, making him promise to bear me in mind if anything should come up. When a planned Asian Grand Prix in Japan was then cancelled at the last minute he offered me the chance to host a revived European Grand Prix in its place.

That was the good news; the bad news was that it would have to be run over the 1993 Easter Weekend, on Sunday, April 11th, which meant I had only four winter months to get the circuit updated and prepared to the latest FISA spec. An awful lot needed to be done in that time because we had called a halt to the heavy on-going financial investment involved in maintaining a full F1 track licence back in 1986, when it became clear that we weren't going to get the 1988 British Grand Prix after all. The deadline we now faced in bringing the circuit back up to grand prix standard was almost impossible, but, even so, I knew it was an offer we couldn't refuse.

Just before Christmas, FISA inspectors presented us with a seemingly endless list of requirements that had to be satisfied. The work involved extensive alterations to the basic infrastructure, the widening of run-off areas, the moving of embankments, the extension of gravel beds and the re-positioning and re-building of retaining walls, crash barriers and debris fencing. We were forced to bring in extra bulldozers and other plant from wherever we could lay our hands on it in an effort to get the job done on time. The task was made even more difficult by terrible weather conditions. And in the middle of all that, the council then popped up again and informed us that the event could not go ahead because it did not comply with the conditions governing the use of the circuit. These stipulated that we could hold only one grand prix a year – and they pointed out that we were already running the British Motorcycle Grand Prix. We managed to get that quashed with the help of local

MPs and other VIPs, but it was a worrying ten days at a point when we were already so far committed that we simply couldn't afford to halt the work.

It got to the end of February and with either rain or snow coming down day after day and turning parts of the site into a sludgy mess there seemed no way that we could get everything finished on schedule, despite working around the clock. Then, at the very height of all this frantic activity, I suffered a completely unexpected blow.

I was on site almost every day at this stage, helping to supervise the work, and as I went to lift a kerbstone one afternoon I noticed a sudden pain in my chest. It brought me up short. I thought to myself: "Ooh! That hurt a bit." I reckoned I must have pulled a muscle. I straightened up and then bent down to have another go at lifting the kerb and bang! It happened again. This time it really did hurt and I had to sit down for a minute or two. I felt absolutely knackered all of a sudden and as it was getting towards the end of the day I decided to go straight home. Lenchen diagnosed indigestion. She made me a cup of tea and I then took an aspirin and went to bed early.

I had an appointment the next day to meet my son Kevin at Donington Park for lunch with some American friends of his. When I got there Kevin remarked that I looked very pale and I admitted that I wasn't feeling too good. As we sat there things got worse and at the end of the meal he insisted that I go to hospital to get checked out and offered to drive me there straight away. I told him not to worry, that I was OK to drive myself, but by the time I got to the Queen's Medical Centre in Nottingham I was seeing double and couldn't breathe properly. I can't remember parking the car. I just about made it to the main reception desk, where I asked if I could see Mr Lyn Jarrett.

Apart from his regular hospital duties as a consultant, Lyn Jarrett was the resident doctor at both Nottingham Forest football club and at Donington Park at this time. He's a brilliant chap – they say that if you've still got a pulse, he'll save you. Anyway, I can't remember much about what happened next because no sooner had I asked for him than I collapsed in a heap on the floor. However, I'm told that an emergency medical team was summoned while somebody in reception called Lyn Jarrett on his pager to tell him: "There's a guy down here who has just passed out after coming in and asking to see you. We've looked at the cards in his wallet and his name is F.B. Wheatcroft. Does that mean anything?"

"It certainly does," said Lyn, without hesitation. "I'll be right down. I'm going to take this over."

It didn't take long to establish that I'd just suffered the third and most serious of three heart attacks, following the two minor ones I'd had on the site the day before without realising it. When I came round in a hospital bed, Lyn told me that I was very lucky, that if it had happened anywhere else I might not have made it. The fact that medical help was instantly on hand had almost certainly saved my life. He added that further tests had revealed that I would need bypass surgery as soon as possible. In the meantime, he said, I had to lose weight, rest and generally take it easy.

All this came as a shock because up until then I had always taken my health totally for granted. Just about the only time I'd had to stay off work through illness was when I jumped off a scaffold without looking and landed on a sharp upturned steel reinforcement rod, driving it right up into my groin. That did make my eyes water a bit, I can tell you, and necessitated several days in hospital. Apart from that, I had never really been ill. Even in my sixties I had remained as fit and strong as a bull, as I proved when, at the age of sixty-seven, I had a run-in with a bunch of tearaways I'd caught trying to nick stuff out of a house we were building.

This was during the housing crash of the late eighties and we had been forced to board up a number of new properties that we couldn't sell. I was checking the site one evening when I heard muffled sounds from the attic and realised there was somebody up there. I shouted out that they could either come down of their own accord, in which case the worst that would happen was that I would sling them out, or I would have to come up after them and give them a good pasting. At this point one of them jumped down out of the attic right in front of me and swung a punch. He missed – but I didn't. Unfortunately, I hit him a bit harder than I meant to and knocked him backwards, so that he hit his head against the door frame. Four others then followed him down and they all got thumped, too. They picked themselves up and ran off and I thought that was the end of it, but the next thing I knew there was a copper on the doorstep. And needless to say, it turned out to be me who was in trouble, not them.

I was warned that I faced possible charges and was asked to go down to the police station immediately. There, I really laid it on. Lawrence Olivier himself would have been proud of my performance as a frail old OAP who had been in fear of his life. I hobbled into the station, leaning on a walking stick and putting on bit of a stoop as I meekly explained to the Sergeant on duty: "I thought these lads were going to give me a real thrashing, officer. I was only trying to defend myself."

"How very fortunate then, Sir, that you were still fit enough to give all five of 'em a good hiding," smirked the Sergeant, raising an eyebrow and struggling to keep a straight face. There was a pause and then he added: "As long as you apologise and promise to be a little less forceful in future I'm sure we can overlook the matter on this occasion".

Given all this, I suppose I found it hard to accept that I was now a seriously sick man. After lecturing me on the need to slow down and take things a bit easier while I waited for major heart surgery, Lyn Jarrett was not at all impressed when I reminded him that I'd got a grand prix coming up in a few weeks' time and that there was no way I was going to miss that. And he was positively aghast when the big day finally arrived and I insisted on driving a few demonstration laps in a Mercedes W154 as part of a curtain raiser for the main event that also featured examples of the winning cars from all four pre-war Donington Grands Prix held between 1935 and 1938. "Don't do it, Tom," he pleaded. "It's the last thing you should be thinking of in the circumstances. Apart from anything else, cold, damp air is going to be forced into your lungs and that's not good for a man in your condition."

I brushed his cautions aside, even though I knew he was right. This was the moment I had been looking forward to for twenty-two years and after all the work and effort, all the legal wrangling and long drawn-out battles with the planners and protesters, all the last-minute set-backs and disappointments and all the frustration, I was determined to make the most of it. It had been made very clear to me that the bypass operation I was facing was a serious one and that, at the age of seventy-one, there were no guarantees that I would come through it. With this in mind, I reckoned that if I was going to go, then I would prefer to go with my boots on.

"I hear what you're saying, but I'm going to take the risk," I replied when Lyn warned that there was a real possibility that I could have another heart attack at the wheel. "Just make sure you don't tell the owners of the car what you've just told me!"

The 1938 Mercedes was actually owned at this time by a bank that reckoned it must be worth $10 million. They had repossessed it from a collector who went bust owing them a lot of money and I had been approached by one of their executives, a young chap called Brent Pollard, who wanted to know if I could help them to find a buyer. I suggested that he bring it along to the grand prix for a demonstration run in the hope that this might generate interest from any wealthy collectors who happened to be among the specially invited spectators. If nobody were to come forward I might buy it myself, I told him – although not at anything like the $10 million he was asking for it.

The original idea was for it to be driven on the day by somebody from the restoration specialists Crosthwaite and Gardiner, but in the end I insisted on taking the wheel myself. And, of course, once I got into the car I soon forgot all about my health problems and almost literally threw caution to the wind. The W154 is enormously powerful and needs to be handled with some care and yet I forgot about that, too, really gunning the old car. Although only scheduled to do three laps, I was enjoying the thrill of it all so much by then that I pretended I hadn't seen the flag marshal and went round one last time.

With over-confidence rising to dangerous levels, I came down the straight at about 140 mph. Just as Lyn Jarrett had warned, the rush of wind at that sort of speed started to blast cold air into my lungs, despite the fancy gold scarf that I'd got wrapped around my face, and as I hurtled through Craner Curves and down towards the Hairpin I felt myself beginning to black out. Fearing the worst, I instinctively went for the brake, momentarily forgetting that the W154 had a central accelerator pedal, which I hit by mistake. In torrential rain, this had the effect of putting the car into a wild spin, which was lucky in a way because it scrubbed off some of the speed and spun me into the gravel run-off at the Hairpin. A marshal ran forward to help me out of the car, instead of which, having quickly recovered my senses, I shouted at him to push me back onto the track. I then set off for the pits in a slightly more gingerly fashion.

Up on the balcony of my suite, Kevin, who was standing next to Brent Pollard, had been slightly alarmed to see how fast I was going on my first lap and as I came round even quicker the second time he had turned to Brent and muttered, only half-jokingly: "You'll be lucky if you ever see your car in one piece again!"

"Don't say that," came the nervous reply. "My job is on the line here!"

Sure enough, no sooner had I disappeared out of sight down Craner Curves on that final, extra lap than the note of the engine suddenly changed dramatically and the crowd at that part of the circuit could be heard going "Ooooh!"

"That's it," cried Kevin, turning away and making a dash for the stairs. "He's stuffed it!"

When I eventually reappeared a few minutes later, the engine was crackling and popping due to the damp air and the valuable car was generally looking much the worse for wear, covered in dirt and gravel and with about £10,000 worth of damage to the underside of the bodywork. Brent groaned, his head in his hands, although he was actually quite relieved to see that his prize asset had survived intact. The same could only just be said about me. Kevin had grabbed hold of Lyn Jarrett and together they came racing down to the pits to meet me as I came in. I had to be helped to the medical centre where I was put on oxygen and attached to a heart monitor.

"You can't keep taking this punishment," said Lyn, clearly losing all patience with me. "At this rate you'll not see the day out."

He wanted to keep me under observation in the medical centre, but I was absolutely determined to watch *my* race from *my* suite – and no way was I going to be carried up there. I climbed the 40-odd steps with

Kevin's ankle-length overcoat draped over my race overalls to hide the oxygen bottle that was strapped to my waist. I also had a hat pulled down over my eyes so that I wouldn't be recognised on the way up. I didn't want anybody there to know how poorly I actually was. Before I went into the suite, where my guests for the day included Princess Diana, Kevin helped me to get out of my race suit and into a jacket and tie so that I could at least make the pretence of being my usual cheery self.

Contrary to everyone's expectations, the race that followed turned out to be one of the most memorable grands prix of all time. What made it so unforgettable was, of course, the extraordinary brilliance of one man – Ayrton Senna.

The omens had not been good. Formula One was going through a strange period, what with Nigel Mansell having suddenly quit and Ayrton's future at McLaren being undecided. Apart from that, the appalling weather conditions had seemed certain to put a complete damper on the proceedings. You have to be prepared for showers in April, but the rain that bucketed down that weekend was even heavier than that which was to cause such havoc at Silverstone in 2000, when the British Grand Prix was held earlier in the year than usual and everybody got stuck in the mud in the car parks. It was positively monsoon-like on Thursday and Friday, a little better on Saturday but foul again on Sunday. Most other circuits would have been flooded, but, fortunately, we had put in very good drainage systems. Even so, there were moments when we began to wonder whether the race would ever actually take place. After everything that had gone before, that would have been the final straw.

As we sat there waiting for the start, which took place during a brief lull in the weather, Robert Fearnall and I were keeping our fingers crossed that no water had got into the electrics, worrying that there could be a major power failure at any moment. Would the starter lights actually work? We held our breath and then, as the two reds turned to green and the cars lurched away, we heaved a sigh of relief. Within the first two minutes, that relief then turned to amazement as we witnessed one of the most spectacular feats of driving ever seen on a racetrack.

Watching the build-up on TV, I had listened as James Hunt, by this time working as a pundit with Murray Walker and the BBC commentary team, confidently forecast that there would not be a lot of overtaking in such appallingly difficult wet weather conditions. Most of us would probably have agreed with him at that point. However, we reckoned without Ayrton Senna's unique talents.

His McLaren-Ford MP4-8 was generally considered to be no match for the Williams Renaults of Damon Hill and Frenchman Alain Prost, who was on his way to his fourth World Championship. In fourth spot on the grid, alongside the young Michael Schumacher's Benetton and behind Hill and Prost on pole, Senna immediately found himself one place further back after Karl Wendlinger got a flying start in his Sauber and shot ahead of both him and Schumacher.

Lying fifth as he approached the first corner, Ayrton made an aggressive move to take the inside line and close out Schumacher. He then drew gasps from the crowd as he went like a madman down the outside of the Craner Curves, apparently taking completely the wrong line through the left-hander. This is absolutely what you are *not* supposed to do there, but Ayrton was a law unto himself. Amid a cloud of spray, he flashed past Wendlinger, while still managing to position himself perfectly for the right-hand Hairpin. It was such a brilliant manoeuvre that there was talk afterwards of renaming this section of the circuit 'Senna Curves' in his honour.

Sitting on Damon Hill's tail as he came up the hill to McLean's, Ayrton once again exhibited the steely nerve, lightning reactions and split-second timing that made him so special. Outmanoeuvring Damon through the corner, he came out ahead, driving to all intents and purposes as if the surface were bone dry. By now, the crowd was buzzing with excitement while, up in the commentary box, Murray Walker was going bananas.

As they came to the Melbourne Hairpin, Ayrton's McLaren was closing rapidly on Prost. Now, the Melbourne Hairpin is definitely the last place at which you would normally even begin to think about overtaking, but while everyone else was understandably twitchy and cautious in the rain, Ayrton took it at speed, out-braking Prost comprehensively and shooting past him on the inside so fast that, as one commentator remarked, he made it look as if the Frenchman were driving an F3 car by comparison.

And so it was that on a day when the experts had predicted that there would be very few overtaking manoeuvres in such extreme conditions, Senna had gone from 5th to 1st inside the first lap, taking out three current or future World Champion drivers in the process! I think it is fair to say that there has never been a lap like it, before or since. Indeed, the readers of *Autosport* voted it 'Lap of the Century' while elsewhere in the motorsport Press it was dubbed 'Lap of the Gods'. And that was just for starters.

With the weather changing continuously throughout the race, drivers kept switching from wet tyres to slicks and back again, but Senna held on to his slicks that bit longer than his rivals, extending his lead to the point where he eventually lapped everyone else in the field except Hill. Damon did just manage to finish on the same lap, although still well over one minute and twenty seconds behind. Altogether, it was a stunning performance by Senna, and one that nobody who was there will ever forget.

Ayrton, conscious of what he had achieved, was in high spirits afterwards. I remember him stopping on his lap of honour to grab a Brazilian flag from a spectator, which he then held aloft in the cockpit of the car. In post-race interviews he recalled how he had had his first ever taste of Formula One at Donington ten years earlier, when he had tested there for Frank Williams in the FW08, remarking on how appropriate it was that he should have come back there to record what he felt was perhaps his greatest victory. He promised me that he would return again some time and I believe he meant it, but tragically, of course, that was never to be.

As I made my way rather shakily up the steps of the podium to present him with his trophy I wasn't sure whether to laugh or cry. I had at last achieved my ambition to hold a Grand Prix at Donington and it had been won in sensational style by the man who will go down in history as one of the greatest and most universally revered drivers of them all – cause enough for celebration. At the same time, it was already obvious by then that the rain-sodden event was going to be a complete wash-out financially.

Advance ticket sales had been disappointing, probably because a lot of those fans who were only prepared to fork out for one major event per season had opted to book for the British Grand Prix instead. The awful weather then ensured that very few people bothered to turn up on the day, with the result that the overall attendance was the lowest ever for a modern grand prix in this country – especially ironic given that it later won the annual award for the best organised grand prix of the season. By the time the race started on the Sunday, I knew instinctively that I was looking at a considerable loss, eventually calculated at nearly £3.5 million.

In view of this, I didn't feel I could afford to splash out on the W154, even though nobody else had come forward to make an offer – not surprisingly, perhaps, given the mess I'd left it in! But Brent Pollard did not go home empty-handed. I paid to have the car fully repaired and later arranged a deal whereby it was sold for a substantial sum to Arturo Keller, the German/Mexican motor industry tycoon who has put together the world's biggest private Mercedes Benz collection.

Aware that I had lost a lot of money on the grand prix, Bernie Eccle-stone was kind enough to make it clear that he would understand if I needed time to pay FOCA the sizeable amount they were owed, a gener-ous gesture that showed a caring side of Bernie's character that the world doesn't often see. He also indicated that I could have the event again the following year, but I had already decided against that. I wasn't ready to take the same risk again so soon and although at that stage I did still hope to have another grand prix at some time in the future, the costs involved soon began to spiral up so high that I couldn't afford even to contemplate it any more. In 2001, when problems at Silverstone and Brands Hatch prompted Octagon to consider the possibility of bringing the British Grand Prix to Donington, the cost of upgrading the circuit to full F1 standard was estimated at £36 million. That gives some idea of the sort of investment required these days to host a major grand prix event.

The main priority once the dust had settled over the European Grand Prix should have been to get my health problems sorted out, but I kept finding reasons to put off the operation. By the summer, I couldn't walk any distance at all without getting breathless and when I announced that I intended to go ahead, as planned, with a visit to the Monterey Speed

Week in California in early August Lyn Jarrett was in despair. He was only mildly appeased when I agreed to be checked out at the world famous Mayo Clinic while I was over there. This was on the advice of my friends Sir Jackie Stewart and the late King Hussein of Jordan, both of whom had been treated there at various times and spoke very highly of the place.

I had known Jackie for years, while King Hussein, a very keen motorsport enthusiast and an experienced rally driver in his own right, was among the select group of friends and VIPs who were invited to join me for special 'play days' at Donington, during which selected cars from the museum and elsewhere would be taken out for spins around the circuit. Other guests at these private get-togethers ranged from ex-King Constantine of Greece to Nick Mason, the Pink Floyd drummer and also one of the country's leading classic car collectors. The atmosphere was always very relaxed and informal. Prince Michael of Kent, a great classic car enthusiast, once asked me what I thought of his driving. "Well, put it this way, Sir," I replied. "I wouldn't give up your day job!" As it happens, he wasn't at all a bad driver.

Not satisfied with driving the classic cars, King Hussein was keen to get behind the wheel of a modern F1 car – and he not only wanted to drive it flat out, he wanted to spin it as well! We arranged to borrow a car from Benetton and to run it at nearby Bruntingthorpe, the ex-USAF base now owned by my close friends, the Walton family. I reckoned that the 1½-mile runway there would allow him the sort of wide-open space in which to spin in relative safety. Jackie Stewart came along to give him a bit of a lecture before he went out, just to make sure he knew what he was doing, and he was then let loose to blast up and down a few times before deliberately spinning the car at high speed. I think we were all a bit nervous, but we needn't have worried. He actually proved to be one hell of a driver – as well as a really warm and friendly man – and it all went off very smoothly.

The King and Sir Jackie between them made all the arrangements for me to be seen at the Mayo Clinic. When I got there, I was subjected to just about every test known to man, after which the doctors confirmed what Lyn Jarrett had already told me.

"We need to operate, Mr Wheatcroft," they said.

"When?" I asked.

"Now, Mr Wheatcroft. You've got so many blockages that we can't quite work out how you're still alive."

When I inquired about my chances of survival I was told that they were only about 50/50. "In that case, thank you very much, but I think I'll go home and have the operation done there," I said. "If I'm going to die, I'd rather die at home in England."

Even then, it was another couple of months before I was eventually admitted to the private BUPA hospital in Oadby. Here, the weather that had plagued me all year once again decided to throw a spanner in the works. I had got as far as having my pre-med injections and was on the point of going down to theatre when a violent thunderstorm caused a major power cut, forcing the surgeon to postpone everything until the following day.

I was finally wheeled into theatre at 1pm. The operation lasted 3½hours, but by 6.00pm I was sitting up in bed having a cup of tea. The first person I spoke to was Rick Hall, who rang up to see how I was, still thinking that the operation had gone ahead as planned the day before. "Don't worry, lad," I said when he realised his mistake and apologised for disturbing me so soon afterwards. "All that stuff they tell you about the pain is a load of bunkum. I ain't felt a bloody thing yet!"

Kevin arrived to visit me in the ward a few minutes later and was equally surprised to hear my distinctive laugh – once described as sound-ing like somebody trying to start a tractor with a flat battery – from half way down the corridor outside. He then came in to find me sitting up in bed with a cup of tea, joking around with the nurses.

Of course, I didn't feel quite so perky once the anaesthetic wore off. However, I said to Kevin: "What's the record for getting out of hospital after an operation like this?"

Somebody in the room piped up: "Nine days."

"Right," I said. "I'm going to beat that."

And I did. I was out in a week – and back in the office not long after that. At that point I then found myself wondering what I was going to do with the rest of my life.

I had gradually been handing over more and more of the day-to-day running of the business to Kevin. His older brother, David, had also worked with me for a time before deciding to strike out on his own, but Kevin had opted to stay on. After leaving school, he first served an engineering apprenticeship before joining the company in 1978, starting right at the bottom as a labourer and learning each individual trade in turn before moving on to manage sites. During the housing crash of the late eighties we then decided not to build any more houses, but to concentrate instead on managing our extensive commercial and industrial investment portfolio. With this ticking over quite nicely, I was free to devote more of my time to other projects. But what should these projects be, now that I had at last realised my ambition of holding a grand prix and given that I had decided against trying to repeat that very expensive experience? First off, I decided to give myself a bit of a treat.

In 1994 I set out with Kevin on what became jokingly referred to as the 'grand tour'. My health scare had convinced me that it was time to start living out one or two of my fantasies before it was too late. High on my wish list for many years in this respect had been the idea of visiting all the best and most famous car museums and collections around the world and with the very generous help of an old American friend, Richie Clyne, that's what I now set out to do.

Originally from New York, Richie Clyne is one of the most colourful characters you could ever hope to meet. A multi-millionaire in his own right from his highly successful dealings in classic cars – among other things, he put together the world's largest private collection of both Rolls Royces and Mercedes 770Ks, the so-called 'Hitler Cars' – he also ran the vast Imperial Palace Collection in Las Vegas for the even richer, multi-billionaire construction magnate and casino owner, Ralph Engelstadt. Richie and I had first met several years earlier through our shared interest in classic cars and we took to each other straightaway, to the point where I would never go to America without looking him up and he would never come to Europe without calling me to see if we could get together. I remember getting on a plane and flying to Luxembourg just to have dinner with him on one occasion.

When I contacted him to see if he might be able to pull a few strings to help me gain access to some of the more exclusive private car collections in America he immediately insisted on taking over the organisation of the whole trip – on condition that he could come too. He then worked out an itinerary, laid on a private Learjet, had a limousine standing by to meet us at every airport and booked all the hotels and restaurants. For ten days we did nothing but eat, sleep, travel and look at cars. We took in up to three museums or collections each day and saw a total of more than 4,500 cars. And that wasn't the end of it. From America we flew on to Japan to see the Hayashi and Matsuda collections and then came back to Europe to take in a few more. Altogether, this incredible whistle-stop tour took us to more than forty separate collections in three different continents in fifteen days.

As a memento of the trip, Richie presented me later with a beautifully bound, six-volume set of photo albums he'd had specially put together, featuring pictures of every single car we'd seen on our travels. The generosity of the man was surpassed only by the wicked sense of fun that helped to make him such entertaining company. At one point, as we were flying across America in the Learjet, he handed me a gin-and-tonic, advising me as he did so to make sure that my seat belt was fastened. The next thing I knew, I had thrown the entire contents of the glass into my own face as the pilot, primed in advance by Richie, flipped the plane upside down. To be honest, it was done so smoothly that I don't think I would have noticed anything untoward if it hadn't been for the gin dripping off my nose and the ice and lemon in my lap.

A couple of years after the Grand Tour, Richie laid on an even more spectacular extravaganza when Kevin and his fiancée, Sarah, decided on a two-stage wedding, starting with a ceremony in Las Vegas and followed by a church blessing in our local village church at home, with his great friend and five times World Speedway Champion Barry Briggs as his Best Man.

Barry, who ran the Speedway Hall of Fame at Donington for a time, is a wonderful character, a big-hearted man in every way and one of the few people I know who could tell Bernie Ecclestone where to stick his contract and still get invited back for lunch! Anyway, as soon as Richie heard about the Las Vegas idea, he once again insisted on taking charge of all the arrangements. It just so happened that he and Ralph Engelstadt were about to open their new $100 million Las Vegas Speedway at the time and he talked Kevin and Sarah into taking their vows in the middle of the oval circuit as a curtain raiser for the inaugural race meeting, watched live on TV and by a sell-out crowd of over 100,000.

As a trio of Elvis Presley look-alikes parachuted in and the American national anthem played, the first car on the circuit that day was the limousine that delivered Kevin and Sarah to the dais in front of the main grandstand, where the crowd whooped and hollered and shouted: "Don't do it! Don't do it!" as a female minister from the famed Little White Chapel prepared to conduct the ceremony. At the very moment when Sarah said: "I do" and she and Kevin were declared man and wife, the lights changed and the inaugural race roared into action. The church blessing back at home was a slightly more restrained affair!

For me, one of the highlights of the Grand Tour had been Ralph Engel-stadt's Imperial Palace collection in Las Vegas, largely put together for him by Richie and featuring more than 1,000 cars. Also very special was Hayashi's collection in Japan. With a fortune made mostly from hair care products, Hayashi himself is almost as colourful a character as Richie, although in a rather different way. Immaculately dressed, impeccably mannered and softly spoken, he carries a silver-topped cane inset with a pair of red ruby eyes and seems to be accompanied wherever he goes by two very pretty girls.

Before personally showing us around his collection, he invited us for lunch in his own private restaurant. As he shook my hand in greeting, he bowed his head and told me: "Mr Wheatcroft, sir, you are my god. It was you who first gave me the inspiration to collect."

That was quite something coming from a man who is himself regarded as a god in his own country and I was quite taken aback. But for the rest of the trip I milked it to death at every opportunity as far as Kevin and Richie were concerned. "God is ready for another drink now if you wouldn't mind fetching it for me," I would announce grandly, with a regal wave of the hand. Or: "Would you mind just carrying god's bags out to the car, please."

Returning home with Hayashi's words still ringing in my ears, I was fired with renewed enthusiasm for my own collection. In the immediate aftermath of my heart operation I had lost some of my interest and had even started to sell off some of my private road cars. Now, with my health fully restored, I decided to set about filling what I considered to be the last few remaining gaps in the Grand Prix Collection.

Top Marques

Achance meeting on a train with a Czechoslovakian refugee, hints dropped by a delegation of Russian civil engineers visiting Donington during the Cold War, large amounts of cash smuggled behind the Iron Curtain in a dummy oil filter, a valuable historic racing car spirited out from the Russian sector of Berlin in a coal barge – as a leading collector of rare grand prix cars I have often been involved in the sort of clandestine operations that you would normally expect to read about in a John Le Carré spy novel rather than in the pages of *Classic Cars* magazine.

There is one very good reason for this. Out of all the great historic grand prix cars, some of the most coveted collectors' items in the world are the pre-war German Auto Unions and Mercedes – the 'Silver Arrows' that dominated motor racing so sensationally in the late 1930s. Given the special connection with Donington, dating back to 1937 and 1938, these cars have always been near the top of my most-wanted list, and yet most of them vanished without trace behind the Iron Curtain after the war.

This was especially true of the Auto Unions, simply because the company – formed through an amalgamation of Audi, DKW, Horch and Wanderer, hence the four-ring logo still used by Audi today – had been based in what was to become part of East Germany. One C-Type Auto Union had been donated to the Deutsches Museum in Munich in 1937, but all the others just disappeared. It is a known fact that eighteen of them were taken out of the works and put on a train to Moscow as soon as the Russians moved in at the end of the war, but exactly what happened to them after that has always been a bit of a mystery. For years nobody really knew for sure exactly how many had survived, if any at all, or where they had ended up. To this day, the vast majority remain unaccounted for. In view of the political situation, finding them during the Cold War years was difficult and getting them out was even trickier. Now it is probably too late, the cars long ago dismantled and the parts scattered far and wide.

The first Auto Union to re-emerge after the war turned up in Prague in the late 1960s and I happened to hear about it before anybody else in the West. This came about quite by chance. I rarely travel anywhere by rail, but for some reason I found myself one day on a train going from London to Leicester and fell into conversation with a young chap sitting opposite me. He turned out to be a Czech who had fled the country shortly before the Russians moved in to crush the uprising of 1968. He was visiting a friend, who lived in a village about twenty miles from Leicester, and leaned across to ask me if I happened to know whether he could get a bus from the station to the village. It was then we got chatting.

His English wasn't too good, so the conversation was a bit awkward, but it gradually emerged that, by some extraordinary coincidence, his father was the curator of the National Technical Museum in Prague, which owned a number of important historic cars, including a Mercedes 154/163. I started telling him about my own collection and my special interest in Mercedes and Auto Unions and, to my amazement, he then revealed that he knew the exact whereabouts of what he claimed was an original 1938 V12 D-Type Auto Union. If true, this would make it the only genuine one of its kind known to exist at that time. I immediately told him not to worry about getting a bus to his friend's house. "I'll drive you there myself," I said.

On the way, I pumped him as best I could for more information and he explained that the car had been on exhibition at the Auto Union dealership in Prague when war broke out and had then found its way into the hands of the pre-war Czech racing driver Zdenek Pohl, who, he said, also owned several rare Bugattis. He added that his father knew Pohl well and would be happy to give me a letter of introduction if I wanted to try and set up a meeting to see whether there was any chance that the Auto Union might be for sale. This could well be a possibility, he thought, since Pohl had fallen on hard times under the Communist regime.

I arranged to meet this chap again for dinner the next night at The Manor in Wigston, my favourite Midlands restaurant for many years until I discovered The Butcher's Arms at Priors Hardwick in Warwickshire, presided over by the wonderful Lino Pires and his family. At the time, The Manor was one of a string of restaurants run by an old friend of mine called Frank Dimbleby, an ex-RAF Squadron Leader who had worked in the British Embassy in Prague as an Air Attaché after the war. Frank, a cousin of the television personality Richard Dimbleby, not only knew his way around Czechoslovakia, but also spoke the language. After talking things over at length and getting as much information as possible from the young Czech, Frank agreed to go over on my behalf to see if he could make initial contact.

Politically, it was obviously a tricky time and Pohl was very nervous at first. However, a meeting at a restaurant was eventually organised and once he was satisfied that he wasn't being set up in any way, Pohl arranged to see Frank at the same place the next day, with the promise that he would then take him to see the car.

Pohl had been a wealthy man before the war and had owned a big estate, but this had been taken over by the Communist government and he had been forced to move out into the gatehouse. However, he had managed to hang on to some of his small collection of cars. As well as the Auto Union, this included three very valuable Bugattis – a Type 51, a Type 13 and one of only three 4.7-litre models ever made. He had them all hidden away under wraps in various sheds and garages in the area.

The message came back to me that he would indeed be prepared to sell the Auto Union and a figure of £45,000 was eventually agreed. However, it wasn't quite as straightforward as that. At that time, the government would automatically take two thirds of whatever was paid in a deal like that, so Pohl asked us to compensate him for this by unofficially paying him the equivalent amount in cash. This was fine by me. After all, the Communists had already robbed him of his family home, so why shouldn't he get something back? The only problem, as far as I was concerned, was how to get the money out to him.

We solved that by fitting a second, dummy oil filter to our transporter and stuffing the cash inside it. Sprayed with oil and dirt, the phoney part looked totally genuine and only a very sharp-eyed expert would ever have spotted that it was false. At the border, the guards literally took the vehicle to pieces, obviously suspicious that something was being smuggled in. They even stripped the lining panels out of the interior to see if there was anything behind them, but they found nothing.

Everything seemed to be going to plan until the very last moment. I had all the papers necessary to take the car out of Czechoslovakia, but just days before we were due to pick it up the authorities apparently twigged what was happening and, maybe realising the true value of the car, impounded it. So, my mechanics came back home without either the car or the cash, which had already been handed over in advance. Pohl himself was an honourable man and I know he didn't try to twist us – the government simply took the car off him. He wrote to me saying that he had got the money and would try to get it back to me, but I told him not to worry about it. I rather felt sorry for him, the way he and his family had been treated, and, apart from that, he did give us a lot of help in trying to trace some other cars, so I did get something for my money.

The next thing I heard was that Colin Crabbe had got the Auto Union. That was several years later. He had acquired it through the German collector, Count Hubertus von Doenhoff. It didn't have a complete engine at this stage – the crankshaft and other internal parts were missing – and von Doenhoff had decided that the restoration would be too expensive, so instead of buying it himself he helped to arrange its sale to Colin. Colin, in turn, then sold it on to the American collector Kerry Payne. I first saw the car shortly afterwards on display at an event in France and I did feel a pang of regret when I thought how close I'd come to owning it myself.

Kerry Payne then had a huge stroke of luck when a genuine original spare engine suddenly turned up out of the blue in Leipzig. A complete two-stage supercharged V12, date-stamped July 1939, it had been discovered in the possession of a clockmaker in the town. He had allegedly got it from the local Technical Museum in lieu of payment for some work he had done there. It was somehow traced to him by Martin Shroeder, an historic car enthusiast from Hanover and a great friend of Colin Crabbe, who managed to smuggle it out of East Germany in what was, by all accounts, a real cloak-and-dagger operation. As a joke at my expense, Colin later put out a press release claiming that it had actually been discovered under a pile of straw in a derelict barn on the Donington Park estate, the story being that it had been left behind there after the last pre-war Grand Prix in 1938. I almost fell for that one until it was revealed that the engine was dated 1939!

Having sold the engine on to Kerry Payne, Colin was then asked by him to carry out the restoration work and, in September 1979, he actually got to drive the car for ten demonstration laps at the Nurburgring on what was the 40th anniversary of its last appearance there. The crowd in the grandstands gave the car a standing ovation as it came howling down the straight. Colin joked afterwards that he half expected to see arms shooting out in a Nazi salute!

Later, American F1 star Phil Hill drove it at Donington as part of a track test for *Road and Track* magazine, only for the exercise to end in disaster. According to Colin, Phil asked him just before he went out: "What can I turn it up to?" – meaning what were the maximum revs he could safely take it up to. Anxious to ensure that he kept well within the top limit of 7000, Colin suggested 5500 through the gears and whatever it would comfortably pull in top, maybe about 4500. After a few laps Phil came in bathed in sweat and announced excitedly: "I just hit 7500! What a car!"

At that very moment water was seen to be pouring out of the exhaust. The engine had blown up and had to be completely rebuilt. Colin never forgave Phil for that. Since then the car has passed through several hands and, last I heard, was owned by a Mr Lee, the chairman of the Korean car company, Hyundai.

Meanwhile, a further two D-types have now been recovered. After years of determined and painstaking detective work, Florida-based enthusiasts Paul and Barbara Karassik found them, in bits, in a barn in the Ukraine. Prior to that, they had apparently been hidden away in a disused salt mine. Karassik himself was born in Yugoslavia and his wife is a White Russian, so they obviously had some very good contacts in that part of the world. Even so, it was an amazing discovery.

The couple took all the bits they had found to top restoration experts Dick Crosthwaite and John Gardiner in Buxted. Basically, what they had got were two engines, one gearbox, one complete chassis, half of another chassis, one car's worth of suspension and other assorted spares. There was no bodywork at all. Out of that, Crosthwaite & Gardiner built two complete cars, one of which was allegedly sold for $7 million to a private collector, who recently loaned it to the museum at Donington on the strict understanding that his identity would not be revealed. Even more generously, he also allowed us to run the car as part of the event we laid on in 2003 to celebrate the 65th anniversary of Nuvolari's victory in the 1938 Donington Grand Prix. It was driven on the Melbourne Loop that day by Rick Hall's son Rob, who rather reluctantly agreed to be dressed up as Nuvolari for the occasion, complete with a trademark yellow jersey, red leather helmet and goggles.

The second car eventually ended up with Audi, who were so impressed with the quality of Crosthwaite & Gardiner's restoration work that they asked them to build six exact replicas from scratch. Audi then exchanged one of these replicas for a genuine hybrid Type C/D V16 hill climber that had turned up in a museum in Riga, Latvia and which was also restored by Crosthwaite & Gardiner.

As it happens, I could have had that Riga car myself. The chance arose when Kevin set about trying to find examples of the winning cars from all four of the pre-war Donington Grands Prix held between 1935 and 1938, with a view to running them in the demonstration laps that featured as a curtain raiser for the 1993 European Grand Prix.

Coming up with an Alfa P3 from 1935 and an Alfa 308 from 1936 was reasonably straightforward, but he always knew that getting hold of an Auto Union was going to be extremely difficult if not downright impossible. It soon became obvious that a 1938 Type D was out of the question and Kevin decided that the Mercedes W154 – the one which I eventually drove on the day – would be a worthy substitute. However, when he heard about the V16 in Riga, he jumped on a plane and went out there to see if he could persuade the museum authorities to let him borrow it. And, to everyone's surprise, he succeeded.

The car wasn't a runner and had to be towed around the circuit rather than driven, but this was the first time it had been seen in the West since the war so it was a bit of a coup just to get it here. When the transporter arrived at Donington it seemed to contain half the population of Riga, along with more suitcases than toolboxes, and we got the impression that they were rather hoping we would buy the car for cash, in which case they probably wouldn't go back to Latvia. Unfortunately, because we ended up losing so much money on the Grand Prix and because I was so unwell at the time, we weren't in the mood for buying anything. So, although we had it at Donington for several weeks and even had it photographed on the lawn in front of my house, we decided we'd have to let it go. But the fact that Kevin had managed to get it out in the first place alerted Audi to the fact that it might be available and very shortly afterwards they did their own deal with the museum in Riga.

Looking back now, I'm disappointed that I missed the opportunity to add such a valuable car to my collection. As it happens, I had already managed to acquire an Auto Union of my own by then, although it was not quite such a significant example, having never actually raced in anger. However, the story of its acquisition is even more dramatic than that surrounding the Zdenec Pohl car. Once again, it came out from behind the Iron Curtain.

Known as a Type E, the car was originally built in 1939 to the 1.5-litre supercharged formula and was intended to run during the 1940 season, only to be mothballed when war broke out. After the war, the chassis was passed on to DAMW, the old BMW racing department at Eisenach, where it was rebuilt as a 2-litre naturally aspirated V12. By the time I got to hear about it in the late seventies it was owned by a Russian, based in Moscow.

Its existence was revealed to me by a delegation of three Russians who had come over to Donington to inspect our circuit before starting to build one of their own back in the USSR. While they were here I took them out to dinner a couple of times. We got chatting about old cars and when I mentioned how keen I was to get hold of an Auto Union they told me about this chap, who, they thought, had two. With their help I managed to make contact with him through an intermediary and although it turned out that he actually had only one, he agreed to sell it to me. The problem, once again, was how to get it out of the country at a time long before the Iron Curtain had started to lift.

A miners' strike in the UK provided the unlikely solution. The government had started buying in coal from East Germany to build up reserves at the power stations and I was tipped off that the skipper of one of the ships that was involved in bringing it over could be bribed to smuggle the car out. And that's exactly what we did. The Russian owner, whom I never met face to face and whose name I never knew, arranged to get it down to the docks and a car that is now worth somewhere between £500,000 and £1 million came over hidden under tons of cheap coal.

In fact, only the chassis came over that way. We decided to have the body sent out separately and by a more conventional route, as a decoy, just in case the Communist authorities were onto us. Sure enough, it disappeared somewhere en route and has never been seen or heard of again. I wasn't too bothered about that because the body was relatively unimportant in terms of the car's authenticity and could fairly easily be replaced. I was so excited about getting the car that I kept it hidden in my garage at home for a year simply because I didn't want to let it out of my sight. I would sneak out to the garage every now and again just to give it a stroke!

There are extraordinary stories of some kind or another attached to just about every exhibit in the Grand Prix Collection. One of the more amusing ones concerns the 1955 Maserati 250F, the works car that I bought from Count Ottorino Volonterio. Shortly afterwards, the Count offered me a spare engine and I decided that I would make a detour on my annual visit to Monaco for the grand prix, stopping to pick it up on the way.

Everything was going according to plan until I had to cross the border from Italy into Monaco. The Italian customs officials at Ventimiglia were fine. I told them that the engine had been to the works to be rebuilt and that I was rushing it back for the grand prix. Being Italian and well into their motorsport, they waved me through enthusiastically. One hundred yards along the road, the Monaco border was manned by the French, who, as we all know, can be very awkward. I gave them the same cock 'n' bull story, but they weren't having any of it.

"Where are the papers?" they demanded.

"I haven't got any," I admitted.

"Well, then, you're not bringing it in."

It seemed I should have had a carnet, some sort of import-export document. I tried to talk my way through, but there was no way. In the end, they impounded not only the engine, but my car as well. And they wouldn't even call me a taxi! I had to walk all the way down to Menton to find one.

At my hotel, I rang the office back in England and got them to sort out one of these carnet things through the RAC and have it couriered out to me as soon as possible. This was duly done and I went back to collect the engine. Still the customs people weren't satisfied. "This carnet proves you own the engine, but it has been raised in the UK and it hasn't been stamped out of the UK and into Italy," they told me. "So how can the engine come out of Italy if it hasn't officially gone in yet?"

They then made me take it back across the border, where I made hurried arrangements to store it in Ventimiglia while I returned to England and tried to sort things out from there.

After much thought, we eventually came up with a plan. It was decided that two of my mechanics would have to go out with a mock Maserati engine, get it stamped out at every border, then do a switch, ditch the mock-up and come back with the real one in its place.

The two mechanics first went to the local breaker's yard and picked up an old Jaguar engine for about £5, ground all the Jaguar names and numbers off it and stamped the 250F numbers on instead. They then loaded it onto a trailer in a packing case, along with the Tec Mec, so that it looked as if they were going to a race meeting and carrying a spare.

The other little difficulty we faced was that there was a restriction at the time on the amount of money you could take abroad – something like £50-per-person. There was obviously no way two people could drive a Land Rover and trailer all the way down to Monaco and back again, staying at hotels along the way, for £100. So I gave them £250 in cash that they hid inside the Tec Mec carburettor.

The two of them eventually arrived in Ventimiglia and went to pick up the Maserati engine. There was a minor hiccup here when the man who had been storing it for me, and who didn't speak a word of English, suddenly became very agitated, gabbling at them in Italian and making angry gestures. They couldn't understand a word he was saying, but, fortunately, a colonial-type English gent made a timely appearance on the scene at this point to help with translation. It seemed the Italian had twigged that there was something a little bit fishy going on and wanted several million lira in return for keeping his mouth shut. "He's mentioned the police and he's mentioned prison," explained the English toff. "It's only about £15 – I'd pay him if I were you."

The mechanics handed over the cash, roped the engine onto the trailer as quickly as possible and headed up into the hills. There they found a remote spot and dumped the Jaguar engine over a cliff, hoping that it wouldn't go crashing through somebody's roof far down below. They then decided that it might be sensible to cross the border back into France somewhere other than at Ventimiglia, just in case the officials there were to smell a rat. However, in the dark and without any decent maps, they got lost up in the mountains and decided in the end that they had no option but to go back the way they had come. There were some anxious moments as they presented their papers, but it was late by this time and the officials gave them only a cursory glance, quickly completing the formalities and waving them through. By the time they eventually got back to our workshops in Aylestone Lane, the pair of them had quite a story to tell.

I'm often asked which of the cars in my collection I would choose if I ever found myself in a situation where I could keep only one. That's an impossibly difficult question to answer. If you were to go purely on monetary value, it would have to be the Auto Union that we have recently had on loan and which must be worth the thick end of £5 million. From a historical point of view, Nuvolari's 1936 Alfa Romeo Bimotore would be high on the list of priorities, along with the 1948 Cisitalia Porsche 360 – one of the most advanced racing cars ever built – and the 1952 Ferrari 500 – the most successful grand prix car of all time, with eleven wins out of fifteen races entered. At the same time, you wouldn't want to lose Stirling Moss's Lotus Climax 18, in which he famously won the 1961 Monaco Grand Prix for Rob Walker's little private team against the full might of the Ferrari works team; or the 1963 Lotus Climax 25, the first ever monocoque design, in which Jim Clark won six consecutive grands prix and his first World Championship.

Fangio's 1948 Maserati 4CLT has a special appeal for me because of the association with my all-time favourite driver and I also have a strong sentimental attachment to the 1934 Maserati 8CM, a genuine Nuvolari car in which I myself have had so much fun as an amateur driver over the years. The 1950 Thinwall Special would have to be in the reckoning, as would the re-created 1931 Type 41 Bugatti Royale that took over 100,000 hours of research and craftsmanship to build. And, for sheer beauty, the classic Maserati 250F is hard to ignore. However, the personalised number plate of my own private road car – V16 BRM – gives a clue as to where my final preference might lie.

I have always had a special interest in BRM, largely for patriotic reasons. Inspired by a desire to challenge the growing Italian domination of the post-war grand prix scene, British Racing Motors was founded in 1949 by Raymond Mays and Peter Berthon, both of whom had previously been involved with ERA back in the 1930s. Later it was owned and financed for some years by industrialist Sir Alfred Owen, chairman of Rubery Owen.

As it happens, the very first prototype V16 was actually built at Donington, in a workshop that stood up near Coppice farmhouse. This later had to be demolished to make way for the new circuit, but I had it dismantled and re-assembled at a local farm I own, where it remains to this day.

The team made its debut at Silverstone in 1950 with the V16 Mark 1, but had to wait until 1959 for its first win before going on to enjoy its finest hour in 1962 when Graham Hill won the World Championship in a BRM P56 ahead of Jim Clark and Bruce McLaren. That very car is in the Donington Collection, along with the P261 in which Hill narrowly failed to win the Championship for a second time two years later, when Lorenzo Bandini took him off in the last race of the season, allowing Surtees, in a Ferrari, to pip him for the title. Thereafter, fluctuating but generally declining fortunes prompted Sir Alfred Owen to withdraw his company's backing in 1973 and although the late Louis Stanley tried to keep the team going, it finally folded in 1977.

I still remain close friends with David Owen, the son of Sir Alfred, and have always been a big supporter of anything to do with BRM, partly as a mark of respect for the family. Shortly after BRM closed down I actually made an offer to buy the whole outfit, lock, stock and barrel, with a view to possibly reviving the team myself. At that stage I still hadn't completely given up on my dream of getting involved in Formula One as a private team owner. However, my offer was refused. Egged on by Christie's, Louis Stanley seemed to think that he could make more by auctioning off the cars, spares, drawings and tools as separate lots, only to be proved wrong when the total proceeds of the auction, held at Earl's Court in October 1981, amounted to less than my original offer.

I was the main bidder at that auction and most of the more important items that went under the hammer during the course of the evening were knocked down to me. When it ended I received a standing ovation from everybody there – as a mark of respect, I suppose, for my heroic spending! Kevin was a director of the company by that time so I got him to write out the cheque for the final amount – a fraction under £250,000. This was a huge amount of money at the time and his hand was shaking as he filled in the figures.

As well as drawings, spares, tools and archive material, the cars I bought that day included a 1969 P139, a 1970 P153, a 1972 P180 and a 1974 P160. The highest price fetched by a single lot was the £160,000 I paid for a 1954 V16 Mark 2 that had been driven by Ken Wharton and Peter Collins. I was also tempted by a 1949 V16 Mark 1 that had been driven by Fangio at Silverstone in 1953, but the car was incomplete and, anyway, I already had one of only three that were ever made, so I passed on that. It went for £100,000 to classic car dealer Dan Margulies, who was bidding on behalf of a syndicate that later sold it to the Beaulieu museum. Margulies also paid £60,000 for a second Mark 2 that was then sold to rock star Nick Mason. It was to be another twenty-three years before this car also joined my Grand Prix Collection, by which time I had to give £1 million for it.

My Mark 1 was re-built by ex-BRM mechanic Rick Hall, using original parts and spares that I had bought direct from BRM over the years. Towards the end, when the team was already struggling to survive, I would regularly go down to the factory at Bourne on a Thursday or Friday, aware that they were likely to be short of the cash needed to pay people's wages at the end of the week and knowing that they would probably be only too happy to sell me a few more bits and pieces to help them out financially. What a sad decline for a once great company.

One way and another I picked up more than sixteen tons of stuff, so that by the time they finally closed down in 1977 I actually had more spares than they did. We have since discovered that we have in fact got enough parts to rebuild the third of the Mark 1 V16s. This was the one that was famously written off after Ken Wharton found reverse instead of top! That was quite easily done because of the design of the gear lever, which was subsequently altered to include what became known as the Wharton modification, a switch that could be flicked over to isolate reverse once you got going.

Although we don't have either the original chassis or body of that Wharton car, we do have the engine, the chassis number and its complete history, as well as enough bits and pieces from the wrecked car to be able to claim that it is a genuine rebuild rather than simply a replica. How we came to find some of the original bits thirty-five years after the car had been totally scrapped and thrown away is another amazing story.

Although based at Bourne in Lincolnshire, BRM had a workshop and test facility ten miles up the road on the old wartime RAF aerodrome at Folkingham and it was here that the V16s were built. When the team then folded and Rick Hall left to set up his own engineering business in partnership with fellow mechanic Rob Fowler, he eventually took over the Folkingham premises. Now partnered by his son, Rob, he still uses those same workshops to this day.

It had always been said that in the early days of BRM there used to be a big pit out the back into which unwanted bits and pieces would regularly be chucked. For instance, if a lathe operator made something slightly wrong he would quietly toss the faulty part into this water-filled crater in order to avoid getting a bollocking. Rumour had it that quite a lot of the wreckage from Ken Wharton's Mark 1 had also been dumped there. However, by the time Rick took over, the farmer who owned the surrounding land had long since decided to fill it in and had been growing potatoes there for years. Every now and again the plough would turn up something quite interesting and when a complete cylinder head popped up Rick got permission to dig the pit out again so that we could have a proper snoop around.

Sure enough, the JCB unearthed a whole lot of discarded odds and ends and when we sifted through it we found that this archaeological treasure trove did indeed include quite a selection of badly damaged bits from the Wharton Mark 1. Altogether, we have now salvaged about one third of the original car, including the engine, gearbox, wheels, brakes and radiator. A new chassis and body have already been made and we hope to have it all finished very soon, at which point I reckon it will be a very valuable car.

Although far from being the most successful of the BRMs – they were always notoriously unreliable – it is the V16s that people remember most fondly. For one thing, the howling scream of those supercharged 16-cylinder engines was quite unique. When Rick Hall was re-building my Mark 1 at Folkingham and wanted to run it on the test bed there, he had to warn people in the locality in advance, because at full throttle it could be heard up to twelve miles away! When we took it out for demonstration runs at Donington, you would see people in the grandstands instinctively clamping their hands over their ears as it went past. It was like watching a version of the Mexican wave!

However, that deafening sound was like music to the ears of Nick

Mason, the drummer with Pink Floyd. Nick is a rather unlikely character. If you didn't know, you would never guess that he was a founder member of one of the most way-out psychedelic rock groups of the sixties. Well-groomed, smartly dressed, quiet and businesslike, he looks more like a successful company executive. He also happens to be a serious collector of classic sports and racing cars.

His V16 Mark 2 had never been a good runner and in the end he rather reluctantly agreed to sell it to me – on the one condition that once I had got it going properly I would let him record the sound of it moving up through the gears for a CD that he was planning to put out with a book about his car collection entitled 'Into The Red'. In the end, the recording was actually made in my Mark 2 rather than his, Rick Hall driving it around the Donington circuit with a microphone strapped between his legs.

I have driven both my BRMs many times, especially the Mark 1, and I have to admit that although they are lovely to look at, they can be maddeningly temperamental. It is always a thrill to get behind the wheel, but you can never be sure from one day to the next whether they are going to start or not. It drives Rick Hall mad. One moment he will have them running perfectly and then, the next time he goes to fire them up, sometimes just a few hours later, he can't get a peep out of them. He reckons he could solve the problem very simply by fitting the engines with modern electronic ignition, but then, of course, the car would no longer be totally authentic, so that's not an option.

As well as the BRMs, the seven Vanwalls in my collection are also very dear to my heart, particularly the 1950 Thinwall Special. I got to know Tony Vandervell very well back in the fifties and sixties. I was just starting to get heavily involved in motor racing at the time while Tony, like BRM, was trying to mount a British challenge to the Italians.

His Vanwalls, developed first from a supercharged 1.5-litre V12 Ferrari 125 and then from a 4.5-litre Ferrari 375, featured the revolutionary Thinwall bearings that he had designed and patented through his company, Vandervell Products. The cars were driven at various times by Stirling Moss, Tony Brooks, Roy Salvadori and also Stuart Lewis-Evans, whose tragic death in 1958 from the burns he suffered in a crash in

Morocco affected Tony as deeply as Roger Williamson's death was to affect me, hastening his retirement from racing.

I was actually with Tony in Monaco for what turned out to be the last grand prix he ever attended before his own death in 1967. He offered me a lift back to England in his private plane and during the trip I told him about my plans to build up my collection and open a museum. It was then that he offered to let me have one of his Vanwalls on permanent loan.

Following his death, Vandervell Products was taken over by GKN and I immediately put in an offer to buy the remaining cars and spares. GKN, however, decided to hang on to everything. I didn't think that much more about it until some fifteen years later when GKN did eventually dispose of Vandervell and the new owners, the American company Dana, put the cars and spares up for sale.

I immediately made what I hoped would be a pre-emptive bid, but the young executive in charge of the sale explained that because his people had no real idea what the stuff was worth, they had decided to ask for sealed bids for each individual car. An enthusiast himself, he was delighted when I arranged for him to test drive some of the cars at Donington and I got the impression then that he, personally, would like to see the whole collection come to us. So, Kevin and I not only put in separate bids for each one of the cars, but also offered a higher overall fig- ure for the whole lot, along with an undertaking that one example of every model would remain on display with the Donington Grand Prix Collection for as long as either one of us was still running the museum.

A few days later I went off to Italy for three weeks with Rick Hall to drive some demonstrations in the BRM V16 and the Maserati 8CM at various events, including a celebration of the 75th anniversary of the Monza circuit. As a rule, I never ring home when I'm away on trips like that – you only get involved in trying to sort out a whole lot of business problems you don't really want to be bothered with – but on this occa- sion Lenchen hadn't been too well so I called to check that everything was all right.

Kevin answered the phone. "What great timing," he said. "I've just walked in through the door after fetching the last of the Vanwalls back from the factory, along with several tons of spares!"

It turned out that although there had been higher bids than ours for some of the individual cars, the fact that we didn't want to split them up had indeed swung things in our favour. It had also been decided that the museum at Donington would be an ideal home for the collection.

When I went down to dinner immediately after making the call, I walked into the hotel dining room to find that, quite by chance, the conversation among the assembled motorsport folk, who were all there for the Monza anniversary event, had turned to the subject of the Vanwall sale. One chap was speculating that it would fetch £3.5 million while at the other end of the table John Surtees was saying that he reckoned not all the cars would be sold. "The little rear-engine VW14 was made specially for me and I'm the only one that's ever driven it, so I think they'll probably give it to me," he predicted confidently.

Somebody called out: "What do you think, Tom?" I don't believe anybody present realised at this stage that I'd even put a bid in.

"Well," I said. "The gentleman who mentioned £3.5 million is way out. And as for John – he's definitely not going to be given the VW14."

"How can you be so sure?" asked someone.

"Because I've just bought 'em myself," I replied.

"I know you've not!" snorted Surtees, as jaws dropped all round the table.

"Well, John," I told him. "You can take it from me that every Vanwall is now in my garage at home – including the little rear-engined VW14, which arrived there about twenty minutes ago."

Surtees has tried to buy that particular car off me several times since then, but I'm not inclined to let him have it. I've never quite forgiven him for that business in America when I bought a drive from him for Derek Bell, only to find when we arrived that the deal didn't include an engine! There is also the little matter of the two works Honda Formula One cars that I wanted to buy from him. He always promised me that I could have first refusal if he ever decided to sell them. Next thing I knew, I was in Tokyo, being given a guided tour of Japanese multi-millionaire Hayashi's incredible collection by the man himself, when suddenly we come upon this pair of Hondas.

"They look like Surtees' cars," I said.

"That is correct," replied Hayashi. "I bought them from him only last year."

I wasn't very happy about that – John had never even bothered to offer them to me. So, one way and another, I'm afraid the chances of him getting that little rear-engine Vanwall are not great.

When I returned home from Italy and we started looking through the large collection of spares that had come as part of the deal we found that it included an unexpected bonus. Many years previously I had found myself driving to London behind a scrap metal lorry and noticed that it was carrying what I instantly recognised as a racing car chassis, along with what turned out to be the radiator, fuel tank and bodywork. I flashed the driver to pull over and he revealed that he'd got it all from Vandervell.

In those days teams routinely scrapped stuff they didn't need any more, never imagining that it would one day have a historical value. I immediately did a deal to buy the entire lorry load and when we got it back to Aylestone Lane we discovered that it actually belonged to the very first 1.5-litre Thinwall Special development car that Tony had built in the late forties. Now, thirty years later, as we sifted through this new lot of spares I'd just bought, we found the suspension and parts of the gearbox from the same car. And that wasn't the end of the story.

Not long after that we had another extraordinary stroke of luck when Count von Doenhoff, one of Rick Hall's regular customers, contacted him to say that he was looking for a 750 Monza Ferrari engine. Rick knew that I had one and thought I might be willing to sell. Von Doenhoff then suggested that instead of a cash deal I might be prepared to do a straight swap with a spare V12 Ferrari 125 engine that he'd got. I was very happy with that, especially when it arrived and we checked the number to find, to our amazement, that it belonged to the chassis I'd found on the scrap lorry all those years before. I now had the complete car, which was later sold to Bernie Ecclestone and rebuilt for him by Rick Hall.

Meanwhile, its big sister, the 4.5-litre version that Tony had also given me on permanent loan and which I then bought outright, is still on display in the museum, together with the 1949/50 1.5-litre Thinwall Special, the 1957 Streamliner and one of the 1958 2.5-litre Vanwalls with the Colin Chapman chassis and the Frank Costin body in which the team won that year's Manufacturers' Championship, Stirling Moss losing out to Mike Hawthorn in the Drivers' Championship by a single point.

I bought this latter car from two ex-Vanwall mechanics, who had built it up from spares that they got direct from Tony and I'll never forget the day they delivered it to me at The Mill. I had a dog called Winston at the time, a cross between a collie and a husky. I've always had a soft spot for dogs with a bit of character and Winston was a real one-off. He was fine most of the time, but he had a look in his eye that suggested he was ready to bite you if you gave him the slightest excuse.

Anyway, the chaps who were selling me the Vanwall were so proud of the car that they stopped in a lay-by just up the road from the house to give it a final polish before handing it over, anxious to present it in absolutely pristine condition. It certainly looked an absolute picture, sitting in the drive in front of The Mill. But as we stood back to admire it, Winston sauntered over, gave it a sniff and then proceeded to cock his leg over each one of the four gleaming, Burani wire wheels in turn. In my mind's eye, I can still see the look of horror on the faces of those two mechanics.

Also in storage at Donington are the remains of the 1959 low-line Vanwall, a lowered and lightened version of the standard 2.5-litre car that only actually ran once in testing and which we hope eventually to restore. And finally, of course, there is the Surtees VW14 – the last of the line.

While the Vanwall and BRM acquisitions remain among the highlights of my career as a collector, one of the bigger disappointments came when I narrowly missed out on the opportunity to buy up the famous Schlumpf collection. What a coup that would have been!

Concentrating at first almost exclusively on Bugattis, brothers Hans and Fritz Schlumpf, owners of a large textile business in Alsace, secretly amassed a vast collection of more than five hundred cars between 1958 and 1975. Having started out with the aim of acquiring one example of every Bugatti ever made, their buying became an obsession that eventually got out of control to such an extent that it eventually ruined them and helped to bring down their entire business.

Not much was known about the full extent of their extraordinary collection until the collapse of the business in the late seventies, when the factory was taken over by the workforce for a time while the brothers took refuge over the border in Switzerland. When the workers then discovered this Aladdin's Cave of valuable cars, hidden away in a secret showroom in a sealed off section of the factory, they were furious, believing that the money spent on them should have been invested in the business instead. One car, an Austin Seven, was actually dragged out and set on fire as a protest. In making this gesture the workers showed that they obviously knew a bit about historic cars, since the Austin was unrestored and of very little value

In the middle of all this, I flew out to Switzerland and met with the brothers to discuss the possibility of buying the museum from them. After a couple of days of negotiation we hammered out a deal for the sale that involved me covering debts amounting to around £3.5 million, allowing them to keep one or two of their favourite cars and otherwise leaving the collection as it was. Although £3.5 million was quite a lot of money at the time, it was still a fantastic bargain, given the cars that the collection contained.

I flew back to England on a Friday having shaken hands on an arrangement whereby the money was to be transferred by the following Tuesday. I'd even got as far as instructing my secretary to type out all the instructions to the bank, a document I still have framed and hanging on my wall. However, almost as soon as I got back to the house at 7.00pm I received an urgent call from my bank manager, warning me not to touch the deal with a barge pole.

He told me that his people had been looking into the matter and had learned that the left-wing French Government of the day were about to issue an order classifying the entire collection as an "historic monument", effectively making it the property of the nation. What's more, he said, the bank's inquiries had suggested that the Schlumpfs had already borrowed money against some of the cars.

I was on the phone to him for over an hour and afterwards I was left speechless with disappointment. Lenchen said to me at one point: "Tom, I've been in the room for forty-five minutes since that call and you haven't spoken a word. Whatever's the matter?"

To be honest, I wasn't worth talking to that night. The bank manager had certainly sown serious seeds of doubt in my mind, but at the same time I had the feeling that if I turned my back on the deal I would be missing out on a great opportunity. Looking back, I still reckon I should have gone ahead. There might well have been a few problems, but, even so, I reckon I would have come out way ahead.

I was only really interested in about forty of the five hundred cars and, with the museum in Mulhouse being only about ten kilometres from the Swiss border, I could have moved them out very easily, one by one, as soon as the deal was done. The rest I would have been happy to leave in the museum, which I planned to open to the public. The Bugatti Royale that was in there would, alone, have been worth around £8 million, going by the price that was paid the last time one went on sale. Altogether I worked out that I stood to make up to £28 million on the deal.

As it was, the entire collection was eventually taken over by the French Association Du Musée in 1981 and is now known as the Musée Nationale de l'Automobile Schlumpfs. Still housed in what remains of the Schlumpfs' textile factory, it is packed with interesting and valuable exhibits. I can't even think about them without a twinge of regret at what might have been if only I had been a bit bolder and had ignored the bank manager's warnings. It remains the only time in my life that I've ever been talked out of a deal instead of going with the gut instincts that have always served me so well in business. I vowed never to make the same mistake again.

It was after failing to get hold of the Schlumpfs' Bugatti Royale, one of only six made, that I decided to build my own replica. This remains probably the most ambitious project of its kind ever undertaken. Twenty-two foot long and weighing four tons overall, with a fifteen-foot wheelbase and a vast 12.7-litre straight eight engine that was nearly five feet long and, by itself, weighed nearly half-a-ton, the Royale was one of the biggest and most extravagant cars ever produced. The chassis alone cost $30,000, a stunning amount of money in 1930.

Designer Ettore Bugatti's wildly over-the-top creation was said to have been inspired by the comment of an aristocratic English lady who remarked that although his cars were the fastest in the world, Rolls Royces were the best. He originally announced that the Royale would be sold only to royalty, although he agreed later that it didn't have to be quite that exclusive.

The full story of how my replica came to be built turned into a ten-year saga, full of twists and turns, chance encounters, secret deals and even a bit of industrial espionage – not to mention a huge amount of time, effort and money.

To start with, I needed to get hold of a full set of drawings. I went first to the Bugatti Owners Club and came to an arrangement with the secretary, Hugh Conway, whereby he agreed to let me have the drawings in return for building a new clubhouse. However, we had to drop that idea when the club couldn't get planning permission for the building. Instead, I simply handed over a cheque for the equivalent amount. Then Hugh Conway died suddenly and the chap who took over from him got very awkward. He demanded all sorts of extra payments, including nearly £3,000 for printing copies of the plans. When I refused to cough up he got really shirty, warning me I that would never be allowed to build the car anyway.

"Call me again in three years' time and you can come and see it finished," I snapped and slammed the phone down.

As it happened, their drawings were no good to me anyway. They were copies of the originals, about sixty years old – in fact, they weren't even copies, but copies of copies, and the reproduction was so poor that the engineers couldn't really work from them. It was in totally unexpected circumstances that I was then presented with a perfect set of originals.

I was at the Retromobile motor show in Paris when I stumbled across a remarkable Polish model maker who had a stand there. What caught my eye as I walked past was a fantastic scale model of a Bugatti Royale chassis, without a body. I was fascinated because it was completely accurate in every detail, right down to the exact number of nineteen bolts on each side of the gearbox.

The model maker knew just enough English to make himself understood, but he couldn't understand me at all – nobody abroad ever does, because of my Leicestershire accent. However, we somehow just about managed to have a conversation. It turned out that he wanted £6,000 for the Bugatti model, which I thought was very good value for money. Even though it was without a body, I actually liked it a lot better than the complete model for which I had previously paid someone £18,000.

I complimented him on the accuracy of the detail and asked him what he'd worked from. He then told me that he'd managed to get some drawings from the Bugatti family. Was there any chance, I wondered, that he might loan them to me?

"As you are buying the model, I will give them to you," he said. "But I am afraid that I will have to charge you for the postage because I am a poor man and I have very little money."

As promised, the drawings arrived a fortnight later and proved to be extremely useful, just what we needed. And, as I recall, the postage amounted to something like £6! I have kept in contact with that man ever since and have bought several other models from him.

Altogether, we spent a solid year researching every aspect of the Bugatti Royale before we started work on it. We read every book and article we could find, trawled through archives, visited the old Bugatti factory, lined up specialist companies that could make all the various components and made contact with the owners of all the existing cars, asking very diplomatically for permission to measure or copy various components.

One man was particularly helpful in this respect. American construction magnate and classic car collector General Lyons not only invited me to visit his museum – a beautiful, domed building that he had put up in the grounds of one of his many homes and which he referred to as his motor house – but also gave permission for my engineers to go over his Royale with a fine tooth comb to see if there were any measurements or other things we needed to double check.

Much to my regret, I never got to meet this gentleman face-to-face and never even spoke to him on the phone, which made his generous offer all the more amazing. He was such a busy man that he was never around on the couple of occasions when I visited his motor house. He had about £60 million worth of cars there and I can honestly say I would love to have just about every one – and it's not often you can say that about another man's collection!

As it happens, he later sold his Royale to the Volkswagen Group for an undisclosed figure, rumoured to have been as high as £8 million.

From conception to completion, it took ten years and cost £1.6 million to build mine. The jig for the front axle alone accounted for £36,000, while the sixteen-layer paint job, all done by hand, took seven months and cost £72,000. Considerable research and experimentation went into matching the exact tones of black and blue of the original Coupe Napoleon on which my car is based and the actual painting process itself involved spraying 2,800 individual items with thirty applications of cellulose paint, including etch primers, primers, primer fillers and colour coats. After each application the solvent had to be allowed to dry out naturally and the layer then rubbed down.

No effort or expense was spared in our bid to achieve absolute perfection. From the horsehair that was used to stuff the seats in order to recreate exactly the right feel, to the ivory billiard balls that formed the gear stick and control knobs, and from the mechanism of the door locks to the precise threads of the nuts and bolts, everything in the car is a faithful reproduction of what was in the original. The result is a car that I regard as much more than just a very good replica. In my view, it is to all intents and purposes the seventh Bugatti Royale, totally authentic right down to the tiniest detail and made with the same care and attention as the original.

The final proof of this authenticity, to my mind, is the fact that it displays some of the very same faults as the original. When mine completed its first road tests I compared the results with the tests done in the early 1930s and there were so many similarities – such as the tendency of the differential bolts to unwind – that it was really quite spooky. It even smokes like an old car should.

Altogether, seven British firms were involved in the project. The engine was built up in Yorkshire by John Bentley and Keith Taylor of Bentley Engineering; the brakes, axles, steering box, gearbox, wheels and all other components were made by Brineton Engineering in Walsall; and the final assembly, paintwork and all the finishing touches were carried out by Vintage Restorations at Ashton Keynes, near Swindon.

I'll always remember the day I finally went down there to pick it up. Keith Bowley and his team had done some of the best restoration work I had ever seen and the car looked absolutely wonderful. I arrived at Ashton Keynes quite late on a wet winter's afternoon and took everybody by surprise when I announced that instead of taking the car up to Donington in a transporter I intended to drive it up there myself. I was so excited – I just couldn't wait to get behind the wheel. However, the look of horror on Keith's face had to be seen to be believed as I waved goodbye in the pouring rain and disappeared into the darkness with £1.6 million worth of classic motor car that had barely turned a wheel up to that point. For a moment I actually thought he was going to burst into tears!

"Don't worry," I called out. "I'm a careful driver!"

The Royale got back to Leicestershire unscathed, turning quite a few heads on the way. And since then I have taken the greatest pleasure in driving it for over 3,500 miles without the slightest mishap. But I have to admit that other cars in the museum have not been quite so safe in my hands.

A Lifetime of Achievement

ONE OF THE prettiest and most famous exhibits in the entire Doning-ton Grand Prix Collection is the Ferrari 500 in which Alberto Ascari won back-to-back World Championship driver titles in 1952 and 1953. With eleven wins out of a total of fifteen starts, it is possibly the most suc-cessful individual grand prix car ever built.

I first acquired it in the late sixties, only for the engine to blow up shortly afterwards as I was preparing to take it on a demonstration lap as part of the build-up to the street circuit event that used to be held in Birmingham at that time. It then languished in the museum for about twenty years before I finally got round to asking Rick Hall to put it back in full working order. Rick did a brilliant job and it emerged from his workshop a few months later looking like a million dollars – and actually worth considerably more.

It was delivered back to Donington in late February 2002, on a day when we were basking in the first really warm sunshine of the year. Rick himself was in Australia at the time, so it was his son, Rob, who actually brought it along. He took it out on the test circuit, made a few minor adjustments and then asked if I fancied a go.

"I'd better not, Rob," I told him. "I'm not really prepared. I haven't got my racing shoes or anything. But I wouldn't mind just sitting in it."

I tucked my trousers into my socks, so they wouldn't get caught up on the gear lever, and climbed in. I was sitting there with my hands on the wheel, blipping the throttle and watching all the instruments on the dashboard and I thought to myself: "Ooh, this feels great!" And I said to Rob: "Perhaps I will have a little pootle with it, after all."

The test circuit at Donington, which we use for shakedowns and also for various ceremonial events and demonstrations, is completely separate from the main circuit. It includes the old original Melbourne Loop, which has been preserved outside the main circuit, and by branching off just beyond the brow of the Melbourne Rise and continuing on around what is now the vast car park that doubles as the site of the hugely successful Sunday Market, it is possible to complete a circuit that provides more than enough room to put a car through its paces.

I set off and it was absolutely beautiful. I went up and down through the gears, just flicking the stick with the back of my hand, and it was like silk, so sweet you'd think it was the latest thing ever been built. I went round a few times like that, ever so relaxed and really enjoying myself, and then I thought I'd just see how quickly I could get her up to 6500 revs.

I was in the Sunday Market car park area, doing about 115mph, when I suddenly realised I was running out of space and needed to make a turn. I put on a bit of lock and that was when I started to lose her. I'd forgotten that she was fitted with a set of narrow, thirty-year-old tyres. We'd got a new set of specially made modern replacements on order, but they weren't going to be ready for another six months. These old ones just wouldn't grip and I felt the car beginning to slide. I was heading straight towards the solid concrete wall that marks the outer perimeter of the main circuit and divides it from the Sunday Market area at that point and I knew I had to get the back round to stop her hitting it full on. That's the last I remember for a few seconds.

Afterwards, nobody could quite understand how I'd managed to make such a mess of the car with my body, while at the same time doing relatively little really serious damage to myself – especially as I had no helmet on and wasn't strapped in. Trying to imagine the sequence of events in slow motion, it seems that as the car smashed into the wall I was thrown forward, hitting my chin on the little glass windscreen and bending it forward. If it had been an inch lower it would probably have cut my throat. At the same time, I was gripping the steering wheel so tightly that it came off in my clenched fists, both of which then smashed right through the quarter-inch-thick bevelled glass of the instrument panel. As the car then rebounded from the initial impact, I was slammed back down into the seat so violently that my elbows dented the inside of the bodywork while my feet were driven clean through the floor.

Seconds later, the first people to arrive on the scene found me sitting there, with the steering wheel still in my hands. I couldn't move because my legs were trapped. My chest hurt and I was finding it hard to breathe. It felt just the same as when I had my heart attack, but all that had actually happened was that I'd been badly bruised and winded when I'd smacked into the steering column. Then, as I sat there in a dazed and confused state, waiting for the ambulance to arrive, everything suddenly seemed to start going dark. "It's going to rain – have we got anything to cover the car with?" I asked. In fact, it was still brilliant sunshine, but the sky seemed to me to change from orange to mauve. The next thing I knew I was in Derby Royal Infirmary, where I spent the next ten days.

I ached all over. It was as if every bone in my body had been very badly bruised, right the way down from my chin, where it had hit the windscreen, to the soles of my feet, where they had rammed the pedals through the floor. My whole body was literally black and blue – black on the side that had taken the brunt of the impact and blue on the other, exactly half-and-half. My legs were skinned all the way up to my knees, where they'd been forced through the floor, while my hands and wrists had been lacerated when they'd smashed through the dashboard. My elbows and knees hurt like hell where they had been banged against the sides of the car, whiplash injuries to my neck and back meant that I could hardly lift my head off the pillow and torn tendons in my left leg have left me with a permanent limp. One way and another, I had knocked myself about to buggery. Miraculously, however, nothing had been broken. Apart from the car, that is!

As I mentioned earlier, the only thought in my mind as I headed towards that concrete wall was: "Oh, shit – and the car's only just been restored! Rick Hall ain't half going to give me some stick when he hears about this!"

By some extraordinary co-incidence, Rick called from Australia at the very moment when I crashed. He knew the car was due to be delivered that morning so he rang Rob on his mobile to see how things were going.

"Fine," says Rob. "I've just let Wheaty have a go. In fact, he's a long time coming round and it's all gone a bit quiet – I'd better go and see what's happened. He's probably broken down. I'll ring you back in a minute."

Rick waited and waited, but the call didn't come so he rang again about half an hour later. "You'll never believe it," Rob told him. "He's crashed the bloody thing into a wall! We're just waiting for the ambulance to come and fetch him. He's a bit shaken but he's OK. I'll pass you over and you can have a word with him if you like."

I hardly knew where I was at this point because I was actually in deep shock, but I vaguely remember hearing Rick's anxious voice saying: "Wheaty! What *are* you doing!"

He might well ask! Three months short of my eightieth birthday at the time, I suppose I should have known better than to be giving it plenty of welly in a very valuable fifty-year-old grand prix car with which I wasn't totally familiar, especially when I wasn't wearing a helmet or any other proper gear. As everybody keeps reminding me, I was very lucky indeed to get away with it.

As it was, the accident left me feeling my age for the first time in my life. For days afterwards I could hardly get out of bed; I was unable to hobble more than a few yards without taking a rest and I had difficulty turning my head properly. Ironically, things then got even worse when I went out to Portugal a few weeks later to recuperate in the sun. I hadn't been there more than a few days when a deck chair collapsed underneath me as I went to sit down on the hotel balcony. I fell awkwardly, hit my head on a balcony rail and chipped one of the vertebrae in my neck.

I spent the rest of the holiday in plaster. Meanwhile, X-rays taken by the doctors there revealed evidence of fourteen separate fractures that I'd suffered at one time or another over the years but had never previously been aware of. These included hairline fractures to five other vertebrae in my neck, quite apart from the one I'd just damaged in the fall. We reckoned that these must have resulted from the accident at Silverstone in the Tec Mec nearly forty years before, when I almost demolished Silverstone Sid's ambulance. As for all the other breaks, I couldn't remember where I might have picked them up. In the Army and on building sites you were always suffering knocks that you tended to shrug off and leave to heal in their own time if they weren't too obviously serious.

After I had limped home from Portugal, some fairly intensive physiotherapy helped to get me back into reasonable shape in time for what was billed as the 'TW80 Celebration of a Lifetime' – a star-studded bash organised by Kevin and John Bailie as a joint celebration of my 80th birthday and the 25th anniversary of the re-opening of the Donington Park circuit in 1977. Held during the weekend of the Vintage Sports-Car Club's British Empire Trophy Meeting on June 8th, 2002, the party was attended by three hundred guests, including Sir Stirling Moss OBE, his former Vanwall team-mate Tony Brooks, Richard Attwood, Willie Green, Lord March, Lord Montagu of Beaulieu and Sir Rodney Walker.

Motorsport journalist and commentator Simon Taylor acted as Master of Ceremonies for the proceedings, one of the highlights of which was a live video link with Eddie Jordan and Ian Phillips at the Canadian Grand Prix. One of the great characters on the modern Formula One scene, Eddie has been a friend since his early visits to Donington for the Irish Formula Atlantic series when, as he recalled in his speech: "I'm not sure whether we did more damage on the track or in the bar at Redgate Lodge!" He must have liked it there because when he decided to throw a massive party of his own to celebrate Jordan Grand Prix's tenth anniversary in September 2000 he chose Donington as the venue, despite the fact that the Jordan team is based at Silverstone. I was chuffed to bits about that and as you can imagine, given Eddie's reputation as someone who really knows how to let his hair down, it was a lively do!

My own party may have been a slightly more restrained affair, as befits an eighty-year-old, but we nevertheless celebrated in style. A starlit marquee had been erected to form an extension to the museum halls and, inside, the main stage was flanked by two cars from the Grand Prix

Collection – the Lotus in which Sir Stirling Moss won the 1961 Monaco Grand Prix and the Vanwall in which he and Tony Brooks, sharing the drive, won the 1957 British Grand Prix. The drinks on offer included Old Tom's Original Donington Ale, specially brewed for the occasion by Everard's, our local Leicester brewer. And a charity auction, organised during the evening by Simon Hope of H & H Classic Auctions, a great friend of Donington, raised in excess of £25,000 for the NSPCC, for whose Full Stop campaign we have promised to help raise a target figure of £1 million.

Among the birthday messages from friends and VIPs who could not be present was one from Prince Michael of Kent, who recalled that his father had dropped the flag to start the 1938 Grand Prix at Donington. He added: "I still have fond and vivid memories of driving some of your magnificent motor cars on more than one occasion, as well as Nigel Mansell's Formula One Lotus."

In characteristic fashion, Bernie Ecclestone couldn't resist taking the mickey out of me over the prang I'd had in the Ferrari 500. Doubting that I could actually be eighty years old, he wrote: "Obviously, this is not true as no-one at nearly 80 would be silly enough to drive a Ferrari at what I am led to believe was bloody quick. So I can only imagine that it was either a tax benefit or a supplement pension."

Special Guest at the party was Murray Walker OBE, who was there not just as a great friend but also to become the first recipient of the Tom Wheatcroft Trophy, which I presented to him during the course of the evening.

It was actually Kevin who dreamed up the idea of the award, to be presented annually to a personality who had shown outstanding lifetime commitment and dedication to motorsport. For my money, Murray has made a huge contribution over the years, not simply with the inimitable style of his commentaries, which established him for a whole generation of fans as the 'Voice of Motor Racing', but also with the warmth of his personality and his sheer enthusiasm, which remains as fanatical today as it ever was.

Apart from that, I had personal reasons for choosing him as a particularly appropriate inaugural winner of my trophy. Murray and I go back a long way and have a lot in common. Exactly one year younger than me, he, too, was among the crowds who flocked to Donington to watch those great pre-war grands prix in 1937 and 1938. And, like me, he went on to drive tanks during the war. Not that we were aware of each other's existence in those days, of course. I first met him when he was the curator of the museum that Dunlop had established at their headquarters in Birmingham and I went to have a look around one day when I was there picking up some racing tyres.

We have been friends ever since then and, professionally, I have always held him in the highest regard. Most people listening to his commentaries would probably not have realised how much hard work he put in behind the scenes. He would always be there in the paddock, doing his homework – chatting to everybody from the team bosses to the mechanics and from the drivers to the officials, forever asking questions and generally making sure he was in the know about everything. In many ways, his actual commentary was just the tip of the iceberg.

Subsequent winners of the Tom Wheatcroft Trophy have included Professor Sid Watkins, Jean Todt and Bernie Ecclestone. As the long-standing, official on-track grand prix surgeon and Chairman of the Expert Advisory Safety Committee of the FIA, Sid Watkins is the man largely responsible for masterminding the dramatic improvement in the safety record of Formula One over recent years, especially since the death of his great friend Ayrton Senna in 1994.

An easy-going, avuncular and yet hugely authoritative and respected figure, known affectionately throughout motor racing circles as 'Prof', he is actually one of the world's leading specialist brain surgeons and yet is probably more widely known for his association with the sport to which he has devoted just about every minute of his spare time over the last forty years.

The ornate, solid silver Tom Wheatcroft Trophy was specially commissioned by Kevin from silversmiths Adam Veevers and Trevor Duncan, with a design incorporating a full size racing steering wheel and a sculpted model of Roger Williamson's 1973 March 731G car. It was presented to Sid by Murray Walker during a dinner held at the Donington Grand Prix Collection in June 2003 as part of a 'Tribute To Ayrton Senna' weekend that marked the tenth anniversary of Ayrton's legendary victory in the European Grand Prix.

This was particularly appropriate as Sid had been especially close to Ayrton, on whom he kept a fatherly eye. In his capacity as the on-track surgeon, he then had the dreadful duty of attending to the stricken driver at the scene of his fatal accident at Imola. That shocking event marked a watershed in motorsport history, galvanising the FIA and Sid himself into launching a determined and extremely effective drive to achieve zero mortality through research and development aimed at improving safeguards in car design, circuit design and driver protection.

Like Sid – and so many other people involved in motor racing – I had the greatest regard for Ayrton Senna. He had both a talent and a personality that set him apart. And, of course, he will be forever associated in my mind with that dramatic European Grand Prix at Donington, the event that represented the pinnacle of my achievement as a circuit owner.

The dinner was the highlight of a whole weekend programme of anniversary celebrations that included the biggest ever display of F1 cars driven by Senna during his career, with several demonstration laps featuring his Lotus 97T and 98T as well as the Williams FW08C in which he had had his first taste of Formula One at Donington while testing for Frank Williams back in 1983. Also on show in the museum was a collection of Ayrton's trophies and other memorabilia plus an exhibition of paintings of him by members of the Guild of Motoring Artists and a selection of photographs taken of him throughout his career by the world famous motorsport photographer Keith Sutton. Keith had been Ayrton's first manager and these photographs from his personal collection, which he kindly loaned to us for display in the Grand Prix Collection, were being seen in the UK for the first time.

Among the special guests who attended the dinner were former Lotus managing director Peter Warr and some of Ayrton's mechanics, including Bob Dance. There was also a live telephone link, from his home in Spain, with Ayrton's legendary McLaren mechanic Jo Ramirez, who was on duty in the pits at Donington for the European Grand Prix.

Two months earlier, on April 11th 2003 – the tenth anniversary, to the day, of the European Grand Prix – a special service of remembrance had been held at the Senna Fangio Tribute, a memorial featuring lifesize bronze figures of the men who dominated two golden eras of World Championship motor racing. Located in our Memorial Garden, just outside the museum at Donington, the Tribute had been unveiled six years earlier in 1997 in the presence of Sir Stirling Moss and the Ambassadors of both Brazil and Argentina.

Fangio and Senna are two of my greatest motor racing heroes, but there is a third who I do believe might have gone on to establish himself in the same league and who will always have a very special place in my heart. I refer, of course, to Roger Williamson. It was on July 30th, 2003, the 30th anniversary of his death and three months after the 'Tribute To Ayrton Senna' weekend, that we unveiled the Roger Williamson Memorial. Standing just a few feet away from the Senna Fangio Tribute, this is again in the form of a lifesize bronze statue, commissioned from Scottish sculptor David Annand.

During a ceremony conducted by Simon Taylor and attended by many leading figures from the world of motorsport, the unveiling was carried out jointly by me and Roger's sister, Barbara Upton, with a dedication and blessing by Canon Lionel Webber, chaplain to the Vintage Sports-Car Club and a former chaplain to the Queen.

Even after all those intervening years since his death, I still found it a very moving occasion – one that brought the most fond and vivid memories flooding back. As I told a reporter at the time, Roger's seasons with my team in Formula 3 and Formula 2 were magical and provided some of the happiest and most fulfilling days of my life in motorsport. He was in a class of his own and I am convinced that he could easily have gone on to become the Ayrton Senna of his day. He was in the same mould.

The older you get, the faster time flies by and the anniversaries seem to have been coming up thick and fast in the last few years – not that I ever need much excuse for a party! The first big one was in 1998, a joint celebration of the 25th anniversary of the opening of the Grand Prix Collection and the 60th anniversary of Tazio Nuvolari's win in the 1938 Donington Grand Prix.

Among other things, this gave me the perfect excuse to take Nuvolari's 8CM Maserati out of the museum for a few demonstration laps. Also taking part in the demonstration were Rick Hall, driving the Alfa Romeo Bimotore in which Nuvolari set two new world records in 1936 (201.98 mph over a measured mile on an Italian autostrada and 200.89 mph over a kilometre) and Jeffrey Pattinson in an old sit-up-and-beg ERA that had actually taken part in the original 1938 Grand Prix.

The ERA had been driven on that occasion by Ian Connell and Peter Monkhouse – drives were often shared at that time – and, at the age of eighty-five, Ian came along to be re-united with the car in which he and Monkhouse eventually finished 8th behind Nuvolari. Just ahead of them that day in 7th place was Wilkie Wilkinson, who was co-driving another ERA with Billy (Wakey! Wakey!) Cotton – a regular and talented driver in the days before he found fame as a bandleader. Looking remarkably fit for his age at ninety-five, Wilkie was there to watch as Rick, Jeffrey and I put the old cars through their paces, actually managing to get them airborne over the old Melbourne Rise, much to the delight of the crowd.

Major John Gillies Shields came wearing the same VIP pass that he had worn as an eighteen-year-old for the 1938 Grand Prix – a leather lapel badge signed by his grandfather. Talking to reporters, he recalled how there had been quite a lot of fatal accidents in the very early days at Donington, mostly involving motorbikes going down towards the old Hairpin, with the injured being taken to the Hall and put in the stables to await the arrival of the ambulance.

"Some of them, I fear, were already dead by then and the odd ghost is supposed to haunt the stables," he said. "In fact, I had to get the vicar of Donington to come out and exorcise the building at one time because we were getting a lot of poltergeists."

As part of the anniversary celebrations, Ian Connell and Wilkie Wilkinson unveiled a commemorative plaque to Nuvolari in the museum, while Mrs Cordelia Brock, chairman of Leicestershire County Council, planted a commemorative Nuvolari rose bush in the memorial garden. There is a lovely story behind that. It was said that a schoolboy among the crowd in 1938 picked up a rose that had dropped from the winner's garland, took it home and gave it to his mother. She planted it in their garden and it grew into a flourishing bush. This was the inspiration for the idea of planting the rose that now grows just outside the entrance to the Grand Prix Collection.

The next big landmark came in 2001 with the 70th anniversary of the first ever event at Donington Park, the inaugural motorcycle meeting held in 1931. Among the many veteran racing motorcyclists who joined us for the celebrations were Titch Allen, Arthur Tyler, Arthur Wellsted, Alf Briggs, Harry Johnson, Dennis Jones, George Geeson, Kel Prince, Ivan Rhodes and Syd Barnett.

Several of these wonderful old boys turned up again in December 2003 for the official opening of a new Heritage section at the Grand Prix Collection devoted to historic motorcycles. Arthur Wellsted, in particular, kept everybody spellbound with his reminiscences about the thrills and spills of pre-war motorcycle racing at Donington, where he regularly rode his JAP-engined Excelsior and then a KTT Velocette between 1935 and 1939, risking life and limb among the trees for a first prize of £40 or £50.

"I first started coming here just as a spectator," he recalled. "The girl who was then my fiancée used to come with me and one day as we were watching I turned to her and said: 'I wouldn't mind having a go at that myself.'

"She replied: 'If you do, I'm going to pack you up!' But I did. And she packed me up! But I never regretted it."

A tiny figure, bright as a button at ninety-four and still riding around enthusiastically on a Yamaha 350, he casually claimed to have had a ton out of it only a few months before. "About 120 mph, actually," he added nonchalantly. "I couldn't really go flat out because I had a girl on the back."

The 'girl', it turned out later, was actually a middle-aged lady member of his local golf club who had asked him to take her for a spin!

At around the same time he had been pulled over by a motorcycle speed cop for doing nearly 90mph on the road between Melton Mowbray and Nottingham. "He was a bit surprised when I took my helmet off and he realised how old I was. He asked me: 'Do you usually travel at this speed?' I replied: 'Yes, I do. Always.' And I told him: 'I was riding motorbikes when you were just a twinkle in your daddy's *daddy's* eye!' We then got chatting and it turned out he was a motorbike racing fan who knew quite a bit about me, so we ended up shaking hands and he let me off with a caution. Mind you, I had already started slowing down a bit simply because you can't trust anybody on the road these days."

A truly remarkable character, Arthur apparently thought nothing of doing a bungee jump off a bridge in New Zealand when he was already in his late eighties. "When you've been through the war as an RAF air gunner, a bungee jump is no big thing," he told us.

Although some six or seven years younger than Arthur, Titch Allen has memories of Donington that go back even further. "Very few people have had the privilege of seeing the birth of Donington, the death of Donington and the re-birth of Donington and of knowing the two extraordinary men who made it all possible," he told the audience. "Fred Craner, whom I knew well, had the vision and determination to create the original circuit and Tom Wheatcroft, who is a similar sort of person, had the same vision that it could be resurrected and the same determination to see it through."

In June 2004, Titch – Charles Edmund Allen to give him his full name – was honoured with an OBE in recognition of his massive contribution to motorcycle heritage over the years and, at his request, the investiture – performed by the Lord Lieutenant of Leicestershire, the Lady Gretton JP – took place at the Donington Grand Prix Collection rather than at Buckingham Palace.

Meanwhile, on March 25th, 2003, two more old-timers, Tom Delaney and Max Turner, had been on hand to help us celebrate the 70th anniversary of the first car races at Donington. Tom had driven his Lea Francis there during that first 1933 season and seventy years later he was still competing in the same car – at ninety-two, by far the world's oldest holder of a current racing licence.

Max Turner, three years younger at eighty-nine, had actually taken part in the very first meeting in 1933 as co-driver in his brother's 750cc

Austin, coming 2nd in their race. One of the highlights of the anniversary celebrations came when Tom Delaney drove himself on a lap of honour around the circuit, while Max was chauffeured round in another Lea Francis owned by racing driver Willie Green, whose father had used the very same car to conduct the assessment laps at Donington prior to that inaugural meeting.

The 30th anniversary of the opening of the museum, the 65th anniversary of the 1938 Donington Grand Prix ... the significant dates keep coming round, giving us yet another opportunity to stage a little celebration of some sort. At the same time, I have been enormously proud and not a little overwhelmed over recent years to find myself being honoured with a string of lifetime achievement awards in recognition of my contributions to motorsport in reviving Donington Park and building up the Grand Prix Collection.

The first of these, the Chrysler Lifetime Achievement Award, came in 1998 and was presented to me during a dinner at the Park Lane Hotel in London by Murray Walker. There was then a similar award from the Historic Grand Prix Cars Association in 2001, followed in 2002 by the Gregor Grant Trophy, awarded in Gregor's memory by *Autosport*, the magazine that he founded and ran for many years. This was presented to me at the annual *Autosport* Awards dinner by Formula One star Jean Alesi.

I had known Gregor well and liked him very much. At one point shortly before his death I even loaned him the money to pay the printing costs of another motorsport magazine that he had launched, stepping in to help him out after his original American backers let him down at the last moment. He insisted on giving me the deeds to his house as collateral. I then forgot all about them until some years after his death when I bumped into his wife, Eva, at Silverstone and she happened to mention that she had decided to sell the house but couldn't find the deeds anywhere.

"Ooh dear, Eva," I confessed. "I reckon I've got 'em!"

She had no idea that Gregor had given them to me.

In July 2003, I received the prestigious Motorsport Industry Association Award for the Most Outstanding Contribution to the UK Motorsport Industry, previous winners of which include Bernie Ecclestone, Sir Jackie

Stewart, Ken Tyrell and David Richards. This was presented to me at the House of Lords by the Rt Hon Peter Hain, Secretary of State for Wales.

Then, in September 2004, I received the Meguiar's Award in recognition of my achievements in establishing the Grand Prix Collection. This was presented to me during a dinner at the RAC Club, held exclusively in my honour and attended by 250 guests. It was the first time that the presentation had been made in England and I was especially proud of the fact that I won it unanimously. Among the speakers who got up to say some very nice things about me was Simon Taylor, a great friend to me and to Donington over the years.

Most recently, in January 2005, I was awarded an honorary Doctorate by the University of Derby – not bad for someone who only went to school for eighteen months and left at 13½!

All such honours and awards are hugely gratifying and I treasure every one of them. But the one that means most to me is the Nigel Moores Trophy that I won as Best Private Entrant with Roger Williamson. That's not just because of the emotional attachment I have to Roger. To be truthful, the reason I've got all these Lifetime Awards is simply because I've spent a lot of money on some very important cars and saved them for the country. To my mind, that doesn't compare with backing a driver, entering a car and winning everything in sight. That is definitely the achievement of which I am most proud.

The other slight problem with Lifetime Awards is that, like the Donington anniversaries, they reflect past glories. And even at my age I am not content just to look backwards. I like to be active and I always need to have new projects on the go to keep me busy, especially now that I have regained my health, strength and mobility following the Ferrari 500 accident.

I had half promised Kevin and the family immediately after it happened that I would stop trying to pretend I was Fangio and that I would never again take one of the cars out on the track. At that stage I really did believe that my high-speed driving days were over and that the nearest I would get to recreating that special thrill would be to ease my creaking bones behind the wheel of a stationary car and simply fantasise.

However, as soon as I began to feel a bit fitter my resolve started to weaken. In August 2004 I organised another of my 'play days' at Donington and although I hadn't intended to have a drive myself, I just couldn't resist the temptation once I saw the others going around. I thought I'd start off by taking the BRM P25 for a little spin and having survived fifteen laps in that with no ill effects I decided to have a go in the Vanwall VW14. I did a further ten laps in that, by which time I was feeling confident enough to climb back into the Ferrari 500.

I could see Kevin looking on rather anxiously, but he didn't say anything. He knew from long experience that it would be a waste of time trying to talk me out of it once I'd made my mind up. I took it out for ten laps and although I treated it with respect, determined to bring it back in one piece, I didn't hold back completely. I actually recorded some quite respectable lap times – and it felt beautiful.

Altogether during the day I drove the equivalent of half a grand prix. Kevin did about the same number of laps, but I was very encouraged to find that, at the age of eighty-two, I wasn't nearly as stiff as he was the next day. I'm now eagerly looking forward to the prospect of some further very special driving treats once our latest restoration projects have been completed.

The first and most ambitious of these involves the 1937 Mercedes W125, still one of the most powerful grand prix cars ever built. Nine of these 600-bhp, 200-mph cars were made originally, but of the six or seven that remain in existence only one is in private hands and that is the one that Colin Crabbe and Neil Corner had and which is now owned by Bernie Ecclestone. Mercedes themselves are believed to have four or five and there is another one, a hill climb version, in the former Schlumpf collection. This was kindly loaned to us by our good friends at the renamed Musée Nationale de l'Automobile Schlumpfs in 2003 for our celebrations to mark the 30th anniversary of the opening of the museum at Donington.

I am currently involved in building a couple of W125s based on spares that I have accumulated over the years, one of which will feature the special streamlined bodywork. The work is being carried out for me by

Crosthwaite & Gardiner, using a set of 2,800 original drawings that belonged to the pre-war Mercedes team manager Alfred Neubauer and which I bought when they were sold off in Austria after his death a few years ago. At the time of writing, each chassis has already been built and all the patterns have been made. I have also seen the first camshaft, machined out of a solid piece of metal, plus the first crankshaft. We hope to have the first complete car up and running very shortly.

The Holy Grail of any historic grand prix car collection as far as I am concerned would have to be the 1932 Mercedes Benz SSKL. Designed by the legendary Ferdinand Porsche, only four of these cars were ever made and all of them were believed to have been destroyed when the Mercedes factory was bombed during the war. Then, a couple of years ago, we heard that a genuine chassis and some other spares had suddenly turned up in Austria and were available for sale. The story was that one of the four original cars had been dismantled in the factory and put aside for spares and that because it was stored separately from the other three, what was left of it had actually survived the bombing.

I was initially very suspicious. There have been many copies made of the SSKL over the years and I was extremely doubtful at first as to whether this treasure trove could be genuine. However, when I arranged to go and see it for myself close inspection satisfied me that it passed all the obvious tests of authenticity.

Two things, in particular, helped to convince me that this was indeed the car that I had coveted all my life. The SSKL was developed from the SSK, the L standing for Leicht, which is German for lightweight. This extra lightness was achieved partly by cutting holes along each side of the chassis. On the originals these holes were stamped, whereas on the copies they are always drilled. When I felt underneath, there, sure enough, was the telltale flange that you get with stamping. I also knew that the original chassis had been made using special lightweight steel and when I went to pick it up I found that it was, indeed, noticeably lighter than you would expect. At that point, I agreed to buy it and any lingering doubt about its authenticity seemed to have been finally removed when we got it back home, cleaned off some of the rust and found the chassis number.

Over the next few months we managed to track down some other genuine SSK and SSKL parts, including both a back and front axle. At the same time we did a huge amount of research to make sure that we knew everything there was to know about the car. We even went so far as to trace an old boy in Austria who had actually been working in the Mercedes factory in 1932 and who, despite his age, was able to give us a lot of useful information. And although we were going to be building the engine, the body and quite a few other parts from scratch, the fact that we had an original chassis and a history to go with it meant that this would be the most authentic SSKL in existence, an unbelievably rare and valuable car.

I was getting very excited at this point, but then came the bombshell – incontrovertible evidence that, just as I had feared when I first heard about it, what we had bought was actually a fake, albeit a very clever and convincing one. It was apparently made sometime in the sixties, although we have not yet established its full history. And I have still not finally made up my mind about what to do with it, although I may well decide to go ahead and rebuild it as what would probably be the most impressive recreation so far.

Almost equally rare and significant is the 1948 Cisitalia-Porsche 360. This will probably be my last full restoration project, despite having been one of the first collectors' items I ever bought – in my possession, in pieces, for more than thirty years.

Like the SSKL, this Ferdinand Porsche-designed car was thought at one time to be extinct and comes with a chequered history. It was commissioned by wealthy Italian industrialist-turned-car-manufacturer Piero Dusio in 1946, but as Porsche himself had been interned by the French after the war, largely because of the work he had done on military vehicles for the Germans, most of the basic design work on the Cisitalia was actually done in his absence by Karl Rabe, his partner in the old Porsche design team, with help from an ex-Auto Union engineer, Eberan von Eberhorst. Incorporating many innovative features, including a dual drive system that allowed the driver to switch from four-wheel to rear-wheel drive at will, the mid-engine car was one of the most advanced for its time ever built.

Dusio had started out with ambitious plans for a six-car team, with Nuvolari as his No 1 driver, but costs then escalated to the point where the project threatened to ruin him financially. Pressed by creditors and sued for arrears of pay by his own workforce, Dusio eventually did an extraordinary deal with President Peron of Argentina in 1949 whereby, in return for having his debts paid off, he agreed to move his whole company to Buenos Aires to form the basis of an Argentinian motor industry. The first Cisitalia 360 was eventually launched in Italy amid a blaze of publicity, only for Nuvolari to take ill very shortly afterwards. As a result, the car never actually raced.

Shipped over to Argentina in 1950, it then disappeared from public view until 1959, when Ferry Porsche, the son of Ferdinand and head of the modern Porsche company, tracked it down and brought it back to Germany. Some ten years later, in the late sixties, I heard that enough spare parts had been discovered in the old Cisitalia works to build a second car and I managed to acquire these.

I then had a body built by John Cole, but, up until now, we have never quite got around to rebuilding the engine and assembling the whole car, so it has remained on display at the museum as a show car, still not fully complete. As it happens, it has the potential to be better than the one Porsche have got. That has never been a runner as far as I know, having been in a seawater flood during its time in Argentina as a result of which it suffered severe corrosion damage. In fact, I gave Porsche a spare gearbox from among the parts that I had bought so that they could replace the one on their car, the casing of which had been eaten away.

With the W125 and the Cisitalia included, I reckon the Donington Grand Prix Collection will be pretty much complete. I also have the satisfaction of knowing that its future is secure for at least the next generation, since Kevin not only shares my passion for motorsport, but also seems to have inherited the Wheatcroft collecting gene, although his special interest is in military vehicles.

This goes right back to his childhood and he reckons it was sparked by the war stories I was always regaling him with. For his fifth birthday present he asked for a German helmet he'd spotted in an antique shop while his mother and I were browsing around one day. For his next birthday he wanted an Iron Cross and by the time he was twelve he already had quite a little collection of World War II memorabilia, most of which he'd got from friends' fathers. At fourteen he then acquired his first military vehicle, using a £100 gift from his grandmother to buy a Willys Jeep.

He ended up getting an amazing deal. He had seen this jeep advertised by a chap who was living up in the Shetland Islands and agreed a price of £50 over the 'phone. I then took him up there to collect it and when we arrived the owner, who was confined to a wheelchair, was quite astonished to find that he had been dealing with a fourteen-year-old who was still too young to drive and yet was so fanatical.

After the three of us had chatted for a while, he handed Kevin two keys and said: "Tell you what – the jeep is yours. Here's the key. The second key fits the lock on that shed over there and anything you find in there is yours too, if you want it."

When Kevin looked inside the shed he found five other identical Willys Jeeps sitting there. This chap let him have the lot for £50. He had bought them at a war surplus auction some years earlier for next to nothing and had been using them to run a taxi service on the islands until crippled by ill health. In the end he was just very happy to see them go to a good home. Later, having done them up, Kevin sold the other five for a handsome profit and used the money to buy his first really serious military vehicles, of which he very soon had a considerable number.

His collection, which specialises in German vehicles and equipment, now numbers over two hundred items, including fifty-five tanks, twenty-five artillery pieces, twelve amphibious craft, fifteen motorcycles, assorted trucks, jeeps, staff cars, demolition vehicles and even a field kitchen.

I am constantly amazed by how valuable some of these things have become. For instance, his recently-acquired 770K Mercedes staff car – known as the 'Hitler Car' – is worth every bit as much as some of my more expensive classic grand prix cars.

Ask Kevin to name his favourite pieces and he will list the big German tanks such as the Panther, the Tiger and the King Tiger. When I hear him talking about their relative capability compared to the sort of things I was driving during the war it makes me very thankful that I didn't know then what I know now.

The Tiger, for instance, was never defeated in one-on-one combat. Virtually nothing could penetrate its 150mm-thick armour plating, even at virtually point blank range. German tank crews apparently used to boast about how they would sit inside listening to the dink-dink sound of shells bouncing off them and think to themselves: "Ah, the British are having a bit of a go again." The only damage it would do was to chip the paintwork! At the same time, a Tiger could kill a Sherman from a mile away. If Ben and I and the rest of us had been aware of that at the time, we might not have trundled round North Africa and Europe quite so confidently. As it was, we were fortunate never to come up against one of these monsters.

I had a poignant reminder of my wartime experiences when, in 2001, I found myself back in Walkenried for the first time in many years. The visit was a very sad occasion, prompted by Lenchen's death after a long period of ill health.

Following our eight-year separation in the seventies, she and I had got back together again and, along with Kevin and the two youngest girls, she had moved into the converted mill at Arnesby, where I was living by then and which is still my home. It was wonderful to have the family around me again. Lenchen still wanted a quiet life and had little interest in going to the events and functions that I inevitably got involved in all the time, although she did accompany me to some of the more important race meetings at Donington and even, occasionally, presented the trophies. Mostly, she much preferred to stay at home, where she kept the house looking beautiful and spent hours working in the garden, always elegantly and immaculately dressed whatever she happened to be doing. At the same time, I made an effort not to spend quite so much time away. We soon settled back into a comfortable routine.

The four older children had already flown the nest by this time. Kevin's elder brother, David, worked for me on the building sites for a few years before branching out on his own in business, while Jill and Sue both worked in the office for a time until they got married. Joy did things the other way round, only joining the business much later. She stayed on and is still with us. Tina and Mandy briefly had jobs as receptionists in a motel that I owned, but they, too, eventually went their own way. Meanwhile, the family was growing steadily and, at the last count, included thirteen grandchildren and two great-grandchildren. We always make a point of getting together at my house on Boxing Day, but there are so many of us now that we have to stagger the meals, with one sitting for lunch and another for dinner!

For twelve years after Lenchen came back everything was fine and we enjoyed some of the happiest times of our entire fifty-seven-year marriage. Then, in 1990 she suffered two heart attacks. We were told that she needed major surgery as soon as possible if she were to have any prospect of long-term survival, but, at the same time, the doctors warned us that the chances of her coming through the operation were no better than 50/50. It was a difficult decision to have to make and we sat down as a family to discuss the options before giving the go-ahead. Happily, it all went well. Lenchen made a full recovery and was her normal self until 1999, when a mini-stroke left her blind in one eye and completely destroyed her self-confidence.

She had always been incredibly house-proud, keeping it absolutely spotless, with everything precisely in its place, but now, suddenly, she felt that she couldn't cope any more. She hid herself away and became more reclusive than ever, not wanting to go out at all. After a while, she then decided that she would actually prefer to live in a residential care home. The family and I did our best to talk her out of it, but she insisted that this was what she wanted to do. We eventually gave in and drove her round to look at various different places until she found one she really liked, an old manor house set in beautiful grounds, with views over open countryside and superb accommodation for just twelve residents.

She loved it and seemed perfectly content with the arrangement, but I felt very awkward and unhappy about it. As an alternative, I eventually suggested to her that if she didn't want to live in The Mill itself, then I would build a bungalow for her in the grounds, with self-contained accommodation for a live-in nurse. We finally persuaded her that this was the ideal solution and I set about filling in the swimming pool and building the bungalow on the site. I had it fitted with every kind of safety device and alarm so that if for any reason she were ever on her own and there was an emergency she could press a button and a blue flashing light on top of The Mill would summon help from neighbours if I myself wasn't around for any reason. We got everything ready for her and then, three weeks before she was due to move in, she had another heart attack and this time there was nothing that could be done for her.

It had always been Lenchen's wish that her ashes should be scattered in Walkenried and it was to perform this last duty that Kevin and I went out there together. Although Lenchen herself had returned regularly while her father was still alive, it was many, many years since I had been back and I barely recognised the place. What had been little more than a village was now a small town, with modern dual carriageways where there had once been narrow mountain roads and with shops and houses on the fields where I had once gone hunting deer and wild boar with a Bren gun.

As I searched for familiar landmarks, the memories came flooding back. I found myself thinking again not just about Lenchen and our rather unusual courtship, but also about Harry Hinge, Witt, Copperwheat, Ben Warr and all the others with whom I'd lived through the most intense few years of my life. Despite all the heartfelt vows we had made about staying in touch when we got back to Blighty after the war, we never did. In a funny way, you wanted to forget it all once you got back, to put it all behind you and start afresh. At least, that's how I felt. I never even had occasion to wear my medals until sixty years later, on VE Day 2005, when I was invited to cut the ribbon at a ceremony to mark the 10th anniversary of the opening of the Arquebus Krigshistorisk war museum in Haugesund, Norway, which is twinned with Kevin's planned military vehicle museum.

Copperwheat and I looked each other up a couple of times after we had all come home and I did, of course, go up to Manchester to see Ben. I came away wishing that I hadn't bothered. The man I had looked up to as a hero in the extraordinary circumstances of the war cut a much less heroic figure in the bar of his local back street pub, where it came as a shock to realise that he was actually just another local hard man, with a police record and not much of a future.

What had seemed like great resourcefulness in the context of the war was revealed back in Civvy Street as little more than low cunning. The contempt for authority that went down so well in the barrack room was actually the hatred of a habitual lawbreaker for the police; the fearsome fighting qualities that were so admirable in the heat of battle were actually born out of a ruthless and innate violent streak.

The last time I saw him, he was still talking about setting up a raid on a cinema box office.

"It's so easy, Wheaty," he insisted. "I've done it before – and this time I won't get caught."

"Don't be so daft, Ben," I told him. "You can't carry on like that. You've got to get yourself a proper job."

I was already starting to do quite well for myself by this time and had driven up with Lenchen in my little two-seater Daimler. The look in his eye when he saw that car made me realise that we were now living in different worlds.

We said our goodbyes and that was that. We never spoke again and I have no idea what happened to him. In my mind's eye, I still picture him as he was in the war – a first-class soldier in every way. Marching, drilling, laying guns, stripping down a Bren and putting it together again blind-fold – whatever it was, he was better at it than anyone else in the unit and in a tight corner he was the one person you wanted by your side. A natu-ral fighting man, he was completely in his element on the battlefield, but outside that environment, he was just a shadow of the man I had so much admired. However, I prefer to remember him as he was at his best – a fearless and loyal friend and a tower of strength at a time of need.

Back in Walkenried, Kevin and I scattered Lenchen's ashes around the war memorial. This is the only memorial of any kind for her brother Gerhard, whose body was never recovered after he was killed outside Stalingrad and who therefore has no known grave. It is my wish that my own ashes will one day be scattered at the same spot.

I never thought I would marry again. I have always believed that marriage is for life and even when Lenchen and I split up for a while, the idea of divorce never crossed my mind. There was no way that anyone could ever replace her in my heart and I still keep up the family tradition whereby we all get together for dinner at The Butcher's Arms every year on December 12th, her birthday. After she died, however, there were times when I did begin to feel rather lonely. At an age when my social life wasn't quite what it used to be and I wasn't going out so much, I seemed to spend a lot of time rattling around The Mill on my own and I found myself longing for a bit more company.

I had known Sheila Andrews socially for many years. When I first met her she was married to a director of Lucas and the motorsport connection meant that we would often bump into each other at race meetings around the world. We shared the same interests and got on well and later, after her marriage had broken up and Lenchen and I were living apart, the friendship became much closer. She was very supportive in the months following Lenchen's death and after a while it seemed obvious that we should get together.

We were married on May 8th, 2004 – my 82nd birthday. The wedding ceremony itself was a very quiet affair. Kevin and Sheila's daughter Debbie were the only other people present at the register office ceremony in Market Harborough. Neither Sheila nor I wanted a big song and dance – and apart from that I was keen to get back home in time to watch the practice for the Spanish Grand Prix on television – so as we went in I took the lady registrar on one side and told her very politely: "We don't want a long job – could you speed it up a bit?" We were in and out of the place in twenty minutes flat and she assured me that it was the shortest wedding she'd ever officiated at. I slipped a £20 note across the table by way of thanking her for doing a good, quick job – and got a rather funny look in return. Kevin said afterwards that he didn't think it was quite the thing to do!

The ceremony was followed later by a party in the Senna Fangio Conference Hall at Donington at which Canon Lionel Webber conducted a marriage blessing. There were exactly eighty-two guests –

one for each year of my life – and one of the highlights of the evening came when Rick Hall got up to propose a toast, making a speech in which he gave me more stick than I've ever had in my life!

He started off by joking: "I thought I'd have to wait for his funeral before I'd get the opportunity to tell you some of the things I'm going to tell you now!" From then on he didn't come up for breath for about half-an-hour! He really did turn it on, getting his own back for all the stick I'd given him over the years. Some of those present were worried that he'd maybe gone too far, but I loved it. I like people who take the mickey out of you to your face – to my mind it shows they're true friends. And Rick Hall is a man I've always admired, both personally and professionally.

I'd like to think that getting married again at eighty-two helps to prove that I'm still very much looking forward as well as back. Despite my love of historic cars, I'm not one for dwelling too much in the past. There are still lots of things I want to do and you'll still find me in the office most days. Apart from the restorations that I'm working on – the latest one involves a six-door Mercedes 600 limousine in which I'll be able to take just about the whole family out to lunch! – Kevin and I have plans to rebuild and extend the whole museum complex at Donington so as to include not only my car collection, but also Kevin's military pieces as well. The continuing expansion of the East Midlands Airport and the accompanying industrial development means that the whole area is assuming a new importance and with talk of big new hotels and even a casino going up around the airport, an extended museum with added restaurant facilities has the potential to become an even bigger interna-tional tourist attraction.

As for the circuit itself, I haven't entirely given up the idea of buying back the lease and running it myself again. A series of take-overs has meant that the lease has passed from Two Four Sports to SFX and, most recently, to ClearChannel, a vast American entertainments conglomerate. Their lease runs until the year 2020, but if they were to lose interest in Donington Park for any reason, Kevin and I have made it clear that we would welcome the opportunity to take control again. We've got some very definite ideas about how the whole circuit could be updated and improved.

During the recent furore, when it looked as though Silverstone might be about to lose the British Grand Prix, Donington Park was again mentioned as a possible alternative venue and, in fact, Bernie has asked us several times over the last few years whether we wanted it. Ironically, given the long and bitter campaign I fought to get the event back in the late seventies and early eighties, I had to tell him that we weren't really interested any more, that it no longer made any kind of financial sense.

We estimate that it would now take an investment of around £60 million to bring the circuit and the facilities at Donington up to current Formula One grand prix requirements. At the same time, you have to accept that you're never going to be able to make the event pay for itself. Apart from the millions that have to go to Bernie as the commercial rights holder, there are other liabilities such as the £100,000 fee you have to pay the RAC, the marshalling costs, increased local authority rates and so on. On top of that, you effectively have to close the circuit for a month to get everything ready, which means that you are sacrificing all that potential income as well. Hosting the event certainly raises your profile, but at that cost you have to ask whether it is really worthwhile.

Whatever happens at Donington in the future, I am enormously proud of what I have been able to achieve there. I receive many 'thank you' letters from motorsport fans, mostly complimenting me on the Grand Prix Collection, but there was one in particular that gave me special satisfaction. It arrived quite recently and came from a local Nottingham man who started off by explaining that his love of motorsport had started when, as a fifteen-year-old, he made his first visit to Donington shortly after we had re-opened it in 1977.

"The sight of fast cars and bikes had a profound effect on me as an impressionable teenager," he wrote, going on to mention that his three sons had inherited his interest and that the eldest of them had become the youngest ever pupil at the Jim Russell Racing Drivers School, driving a Formula Vauxhall Junior at the age of eleven. He added that he and his family had travelled all over Europe and America to watch events and to visit museums and ended his letter by saying: "I just wanted to take a few moments to record my personal and heartfelt thanks to you for enriching my life with all of the hard work you have put into Donington Park over the last 25 years or more. Your legacy will be a monument to British motorsport that stands head and shoulders above any other racing collection I have ever visited in Europe or the United States."

Comments like that make all the hard work worthwhile, reflecting my own hopes and aspirations. With Kevin ready to take over, I know that that legacy will be in safe hands. My greatest hope is that it will continue to be enjoyed by many future generations, a lasting monument not so much to me, personally, as to the whole history of motorsport in this country. And, in particular, to those great pioneering days of British grand prix racing when, for the first time, Donington Park echoed to the sound of thunder.

Tom Wheatcroft – A lifetime in motorsport

1935-1938 Tom Wheatcroft attends Donington Grands Prix.

1950 Tom Wheatcroft attends first post-war British Grand Prix. He has attended every one since then.

1971 Wheatcroft Racing Team established: Tasman Series entrant and race winner.

Donington Park acquired.

Wheatcroft Racing Team Formula 3 entrant and winner.

Roger Williamson wins Grovewood Award as the most promising young driver of the year as well as being named BP 'Superman of the Year' and also 'Driver Of The Year' by the British Racing and Sports Car Club.

1972 Wheatcroft Racing Team Formula 2 and Formula 3 entrant and winner.

Roger Williamson presented with the annual John Cobb Award for Best British Driver by the British Racing Drivers Club while Tom Wheatcroft is awarded the BRDC's Nigel Moores Trophy as Best Private Entrant in International Motorsport.

1973 Wheatcroft Racing Team Formula 2 and Formula 1 World Championship Team entrant.

Donington Grand Prix Collection opened.

1976 Wheatcroft Racing Team Formula Atlantic constructor and entrant. 50th race win.

1977 Racing recommences at Donington Park.

1978 Wheatcroft Racing Team records 75th race win.

1980 Circuit at Donington extended to Grand Prix specification.

1982 Over 100 cars in the Donington Grand Prix Collection.

1993 The realisation of a dream: Donington Park stages F1 World Championship Grand Prix – won by Ayrton Senna.

1996 Wheatcroft Racing Team Formula Classic Retro Series launched.

1997	Senna Fangio Tribute unveiled. Donington Grand Prix Memorial Garden opened.
1998	Chrysler Lifetime Achievement Award presented to Tom Wheatcroft.
	Joint celebration of the 25th anniversary of the opening of the Grand Prix Collection and the 60th anniversary of Nuvolari's victory in the 1938 Donington Grand Prix.
2001	70th anniversary of the first race to take place at Donington Park in 1931, a motorcycle event.
	Historic Grand Prix Cars Association Lifetime Achievement Award presented to Tom Wheatcroft.
2002	TW80 'Party in the Park' – Tom Wheatcroft celebrates his 80th birthday and the 25th anniversary of him bringing racing back to Donington with an event at the Donington Grand Prix Collection attended by Sir Stirling Moss, Lord March, Lord Montagu of Beaulieu, Tony Brooks, Richard Attwood and Willie Green. Event includes a live link with Eddie Jordan at the Canadian Grand Prix and the presentation of the inaugural Tom Wheatcroft Trophy to Murray Walker.
	Gregor Grant Trophy presented to Tom Wheatcroft by Jean Alesi at the annual Autosports Award Dinner.
2003	The 30th anniversary of the opening of the Donington Grand Prix Collection. Acknowledged for many years as the largest collection of grand prix cars in the world, with over 130 cars on display, and it continues to expand, attracting visitors from all over the globe.
	Tom receives the prestigious Motorsport Industry Association Award for the Most Outstanding Contribution to the UK Motorsport Industry, presented to him at the House of Lords by the Rt Honourable Peter Hain, Secretary of State for Wales.
	70th anniversary of the first car races at Donington. Those attending include 89-year-old Max Turner, who drove at that first meeting, and also Tom Delaney, at 92 the world's oldest holder of a current racing licence.
	Tribute to Ayrton Senna weekend, marking the 10th anniversary of his historic win in the 1993 European Grand Prix at Donington.

2003   Tom Wheatcroft Trophy presented by Murray Walker to Sid Watkins, official on-track grand prix surgeon and chairman of the Expert Advisory Safety Committee of the FIA.

Unveiling of the Roger Williamson memorial statue in the Memorial Garden at Donington by Tom Wheatcroft and Roger's sister, Barbara Upton.

2004   Meguiar's Award presented to Tom Wheatcroft in recognition of his achievements in establishing the Donington Grand Prix Collection.

Tom Wheatcroft Trophy presented to Jean Todt of Ferrari.

2005   Tom Wheatcroft receives an Honorary Doctorate from the University of Derby.

Tom Wheatcroft Trophy presented to Bernie Ecclestone.

Index